Taking Assimilation to Heart

Taking Assimilation to Heart

*Marriages of White Women
and Indigenous Men in the
United States and Australia,
1887–1937*

Katherine Ellinghaus

University of Nebraska Press   •   Lincoln & London

Acknowledgment
for the use of previously published material
appears on page 221, which constitutes an
extension of the copyright page.

⊚

Library of Congress
Cataloging-in-Publication Data

Ellinghaus, Katherine.
Taking assimilation to heart : marriages of
white women and indigenous men in the
United States and Australia, 1887–1937 /
Katherine Ellinghaus.
p.   cm.
Includes
bibliographical references and index.
ISBN-13: 978-0-8032-1829-1 (cloth : alk. paper)
ISBN-10: 0-8032-1829-x (cloth : alk. paper)
ISBN-13: 978-0-8032-2487-2 (paper : alk. paper)
1. Interracial marriage
—United States—History—19th century.
2. Interracial marriage
—Australia—History—19th century.
3. Indians of North America—Cultural
assimilation—History—19th century.
4. Aboriginal Australians— Cultural
assimilation—History—19th century.
5. Indians of North America—Social
conditions—19th century.
6. Aboriginal Australians
— Social conditions—19th century.
7. Women, White—United States—Family
relationships—History—19th century.
8. Women, White—Australia—Family
relationships—History—19th century.
9. Indians of North America
—Education—Social aspects.
I. Title.
HQ1031.E54 2006
306.84′608997—dc22
2006007395

Designed and set in Palatino
by R. W. Boeche.

Contents

Illustrations

Acknowledgments

I have had tremendous support while writing this book, which began as a doctoral thesis. The History Department at the University of Melbourne provided an enriching environment in which to learn the practice of history. I thank my supervisor, Patricia Grimshaw, for generously sharing her ideas, for expressing her faith in my ability, and for being the best mentor anyone could ask for. David Goodman, my associate supervisor, read numerous drafts with patience, insight, and attention to detail. I was fortunate to find some good companions among my fellow "postgrads" and, later, colleagues. I couldn't have asked for a kinder or more knowledgeable friend than Frazer Andrewes, with whom to share the fraught experience of doctoral candidature. Peter Sherlock came up with the title almost before the project itself had begun, and he has been an important source of encouragement, camaraderie, and coffee breaks. Glenn Moore taught me how to travel in the United States, infected me with his enthusiasm for teaching its history, put up with many years of sharing an office, and in the process became a good friend. Joy Damousi's enthusiasm, support, and good advice have meant more than I can say. I'm indebted to Kalissa Alexeyeff, Tony Birch, Jane Carey, Martin Crotty, Monica Dux, Jo Leahy, Ann Standish, Ellen Warne, and Elizabeth Nelson, who also alerted me to some wonderful references in the Victorian offices of the Australian Archives.

Outside the University of Melbourne there were many scholars who commented publicly and privately on my work. Ann Curthoys and Glenda Gilmore gave me wise advice about turning this thesis into a book. I'm grateful to Donna Merwick, who reminded me to tell a story; to Aileen Moreton-Robinson, whose uncompromising opinions got me thinking; to Patrick Wolfe, who has always been enthusiastic about this project; to Lyn Riddett, who gave advice very early on in the piece; and to the anonymous readers engaged by the University of Nebraska Press. Cathy Dunn was kind enough to contribute some of her research into the Governor family. Margaret Jacobs and Theodore Sargent have generously shared with me their work on, and enthusiasm about, Elaine Goodale Eastman. Tracy Spencer gave me valuable information about Jack and Rebecca Forbes. Barb Landis kindly shared her expertise on Carlisle with me, and Elaine Otto combed through the text with professionalism and enthusiasm for the topic. I was kindly assisted by archivists and librarians across two continents, and I have been a grateful recipient of a Melbourne Research Scholarship and two Arts Faculty travel grants, a Barra Foundation International Fellowship, and an Australian Research Council postdoctoral fellowship.

Outside the academy, my dear girlhood friends Samantha Benton, Winnie Jewell, and Emma Martin kept me laughing and, with constant phone calls, taught me much about the rewards of friendship. Alec and Felicity Ross provided crabs and conversation for a lonely researcher. The "dancing girls" bore the brunt of my need to get away from the computer and were far more important to the completion of this work than they realized. The Hanley and Jenkinson families, particularly Betty Jenkinson, were sources of endless welcome and encouragement. Each member of my own family has, in his or her own way, given support, comfort, and inspiration. Finally, I wish to express my gratitude to Kristian Hanley. I could never have done this without his constant reminders that challenges bring their own rewards and that what I choose to do should always be something to enjoy. I am lucky to have him by my side.

Introduction

*When, only a few weeks after our first meeting, I promised to marry Dr.
Eastman, it was with a thrilling sense of two-fold consecration. I gave myself
wholly in that hour to the traditional duties of wife and mother, abruptly
relinquishing all thought of an independent career for the making of a home.
At the same time, I embraced with a new and deeper zeal the conception of
life-long service to my husband's people.*

      Elaine Goodale Eastman, Sister to the Sioux

When white, middle-class schoolteacher Elaine Goodale made the decision to marry Dakota doctor Charles Eastman in 1891, she did so, she later remembered, with "a thrilling sense of two-fold consecration." Eastman was aware that her marriage was more than simply the natural
consequence of strong feelings between a young man and woman. It was
also part of the United States' project of finding a long-term solution to
its "Indian problem." While she loved Charles, she was also conscious
that her marriage would be a public demonstration of the possibilities
of Native American assimilation. More than that of most white women
at the time, her marriage had meaning in both the private and public
spheres. As Kevin J. Mumford has pointed out, "Sex across the color line
always represents more than just sex."[1] This book explores what marriages between white women and indigenous men reveal about race relations in two settler societies, the United States and Australia, in the late
nineteenth and early twentieth centuries, a period in which both nations
were imagining ways in which indigenous people were to be assimilated into the mainstream. Finding out who participated in such marriages,

what happened to them, and what others thought about it enlightens us with a peculiar directness about the racial, social, and national contexts in which they took place.

Scholars have paid increasing attention to the history of interracial sex, particularly the shameful story of the casual, often exploitative, relationships between white men and indigenous women, but there have been few in-depth studies of interracial relationships that involved white women.[2] Apart from Martha Hodes, who has written an influential history of nineteenth-century marriages and sexual relationships between white women and black men in the American South, few American scholars have focused with any detail on relationships between white women and nonwhite men.[3] In Australia, too, histories deal with the subject of interracial relationships mainly in terms of the exploitative sexual relations between Aboriginal women and white men.[4] Many historians have recognized how seldom relationships involving white women and indigenous men occurred. Australian historian Henry Reynolds, for example, has described the "almost impenetrable barriers of prejudice preventing intimacy between Aboriginal men and European women." Future research "may uncover evidence of relationships of even marriages between Aboriginal men and European women, but they seem to have been rare."[5]

This book proceeds from the premise that rare events and exceptions to the rule such as marriages between white women and indigenous men can tell historians much about the rules themselves. I am, of course, not the first to argue this about cross-cultural associations. A number of studies of interracial relationships explore their role in the colonial project, and there is a growing body of scholarship on the ideology of miscegenation in general.[6] Postcolonial theorist Ann Laura Stoler has recently identified a need for scholars to address "how intimate domains—sex, sentiment, domestic arrangement, and child rearing—figure in the making of racial categories and in the management of imperial rule."[7] Interracial relationships have much to tell about racial hierarchies, colonial culture, and social mores.

My aim, then, has been to investigate marriages of white women and indigenous men in Australia and the United States and then employ them to explore and compare the settler societies in which they took place. I have not tried to comprehensively unearth examples of relationships between white women and indigenous men in a certain time or place, nor to write a broad history of sexual relations between colonizers and colonized. This book, I hope, is more than an exploration of individual lives or a tally of couples who came together despite the odds. I have made some deliberate choices about how to approach this topic. While there are moments in the book where marriages of white men and indigenous women are touched on, I have deliberately restricted my broader discussion to the particular characteristics of marriages of white women to indigenous men. This is because interracial relationships involving white women bring to light particular aspects about the histories of the United States and Australia. They were, for example, caught up in specifically gendered ideas about race and citizenship. "Throughout the history of the United States," says Linda Kerber, "virtually all married women's identities as citizens were filtered through their husband's legal identities."[8] Until the mid-1930s, when American women married "foreign" husbands, they almost always lost their citizenship, and from 1907 legislation ensured that they did so.[9] Until the late 1930s, an Australian woman's citizenship was in danger if she married an "alien."[10] White women's sexual relationships were also inextricably bound up in their financial and social standing. As feminist historian Mary Ryan has suggested, brides in the nineteenth century "entrusted their material destiny to the business acumen of their grooms."[11] Thus when white women married across racial boundaries, the status of their husbands became crucial to their own standing in white society, much more so than white men who married indigenous women. Intermarriage was often understood as a means of assimilation into the dominant society, not the other way around. When the white partner was a man, this could make perfect sense. But women, seen traditionally as following their husbands' nationalities and social and economic status, faced a more complicated prospect, and the way their relationships were viewed is revealing of the inherently gendered and raced notions of national belonging.

The United States and Australia had their beginnings in the impulse of colonialism. Focusing on relationships of white women and indigenous men, therefore, is especially revealing of how each of these groups was seen by colonial discourse. In the last decade, many scholars have concentrated on the role of white women in the colonial encounter, and this book is also a contribution to a field that asks specific questions about how race and gender have operated in settler societies.[12] As Ania Loomba has argued, postcolonial theorists have explored how women "on both sides of the colonial divide demarcate both the innermost sanctums of race, culture, and nation, as well as the porous frontiers through which these are penetrated."[13] Colonial or "frontier" conditions meant that white women and indigenous men encountered each other relatively rarely. Most white colonists, then, assumed that white women, unlike white men, were not drawn sexually to nonwhite people. The possibility that this could be so was met with intense fear and anxiety. In addition, it is nearly impossible to deny maternity (unlike paternity) of a child of mixed descent. A white man, therefore, could escape relatively unscathed from a sexual relationship across racial lines; a white woman had much less chance of doing so. Also, as Richard Dyer has pointed out, white women carried, through their role as reproducers of white children, the "hopes, achievements, and character of the race"—hence the special anxieties associated with their sexuality.[14] White men's dominance was sorely threatened should their wives, sisters, and daughters participate in relationships with men from a colonized or enslaved group. When such liaisons did take place, especially when they were tolerated or understood as part of an ideology such as assimilation, they exposed the sometimes invisible imaginings by which colonial societies justified their existence.

For this reason, I have deliberately chosen to focus on marriages, not casual liaisons. My case studies thus had an aura of respectability that tested the limits of the societies in which they occurred. Nancy Cott has alerted us to the way in which the institution of marriage is both a private and a public relationship. "To be marriage," Cott says, "the institution requires public affirmation."[15] By taking public marriage vows, the couples I examine implicated themselves, if only in a small way, in the structures of the societies in which they lived. A broad and revealing spectrum of toleration greeted these relationships, which ranged from marginalization to acceptance.[16] This spectrum helps us to understand better how indigenous people were imagined as part of the body politics of the United States and Australia in the late nineteenth and early twentieth centuries. In an assimilationist context, white women, with their particular gendered and raced identity, and with the permanent act of marriage, to some extent could bring indigenous husbands "inside" the boundaries of mainstream society. They gave their husbands a stronger push up the ladder of social status than white men did when they formed a relationship with an indigenous woman. Their relationships were not fleeting and dismissible. To some extent, they subverted the hierarchies of race and gender by which settler societies operated, but they were also caught up in the tangible and defining mores of tolerated social behavior. They played a significant role in the story of race relations and the intimate ways in which colonialism could operate in settler societies.

Marriages between white women and indigenous men were rare occurrences. Therefore, this study has also been shaped by a basic absence of archival evidence. Martha Hodes described her experience of researching relationships between white women and African American men as "searching for stories." "No archive contained any sort of index on the topic of sex between white women and black men," she has written, "and only rarely did a catalog heading for 'miscegenation' or 'interracial marriage' lead to one or two brief references."[17] My experience has been equally challenging. For this reason, readers might expect to find some imbalances in the pages that follow. Perhaps the most obvious is the contrast between the detailed information I was able to unearth about the lives of several educated couples in the United States and the more fragmented information available about their equivalents in the Antipodes. There is a simple, fascinating explanation for this inequity. The Native American men who married white women were often almost part of the educated middle classes: Thomas Sloan, who married a white woman in 1891, was a lawyer, and Charles Eastman (also married in 1891) and Carlos Montezuma (1913) were physicians. Some of their wives were well educated; perhaps the best example was Elaine Goodale Eastman, who was a teacher and a published poet. As aspiring members of the literate and relatively leisured middle class, these couples often left rich and copious written records of their lives. On the other hand, Australian white women who married Aboriginal men were usually working-class women who left behind few sources for the historian: Rebecca Forbes, for example, was a cook, married to a horse breaker; Catherine Sharp was a domestic servant; and Ethel Governor was a miner's daughter who was sixteen and pregnant when she married an Aboriginal laborer in 1898. Thus the richness of my American archives could not be matched in Australia, and at the beginning of this project I struggled to make sense of this irregularity. Finding out why it existed has been a long and fruitful process, and in the end this formed the basis of my broader comparative argument about the differences between assimilation policies in the United States and Australia.

The absence of educated Aboriginal men for white middle-class Australian women to marry is central to the comparative insights provided by this book. In order to sharpen my comparative argument, therefore, I chose to focus on the kinds of marriages that most epitomized the assimilation policies of each country. In Australia I was in any case restricted to marriages of white women and uneducated Aboriginal men. To my knowledge, there were no equivalents of the "middle-class" marriages of the United States in the period I researched. In the United States, therefore, I opted to focus on marriages to the most educated Native American men, those who in most cases were involved with eastern boarding schools and reformers, not on white women who married relatively uneducated Native American men and lived with them on reservations. Many such marriages existed, and they remain a promising subject for future research. They have not, however, been the subject of this book.

These choices about how to focus this study have been made in order to best illuminate and compare the contexts in which they took place. There is no doubt that this study has been vastly complicated by its comparative focus, but it has also been immeasurably enhanced by it. The value of comparative, transnational, or global history lies in the insights it can provide into the uniqueness of nations while still recognizing the elements of their histories that they have in common.[18] Looking across national borders is as rewarding as it is complex. It may seem to reveal a minefield of diversity, across which comparisons are only made with difficulty. But once such comparisons are made, they can capture the complexity, diversity, and multiplicity of the past. For this reason, the remainder of this introductory chapter will be dedicated to beginning the story of interracial relationships and their role in assimilation policy in the United States and Australia.

Although scholars have tested the boundaries of traditional comparative history—tracing themes and ideologies across national borders rather than using differences and similarities between two societies to prove a point—by its very nature a comparison must begin with a recognition of likeness and particularities.[19] While there are many differences in the histories of Australia and the United States (most notably the reasons for, patterns, and times of first settlement, the enormous difference in population size, the different political events and traditions, and the presence in America of ex-slaves), scholars have found several areas of similarity between Australian and American history worthy of comparison.[20]

For this study, the most important similarity is the clash between people of European/British extraction and an indigenous population. Both the United States and Australia were settled by British colonists, although at different times (1607 and 1788) and for very different reasons (escape from religious persecution and the hope of profits in the United States, a dumping ground for English convicts in Australia), but both settlements displaced rich and well-established indigenous cultures. Comparative history on this subject is not new to either Australian or American history. When Frederick Jackson Turner "began" the written history of the American West with his frontier thesis, he himself suggested that it might be applied to other countries.[21] A number of mid-twentieth-century scholars have attempted to "test" Turner's theories about the development of democracy using Australian history.[22] Still others have either written or recommended a comparison of the contact history of the two countries.[23] The comparative study most germane to this book is Patrick Wolfe's comparative analysis of the relationship between motivations for colonization and racial oppression and the diverse attitudes toward interracial relationships in the United States, Brazil, and Australia.[24] I have followed Wolfe's lead in exploring the ways that crossnational comparisons help us to see exactly how race was understood in the context of colonialism.

By the middle of the nineteenth century, for example, European settlers of the North American and Australian continents had both begun to find ways to deal with the indigenous people they had displaced. For decades they had clung to a pseudoscientific notion that contact with a "superior race" had conveniently sealed the fate of indigenous people. But Native Americans and Aborigines had stubbornly insisted on not "dying out," and politicians, reformers, anthropologists, educators, and commentators had begun to imagine a new fate for them. If they were not going to disappear altogether, they could at least be taught to live like their dispossessors, thus removing the need for any special treatment that white governments had grudgingly conceded. This was the basis of the ideology of assimilation, pursued with increasing energy by policy makers in both countries in the late nineteenth and early twentieth centuries. It had emerged from an Enlightenment faith in human equality that at first glance differed from the outright derogatory racism prevalent at the time. Articulated in Christian terminology, assimilation was given impetus in sites of British colonization by increasing evangelistic efforts in the early to mid-nineteenth century.[25] There had been early attempts by missionaries to "civilize" indigenous people in both Australia and America, but the idea gained in secular popularity. In 1857, for example, the commissioner of Indian affairs argued that alternative destinies awaited the Native American nations. Either, he said, they "must advance and improve, and become fitted to take an active part in the ennobling struggles of civilization; or, remaining ignorant, imbecile and helpless . . . they must sink and perish."[26] Although some form of cultural change is always the inevitable outcome of contact between cultures, in the period encompassed by this study white people attempted to control the process, forcing cultural change to occur in specific ways and with a particular end in mind—the disappearance of the indigenous people as a separate, distinguishable group whose members might claim some form of financial recompense for their loss of land. Despite its humane beginnings, assimilation became an ideology that inspired many cruel and inhumane policies and practices, so much so that in both countries some scholars and activists have recently identified assimilation as a form of "ethnocide" or cultural genocide.[27]

Comparative historians, however, must be aware of assuming that "because they bear the same label, ideas, institutions, or groups . . . perform the same function everywhere".[28] This book is as much about how the word assimilation meant very different things when annunciated by white Australians and white Americans as it is about a particular kind of interracial marriage. The word assimilate suggests the absorption, dissolution, or incorporation of a discrete racial subjectivity into the mainstream. Most dictionary definitions of assimilation describe it as a process of acculturation, by which individuals or groups of differing ethnic heritage acquire, or are brought into conformity with, the basic habits, attitudes, and customs of a dominant national culture. A focus on interracial marriage, however, reveals a very different aspect of assimilation. Interracial relationships produced children of mixed descent. This process was sometimes perceived by white Americans and Australians as a means by which Aboriginal and Native American physical characteristics could be replaced by Anglo or white features. Children born of indigenous and white parents were denied an indigenous identity by ideas about degrees of "blood" and "caste."[29] Interracial relationships could thus be perceived to be a way of getting rid of a distinct group of people by "absorbing" their indigenous identity. Seeing interracial relationships as a means of indigenous extinction was an idea predicated on the belief that indigenous people of full descent were doomed to "die out," an expectation that stemmed from Enlightenment theories of progress, evolution, and natural selection. "The passing of the Aborigines," Henry Reynolds has argued, was a widely held belief among white Australians from 1788 onwards and was often seen as a measure of colonial achievement.[30]

Australian historian Anna Haebich has argued that assimilation was a "powerful act of national imagining."[31] It is important to understand, therefore, that as a category of analysis, "assimilation" is defined by time and place. Its meaning depends on when, where, and by whom the term is annunciated. For my purposes it could mean teaching indigenous people to live and support themselves as white people (cultural assimilation), or it could mean the loss of indigenous physical characteristics through interracial relationships (biological absorption). In most cases Australian and American reformers, politicians, and public servants involved in solving the "Indian problem" were cryptic when they referred to the future of Native Americans or Aborigines. They rarely explained whether they envisioned assimilation by hastening the births of mixed-descent children who did not appear indigenous, or whether they only wanted indigenous people to live in the manner of white people.

In the Australian context, a number of historians, notably Russell McGregor, Robert Manne, Patrick Wolfe, and Warwick Anderson, have described how biological absorption was used as a solution to the "Aboriginal problem."[32] In 1997 the Human Rights and Equal Opportunity Commission released a report into the removal of indigenous children from their families and the genocidal absorptionist ideology underlying Australian assimilation policies, bringing the issue to the attention of the Australian public.[33] In 2001 Phillip Noyce's feature-length film Rabbit-Proof Fence also described the issue of biological absorption for mainstream audiences.

There has not been a similar public discussion in the United States. Although U.S. scholars have recognized the varying meanings of the term assimilation, few have explored the extent to which biological absorption played a part in the ideas espoused during this period.[34] There have been some exceptions. Patricia Limerick, for example, has summed up the logic behind some of the policies put in place by nineteenth-century white Americans as follows:

> Set the blood quantum at one quarter, hold to it as a rigid definition of Indianness, let intermarriage proceed as it had for centuries, and eventually Indians will be defined out of existence. When that happens, the federal government will finally be freed from its persistent "Indian problem."[35]

Similarly, the literature on Native American identity often lists intermarriage alongside assimilation and acculturation as one of the reasons for the complexity of indigenous identity today.[36] Circe Sturm, for example, argues that present-day Cherokee identity is "embedded in ideas of blood, color, and race that permeate discourses of social belonging

THREE GENERATIONS
(Reading from Right to Left)
1. Half-blood—(Irish-Australian father; full-blood Aboriginal mother).
2. Quadroon Daughter—(Father Australian born of Scottish parents; Mother No. 1).
3. Octaroon Grandson—(Father Australian of Irish descent; Mother No. 2).

1. Auber O. Neville, the Western Australian chief protector of Aborigines from 1915 to 1936, included this illustration in his 1947 book about Australian race relations as a striking visual argument for the efficacy of biological absorption. From Neville, *Australia's Coloured Minority: Its Place in the Community* (1947).

in the United States."[37] M. Annette Jaimes's work on blood quantums proposes that the federal government's efforts to proclaim who was or wasn't "Indian" in legislation such as the Dawes Act were an ingenious way of reducing the Native American population and correspondingly the amount of land and financial assistance promised to it. She sees later policies such as the so-called checkerboarding of reservations and the relocation programs of the 1950s as "virtually ensuring that intermarriage would steadily result."[38] Ward Churchill has labeled this process "arithmetical genocide." "Obviously involved," he says, "is a sort of 'statistical extermination' whereby the government seeks not only to keep costs associated with its discharge of Indian Affairs at the lowest possible level but to eventually resolve its 'Indian problem' altogether."[39]

It is clear then that white Americans, too, had ideas about the uses to which an imagined process of biological absorption could be put. Nonetheless, it is also clear that the idea resonated differently in the United States than it did in Australia. In particular, the particular multiracial populations of each country directly shaped how indigenous assimilation played out. Native American assimilation policy was, for example, not enacted in a vacuum. Perhaps more than any other time in its history, in the late nineteenth and early twentieth centuries North America played host to more diverse ethnic groups than ever before. More often they were physically distinctive peoples with very different ways of living who did not speak English. The government policies directed at Native Americans were just some of the many ways in which white Americans struggled to come to terms with the multiracial nature of American society during this period. The ideology of assimilation, therefore, cannot be understood except in terms of the racial context in which it was developed: a landscape that included newly freed African Americans and immigrants from Europe and Asia, as well as white people and Native Americans.

American ideas about Native American assimilation must therefore be considered in the context of the history of race relations of the late nineteenth century: Reconstruction and the Jim Crow period in the South, and the significant influx of European immigrants into the nation's cities. At the same time, America's ideas about all interracial relationships had been enshrined in the enormous body of antimiscegenation legislation passed by the majority of states at various times from the early colonial period through the twentieth century. The increasingly popular "science" of eugenics continued to emphasize the importance of controlling interracial relationships. Evident in all these phenomena are two hostile discourses of separation and assimilation directed at the various nonwhite populations of America. As the plight of Native Americans became a focus in the late nineteenth century, there were already two options about the ultimate fate of nonwhite people available that could be utilized by reformers. As we shall see, it was the discourse of cultural assimilation that, in the main, would be directed at Native Americans.

Having recently justified a civil war on the basis of concerns about the humane treatment of African Americans, it is no wonder that some white people in the reunited states were also willing to accept humanitarian ideas in regard to Native Americans. David Wallace Adams argues that several factors—the end of Reconstruction, the closing stages of large-scale Native American military resistance, the corruption of many employees of the Bureau of Indian Affairs, and the sympathy generated by publicity about the plight of several individual Native Americans—culminated in "something approaching a consensus" by the 1880s.[40] This consensus was most loudly expressed by well-educated, middle-class eastern men and women who, guided by the tenets of evangelical Protestantism, moved enthusiastically to lobby for the reform in Native American policy. These reformers formed several important organizations, most notably the Indian Rights Association in 1882 and the Women's National Indian Association in 1883, which had impressive influence over both government policy and public opinion.

Although these reformers argued persuasively about the capacity of the Native American to become civilized, they struggled to overcome the racial divisions that characterized American society. Although African Americans were legally free, white people certainly did not view them as suitable to mix with socially. Jim Crow laws, which officially kept the two races physically separate, and the emergence of the Ku Klux Klan, which ensured that anyone who crossed racial lines would be violently punished, guaranteed that African Americans would remain a separate and oppressed group. Reformers concerned with the "Indian problem" had to work hard to dispel such racist philosophies in their efforts to promote assimilation. They were also, ironically, assisted by the intensity of racial hatred directed at African Americans, whom so many white people saw as somehow "below" Native Americans in the racial hierarchy. At least, they argued, the assimilation of Native Americans was not as radical a notion as the absorption of African Americans into the white population would be.

The significant influx into the country (mostly the North) of immigrants from southern and eastern Europe in the late nineteenth century was met with a very different set of ideas. While seen as not yet equal to the white people who had arrived before them, immigrants were confidently expected to "Americanize" and "assimilate" into the mainstream population. White people did not anticipate that migrants would remain a separate group once they were able to speak English and work hard in factories, shops, and on building sites to realize the "American dream." Instead, in one generation or two, they would be indistinguishable from mainstream Americans, intermarrying and living among white people whose families had been in the country for decades. Reformers often applied this idea to Native Americans in the late nineteenth century.

Just as these ideas were being expressed, English scientist Francis Galton proposed raising the "standard" of humanity by utilizing Darwin's evolutionary process, a concept he eventually called "eugenics." Eugenics aspired to control the genetic quality of the white population by preventing people judged "inferior" from having children. The physically and mentally disabled bore the full brunt of the policies stemming from eugenic ideas, but nonwhite people were also an obvious target. Although Native Americans were seen as racially inferior to white people, the stereotype of the "noble savage" helped to raise their eugenic standing among some white Americans.

Eugenicists did not need to lobby for policies controlling interracial marriage—these had already been in place for decades. In 1913 the secretary of the Committee on Eugenics of the American Genetic Association and director of the Eugenics Record Office, Charles B. Davenport, made the obvious connection between eugenic philosophy and the already extensive anti-interracial marriage legislation and studied the latter at length to discover its uses for the eugenics movement.[41] Laws restricting various kinds of interracial relationships had been passed by forty-one American states, in most cases long before eugenics became popular. These laws dated from 1661, when the Maryland General Assembly passed the first colonial antimiscegenation statute, and were operational until 1967, when the U.S. Supreme Court declared such laws unconstitutional.[42] Created to keep the white race "pure," the laws varied greatly in terms of the restrictions and punishments put in place and the groups targeted. As Nancy Cott has pointed out, however, they targeted only interracial marriages that involved a white participant.[43]

Native Americans were one of the groups least often included in antimiscegenation laws passed across the United States. Only twelve states legislated against white–Native American marriages. Even the Chinese, Japanese, and Filipinos, whose populations were relatively tiny, were targeted by anti-interracial marriage laws more often than were Native Americans.[44] The laws that applied to Native Americans were passed during two periods. They were included in early laws passed during the colonial and early national periods in Maine, Massachusetts, North Carolina, Rhode Island, South Carolina, Tennessee, and Virginia. Many of these states repealed their laws or removed Native Americans from their ambit in the late nineteenth century. Then, during the period of expansion in the West in the mid-nineteenth century, Arizona, Idaho, Nevada, Oregon, and Washington passed laws that applied to Native Americans, many of which were not repealed until the twentieth century.

The antimiscegenation laws passed in western states during the 1860s were a response to the multiracial characteristics of nineteenth-century American society. While Native Americans were included, they were not the main focus. In an era that created the Jim Crow laws, restricting all kinds of contact between racial groups in the South, white people no doubt felt anxious about the growing numbers of newly freed African Americans who traveled to the western states. Western laws did, however, reflect "frontier" anxieties similar to those found in the colonial period, either about a shortage of white women or about violent confrontation between white people and Native Americans. While acknowledging that antimiscegenation laws were created in a vain attempt to keep racial groups enclosed within neat boundaries, historian Peggy Pascoe has also pointed out the relationship of these laws to property. After all, she has argued, legislatures targeted marriage more regularly than casual sexual relationships.[45] Marriage, with its links to respectability, economic status, and property ownership, was far more threatening to racial boundaries than were short-term, casual relationships.

It would be tempting to see the inclusion of Native Americans in antimiscegenation laws as a simple consequence of their status as nonwhite and to infer that when legislators made up laws, they included Native Americans with African Americans and other groups simply for good measure. Indeed, as the century drew to a close, Native Americans continued to lose land at a rapid rate. They were no longer the threat they had been when the laws including them had been passed, and they were mostly segregated on small reservations and suffering from intense poverty. There were few reasons to require them to remain sexually separate, except for those worried about racial "purity." By the end of the

First World War, four of the five states had either repealed their laws or removed Native Americans from their antimiscegenation statutes. At no time was a law ever enacted that exclusively prevented the marriages of white people and Native Americans, and comparatively few states bothered to legislate against such marriages. It seems that white people were less anxious about, and even more accepting of, relationships with Native Americans (as with immigrants) than with people of other cultures such as Asians or African Americans. The essential difference between these groups, it seems, was that Native Americans were seen as weaker and less threatening and as more acceptable candidates for biological absorption. This attitude is reflected in the ideas of some government officials and reformers who saw nothing terrible in the prospect of the biological absorption of Native Americans.

But in the records left behind by the four main bodies who commented on and shaped Native American assimilation policy in the late nineteenth and early twentieth centuries, the Lake Mohonk conference of the Friends of the Indian, the commissioner of Indian affairs, the Board of Indian Commissioners, and the Indian Rights Association, assimilationists talked about assimilation with no allusion to biological or reproductive aspects, envisioning Native Americans becoming "Americanized" in terms of ways of living only. The reports made by the commissioners of Indian affairs to Congress in particular, concerned as they were more with matters of economics and practicality than far-reaching philosophy, rarely even hinted at biological absorption. More often, commissioners such as Francis E. Leupp, who filled the position from 1905 until 1909, believed in "improvement" rather than "transformation."[46] Leupp argued in 1907 that "ethnically [the Indian] will always remain an Indian, with an Indian color, Indian traits of mind, Indian ancestral traditions and the like; and I see nothing to deplore in that.[47]

At the very first meeting of the Lake Mohonk conference in 1883, at which the group outlined its assimilationist program, the means of culturally assimilating Native Americans were at the top of the agenda. Over and over again the participants itemized what was required to prepare the "Indian" for citizenship. They emphasized and reemphasized that education was "essential" or "the only sure road" to the achievement of their goals for Native Americans, advocating both industrial and academic education, day schools, boarding schools, religious instruction, and various practical means designed to force or encourage Native Americans to live in the white way.[48] In its first annual report, the Indian Rights Association directed its efforts toward the extension of all laws of states and territories over reservations, the "wise division of land in severalty," and the question of education, which it saw as "a matter of the highest moment."[49] Indeed, in a later report the organization reiterated that there was "no more vital force in relation to our effort for lifting the Indian into civilized life than that of education."[50]

In 1887 the Dawes Act, shaped by a rhetoric of improvement, citizenship, and education, attempted to turn Native Americans into self-supporting farmers by dividing up and allotting reservation lands. From a legislative perspective, as historians David Smits and Brian Dippie have argued, biological absorption was a side issue to the main thrust of white America's vision of the future of Native Americans.[51]

When compared with Australia in roughly the same period, from the late 1880s to the late 1930s, the United States' relative distaste for biological absorption is thrown into even greater relief. In most instances the politicians, public servants, and anthropologists involved in solving the "Aboriginal problem" were just as cryptic as their American counterparts when they referred to the future. A full explanation was never given about whether they envisioned assimilation being hastened by the births of mixed-descent children who did not physically appear to be indigenous, or whether they simply wanted to teach indigenous people to live in the manner of white people. But compared with the United States, where legislation such as the Dawes Act attempted to turn Native Americans into self-supporting farmers and significant government funds were spent on setting up a comprehensive system of Native American education, Australian meanings of assimilation come into clearer focus. The rhetoric of improvement, citizenship, and education that shaped the Dawes Act (which, it should not be forgotten, caused immeasurable suffering and loss of land to Native Americans) was completely absent from Australian legislation. The legislation passed by each Australian state and colony in the late nineteenth and early twentieth centuries rarely if

2. Tom Torlino (Navajo). In publicity photos designed to promote their ability to convert "savages" into "civilized" Americans, institutions such as Carlisle Indian School focused on achieving an immediate, visible external transformation in one generation, as depicted here, rather than on the biological, cross-generational process advocated in Australia by proponents such as A. O. Neville. From Carlisle Indian Industrial School Student Records, 1879–1918, RG 75, Tom Torlino (Navajo) file. Courtesy of National Archives and Records Administration, Washington DC.

ever mentioned cultural assimilation or put in place policies aimed at educating Aborigines. In addition there is evidence that, as Barry Morris has discovered in rural New South Wales, Aboriginal families who attempted to farm and become self-sufficient (as the Dawes Act encouraged Native Americans to do) were often discouraged and undermined in various ways.[52] Nor did the legislation ever allocate land for Aborigines' own use. There were no treaties equivalent to those signed between Native Americans and white Americans in the United States; instead, the doctrine of terra nullius (which presumed that the land was empty) left Aboriginal people little legal status under the law and certainly much less of a basis from which to claim sovereignty than the Native Americans' admittedly limited position as "domestic, dependent nations."

Perhaps the biggest reasons why this was so was that Australia lacked the federal control of indigenous affairs and the influential and well-organized humanitarian reform movement of the United States. Responses to the "Aboriginal Problem" were consequently more fragmented. The numbers of both nonindigenous and indigenous people were, of course, markedly fewer. Instead of a nationwide policy, beginning in 1869 each colony or state created its own series of legislative acts to control the lives of the Aboriginal people living within its borders in slightly different ways. Few contained measures designed to integrate Aboriginal people immediately into the mainstream, such as the Dawes Act had enacted in the United States. Australian colonial or state governments were allowed to enact their racist policies and adopt a laissez-faire attitude toward Aboriginal education without any intervention from the federal government. The constitution of 1901 had strained to appear "race-blind," and indeed it contained only two explicitly discriminatory clauses. Aborigines would not be counted in the censuses; that is, they would not be counted for the purposes of distribution of electorates for the lower house. Second, the Commonwealth would not be empowered to make laws for Aborigines. The constitution, however, contained no bill of human rights, an ominous omission noted by humanitarians at the time. A settler majority, therefore, could readily make laws that contravened the human rights of the Aboriginal minority.[53] Humanitarian lobbyists in the United Kingdom protested, but settlers needed to pay little attention to the few local Christian, humanitarian voices which, in any case, as historian Henry Reynolds has documented, usually fell on the unsympathetic ears of the general population.[54]

Because it was a British colony, most humanitarianism in Australia was prompted by organizations based in England, such as the Aborigines Protection Society, which was formed in 1837.[55] Humanitarian influence from Britain led to some shocked reports of settler violence that were disseminated both at home and abroad and the appointment of public servants or "protectors" who were charged with shielding Aboriginal people from violent behavior in some colonies in the nineteenth century. Locally organized humanitarian groups, however, which were able to mount a watching brief on the actions of the individual state or colonial governments, did not appear until the 1920s. Even then they were much smaller than those in the United States and had little influence on government policy.[56]

It was not until 1937 that the federal minister for home and territories gathered together officials and administrators to discuss a national policy.[57]

The conference was prompted, according to historian Andrew Markus, by international criticism of Australian policies and by the dawning realization (decades after the United States) that Aborigines were stubbornly refusing to become extinct as expected.[58] During the proceedings, however, these concerns were masked by the benevolent theme of "Aboriginal Welfare." Policies aimed at teaching Aborigines to become "civilized" were discussed. They were overshadowed, however, by anxieties about the threat posed to white Australia by the growing mixed descent population in the Northern Territory and Western Australia. Four small humanitarian organizations attempted to contribute to the 1937 conference. In the end their submissions were considered, but their representatives were not permitted to attend, and the conference resolved that in future they would not be asked to contribute. This decision was made to prevent "warring factions" from jeopardizing the "unanimity" of the government departments. Or, as the chief protector of Queensland put it more openly: "If we extended the scope of representation, the Conference would be swamped with arm-chair experts who would take control of proceedings out of the hands of the representatives of responsible departments."[59]

In contrast with the United States, Australia had no influential reform movement. In the United States, it seems, the larger white population with a longer history of settlement developed a significant internal humanitarian movement that consisted of men and women who had ideas based on the equality of all humankind derived from the Enlightenment and evangelical Christianity. American humanitarianism had a significant effect on the government's actions. Instead, financial matters were a priority for Australian politicians in charge of Aboriginal affairs, and in their attempts to be reelected they appear to have acted with the knowledge that the white Australian population had little sympathy for the plight of Aboriginal people. Although there were scattered individuals, clergy, and missionaries who attempted to spread humanitarian sentiments and to support attempts by British organizations to impose such ideas on Australian colonists, white Australian humanitarians never managed to organize a critical mass sufficient to exert a real influence on government. These differences between the United States and Australia impacted sig-

nificantly on how the ideology of assimilation framed the rare phenomenon of marriage between white women and indigenous men.

The popularity of biological absorption in Australia is more evident
in some states or colonies than others, but except in Queensland, it was
an assumption underlying all Australian state legislation pertaining to
Aboriginal people. In Western Australia and the Northern Territory, chief
protectors were empowered by legislation to control whom Aboriginal
women could marry, and they did so with growing emphasis on encouraging biological absorption. In nearly all Australian states, children of
mixed descent were targeted for removal and absorption into mainstream Australian society throughout the twentieth century. Although
white Australians engaged in the rhetoric of cultural assimilation, they
provided few practical measures to help Aboriginal people to become
self-supporting. For Aborigines in the late nineteenth and early twentieth
centuries, opportunities to become educated were few and the chances
of owning a piece of land almost nil. The goal of biological absorption
was the sinister subtext of the majority of the Australian government
policies enacted in the name of cultural assimilation.

Two crucial aspects of policies of cultural assimilation were lacking in
Australia. As John Chesterman and Brian Galligan have argued in their
comprehensive history of Aboriginal citizenship in Australia, it was not
until after the Second World War that the states began to confer on Aborigine people what is the political basis of cultural assimilation—equal citizenship.[60] Earlier legislation had denied Aborigines equal citizenship
rights in ways that hardly encouraged cultural assimilation: keeping
them separate on reserves, restricting their employment, and limiting
their movement around the country. The Australian National Dictionary
records that one of the earliest uses of the word assimilation occurred
in a discussion of the integration of Aborigine people into mainstream
society that took place in federal parliament in 1951.[61] Although my own
research has discovered earlier uses of the word by the New South Wales
Board for the Protection of Aborigines in the late 1930s and early 1940s,
this is telling linguistic evidence that it was not until the second half of
the twentieth century that a widespread policy of cultural assimilation
of Aboriginal people became prevalent in Australia.[62]

Just as the entire racial landscape is seen to have influenced white ideas about Native American assimilation in the United States, the different racial groups that existed in Australia and the attitudes toward them can be seen to have a considerable influence in shaping Aboriginal policy. Unlike the almost open-door policy on immigration that resulted in a large, multiethnic population in the United States, white Australians' immigration policy attempted to keep their largely British population racially homogeneous. Early concerns about the numbers of Asian immigrants (characterized as the "yellow peril") in the late nineteenth century consolidated as Australia became a federated nation in 1901. The first government in power after Federation, led by Edmund Barton, placed great emphasis on restricting the immigration of nonwhite groups. Indeed, as eminent Australian historian Manning Clark has argued, "White Australia" was "the first principle by which the Commonwealth was to be administered and guided."[63] In its first year the Commonwealth of Australia put in place the Immigration Restriction Act of 1901, which combined the various measures the colonies had already put in place into a system of restrictions based on a hierarchy of desirable (European, especially British) and undesirable (Asians, Indians, Pacific Islanders) immigrants. The goal of a "White Australia" was openly stated.[64] What was rarely if ever mentioned in the debates surrounding this policy was the fact that Australia was not completely "white" to begin with—instead, significant populations of Aborigines lived in the northern and western states, including growing numbers of people of mixed descent. The ideology of biological absorption helped Australian society reconcile the existence of these populations with the objective of a "White Australia."

These differences between the two nations had far-reaching implications for interracial marriages between white women and indigenous men. The American emphasis on cultural assimilation led to more rigorous efforts to provide schools in which to educate Native Americans, some offering a level of education high enough to allow entry into college or institutions of higher learning. Consequently, some Native American men were able to make themselves into eligible partners for middle-class white women by earning higher degrees and undertaking professional work. Although these opportunities were in no way available to the majority of Native Americans who were taught little more than manual skills and the essentials of reading and writing English, they represent the quintessence of the reformers' aims. Thus they are the focus of my American chapters. This aspect of assimilation was missing from Australian policies until the 1960s or even later, when the first Aboriginal students began to attend Australian universities. Aborigines received few if any opportunities to gain more than the rudiments of a European-style education; Australian policies left little room for social mobility through education or, indeed, through interracial marriage.

Thus the underlying comparative argument of this book explains why there were no equivalents of middle-class marriages like that of Elaine and Charles Eastman, with whom I begin this book, in Australia. The predominant focus in the United States on cultural assimilation created a system of assimilation that allowed some Native Americans to obtain a kind of middle-class status. The first half of this book describes some of these marriages and how they fitted into the ideology of the day. In Australia, the emphasis on biological absorption as the principal means of assimilation left most Aborigines on the boundaries of the working class. The second half of this book explains how white women who married Aboriginal men were, in the main, marginalized. I have framed this study between an important date in United States assimilation policy (the 1887 Dawes Act) and the defining moment of Australian assimilation policy (the 1937 Aboriginal Welfare conference), but readers will find a mismatch of the time frame studied in each nation and moments when the text moves outside this span of years. This is a reflection of the different periods in which each country put into practice its own version of assimilation. While each nation had a kind of legislative beginning that corresponds with the other quite neatly (in 1886 the Australian state of Victoria put in place an act that is arguably the earliest attempt at biological absorption; in 1887 the Dawes Act brought the philosophy of cultural assimilation into legislative reality), an analogous endpoint is not so easily found. While in the United States the Indian Reorganization (Wheeler-Howard) Act of 1934 reversed the assimilation policies put in place by the Dawes Act, in Australia in the 1930s absorptionist policies in the northern and western states were at their height.

It became increasingly clear during my research that slightly different versions of assimilation ideology were maintained not just at a broad national level but also at a more local level by individuals or groups centered around a specific area. Marriages between white women and indigenous men were treated very differently according to the diverse assimilation policies that can be found not just on a national level but also in smaller and more specific geographical contexts. In order to highlight this important aspect of assimilation, my analysis at times moves broadly across my time period, drawing on national comparisons to highlight the particularities of each nation, and at other times focuses closely on one location at one particular time. This history of assimilation has three levels—the wide view of government policy at the federal and state levels, a slightly tapered look at specific locations in particular times, and the narrow perspective afforded by attention to the lives of individuals. It seems impossible to examine the links between interracial marriage and assimilation policy without such a multilayered approach.

Chapter 1 describes three relationships between educated, middle-class white women and Native American men that were formed at the Hampton Normal and Agricultural Institute when it enrolled Native American students between 1878 and 1923 and the way in which these unions were the product of the nationwide methods of cultural assimilation put in place by humanitarians to solve the "Indian problem." Chapter 2 focuses on the complex ways in which assimilation and interracial marriages of male students was envisioned and strategized by the Carlisle Indian School, using alumni questionnaires that provided information about the early 1910s. Chapter 3 examines a group of "leaders and examples" created by U.S. assimilation policy, a group that had no equivalent in Australia. In particular, it details the lives of two high-profile Native American men, Carlos Montezuma and Charles Eastman, who married white women in 1913 and 1891, respectively, and what marriage meant to their public and private lives. In chapter 4 I examine the life of one extraordinary white woman, Elaine Goodale Eastman (1863–1953), to uncover the vision of assimilation that accompanied her decision to marry a Dakota man.

In chapter 5, I turn to Australia and explore the substandard Aboriginal education system that operated during the years this book encompasses and, in stark contrast to Hampton and Carlisle, offered no opportunities for Aboriginal people as a stepping-stone to higher status within settler society. In chapter 6, I examine Australian attitudes toward interracial marriages of white women and Aborigines at a local level in the colony of Victoria between 1886 and 1910, and in chapter 7, I explore how mainstream Australia's responses to three marriages between white women and Aborigines that took place in 1898, 1907, and 1914 situated them firmly outside the boundaries of normality, repositioning the women outside the normal bounds of femininity.

In the concluding chapters I consider the significance of the comparative differences thrown up in my case studies in separate discussions of the assimilation policies of the United States and Australia. These final chapters demonstrate that far from being a history of exceptions that prove the rule, this discussion of the experiences of white women married to indigenous men reveals critical differences in the assimilation policies of two settler societies, differences that allow us to better understand the history of the displacement of indigenous people in each context.

What assimilation meant exactly to the individuals who lived in Australia and North American during this period is impossibly elusive. No doubt its meaning shifted according to personal opinion and experience, locale, political affiliation, religiosity, ethnic background, and time. But at its heart, assimilation was a solution to the problem of the presence of the original owners of the North American and Australian continents. It was one of two ways whites could imagine the future. Unable to envision a time when they might not be completely dominant, when they might have to share, to learn from another culture, to stand aside rather than overrun, they saw indigenous culture as either dying out or being absorbed. Thus assimilation was an end of indigenous culture as a separate entity. How this ending would take place, whether it be through changes in people's lifestyles, or in the color of their skin, or both, was often ill-defined, and I suspect that many people thought that the two versions went together, even if they did not say so out loud. After all, the average white American or Australian could not have been completely unaware of the interracial mixing taking place, even as they put together policies and built schools that espoused a different kind of solution. These ideas were linked together by invisible ties of half-thought-through logic, the kind that suffices when the hazy possibilities of the future are the topic at hand.

Therefore, although this book describes a plethora of particular versions of assimilation, from those proposed at a federal governmental level, to the particular ideas of the white mother of six mixed-descent children, at the back of every policy proposed and every answer elucidated was the idea of cultural annihilation. When I use the word assimilation, I use it to refer to a group of ideas that had some form of transformation at their heart, transformation of indigenous people into whites. What I don't mean when I use the word assimilated are the characteristics of any individual—I hesitate to designate any of the people discussed in this book as "assimilated." While some were certainly acculturated, in the sense that they had learned much about white culture, there is little evidence, and certainly no way of knowing, that they had lost their connection with their indigenous identity. Thus assimilation in this book refers to the ideas and imaginings of whites only, not the experiences or attributes of an individual personality.

Exploring interracial marriage is an enterprise fraught with the potential of making ill-informed judgments about other people's personal lives. The topic does not have the distance from intimate detail that many historical subjects enjoy, and I am aware of the presumptuousness of making inferences about members of indigenous communities to which I do not belong. This is nevertheless a history of personal relationships, an account of people who willingly and unwillingly on some level "took assimilation to heart." I hope I have done them justice.

1. Native American Education and Marriages at Hampton Institute

Samuel Chapman Armstrong founded Hampton Normal and Agricultural Institute in Virginia in 1868 to instruct newly freed African American
children according to an ideology ruled by three principles: the "gospel
of work," "the demand of unselfish love," and the doctrine of Protestant
Christianity.[1] Although Armstrong had never intended the school to
cater to any group other than ex-slaves and their children, a decade later
Richard Pratt, a U.S. Army officer with a burgeoning interest in Native
American reform, persuaded him to change his philosophy. Hampton
was thus the first eastern boarding school to accept Native American
students and was an early example of the application of reformers' ideas
about Native American assimilation and education.

Scholars have examined the crucial part that boarding schools played
in the coercive cultural assimilationist program run by the U.S. government in the late nineteenth and early twentieth centuries. Procedures
such as haircutting, renaming, forbidding students to speak their language or practice their religions, military-style discipline, and instruction in reading, writing, and white methods of farming have all been
identified as tools with which reformers taught Native American children the white way of life at institutions far from their homes and communities. One aspect of boarding school education, however, has not
yet been examined: the importance placed by white authorities on students' choice of spouse.

The history of Hampton Institute offers an especially valuable point
from which to examine attitudes toward Native American interracial

marriage during this period and the ways in which these marriages operated in an ethnically diverse and assimilationist context. Not only did members of three cultural groups mingle on the Hampton campus, but it was also the site of a number of interracial relationships between students and, most remarkably, of two marriages and an engagement between white teachers and Native American men. These three unusual unions occurred despite Virginia's long history of strong social and legal restrictions on racial "commingling," especially between white women and black men.[2] It is intriguing to ask exactly which aspects of the environment at Hampton Institute allowed these interactions. The answer lies far beyond the boundaries of the school in the assimilation policy vaunted by American humanitarian reformers and the importance they placed on the spouse chosen by Native Americans who had been educated by white assimilationists.

Hampton did not see these relationships as conduits of the loss of indigenous identity through biological absorption. Rather the school's tolerant reaction to marriages of white women and Native American students was the result of the emphasis on cultural assimilation that defined this period in the United States, an emphasis that began in part on Hampton's campus. The first half of this chapter will describe how ideas about assimilation at a local level were shaped by the multiracial context in which they were formed. The relationships of middle-class white women and educated Native American men at Hampton Institute, on whom this chapter focuses, cannot be understood without paying attention to the school's tri-racial population. The second half of the chapter traces the development of particular educational policies that led to the possibility of relationships between middle-class, educated white women and educated Native American men, a combination that had, I believe, no equivalent in Australia.

Twenty-two Years' Work of the Hampton Normal and Agricultural Institute, a book published in 1893 and designed to publicize the school by describing the successes of former students, recorded a number of interracial marriages. Along with the marriages of at least eight female Native American students to white men, it documented six marriages of male Native American students to white women. The latter included 1889 valedictorian Thomas Sloan (Omaha), who declined admission to Yale Law School in order to return to the West to read law with another Omaha lawyer called Hiram Chase. Just before being admitted to the bar, he married "a young white woman from St. Louis."[3] Sloan was an active member of the Society of American Indians (SAI) and a successful lawyer. George Bushotter (Oteri), a Lakota, became engaged to a white woman while employed by the Bureau of Ethnology to assist a white ethnologist in a study of what proud school administrators called the "Tetonwan dialect of the Dakota language." Other students who married white women included Alexander Peters (Peyan), Menominee, Thomas Miles (Much-u-ter-wi-shek), Sauk and Fox (of whom it was reported that "both he and his wife, particularly the latter, have tremendous color prejudice, and seem to regret his Hampton education" because of the proximity to African Americans), Wesley Huntsman, presumably a Lakota from the Lower Brulé reservation (whose wife was reportedly "a great hustler, a foreigner"), and Frank Gautier, a Menominee from the Green Bay Agency in Wisconsin. The booklet touted all these men as Hampton "success stories" with "pleasant" homes and acceptable professions and expressed no shock or disapproval of their choice of marriage partner.[4]

The three instances in which female teachers married or became engaged to Native American men offer a far more telling indication of a level of toleration at Hampton of this form of marriage. Most Hampton instructors were single and missionary-oriented, believing in the inherent equality of all peoples under God, a characteristic which must surely have been fundamental to a decision to marry a Native American man.[5] Their spouses also had important traits in common. The three teachers selected men who had proved themselves not only outwardly to have absorbed white culture but to have become successful within it. Elaine Goodale, who taught at Hampton between 1883 and 1886, married Charles Eastman, a Dakota employed at Pine Ridge, South Dakota, as an agency physician. Eastman had not been a student at Hampton, but he had studied at missionary schools in the West, then at Dartmouth College and Boston University.[6] The Eastmans' marriage will be fully explored in chapters 3 and 4. Rebecca Pond, who was a teacher during the First World War, in 1919 married George Owl, a Cherokee (Eastern Band) who had fought overseas

3. Elaine Goodale (standing) when she was a teacher at Hampton, with colleague Jane E. Davis. Courtesy of Hampton University Museum Archives.

in the U.S. Army. Finally, Caroline Andrus, who held the position of "Indian correspondent" in the records office, was engaged to William Jones (Megasiawa; Black Eagle) until his death in 1909. Jones, a Fox student from the Sauk and Fox reservation, earned a PhD in anthropology under Franz Boas at Columbia University.

Students and teachers at Hampton Institute were not allowed to mix socially. Nevertheless, after arriving at Hampton in 1911, George Owl remembered cleverly opting to work for his keep in the teachers' garden so that he could become acquainted with faculty member Rebecca Pond, a member of the Heinz-Pond cosmetic family. While he was a student, however, Owl and Pond developed nothing more than an "interested friendship." In December 1917 the Hampton school newspaper, the *Southern Workman*, reported that Owl, who would have been a member of the graduating class that year, had been drafted and had reported to a training camp in South Carolina in early October. The paper went on to quote extracts from some of Owl's letters, in which he enthused about

4. The Owl Family. Courtesy of Hampton University Museum Archives.

army life: "You cannot realize how much I enjoy staying here. I have heard talk of the army camps, but I don't want to hear any more, for Camp Jackson is the most wonderful place I have seen so far."

During the First World War the Hampton press proudly kept track of the contributions of its students to the war effort. In January 1918, Owl was reported as one of seventeen Native American students in the services, and by May 1919 the *Southern Workman* had received letters from him from abroad. Soon after his return, Owl and Pond were married. In its column on "Graduates and Ex-Students," the *Southern Workman* reported, "On October 6, George A. Owl, a former Cherokee student, was married to Miss Rebecca Pond at the home of the bride in Washington, Connecticut. Mr. Owl has recently returned from overseas where he remained for over a year with the 'Wildcat Division.'" A little less than a year later the paper announced the birth of a son. Having played baseball successfully at Hampton, Owl was recruited by the American Brass Company for its company team. The couple made their home in Connecticut until Rebecca died giving birth to their third child. Dividing the children among his and Rebecca's families, George struggled to rebuild his life, hampered by a drinking problem. He returned to his family in Oklahoma and began making money taking sightseers on tours. He remarried, this time to a white anthropologist who had come to study the Cherokee language in 1942. He also joined Alcoholics Anonymous and formed a chapter near his home in Oklahoma. He was the first vice president of the Cherokee Chamber of Commerce and a member of the executive council of the National Congress of American Indians.[7]

Caroline Andrus dedicated a large part of her life to Hampton. From 1895 until her retirement in 1922 she maintained the school's extensive records of its Native American students. William A. Jones was the son of a Fox man of mixed descent and an English-Welsh woman. According to some sources, his father could not get the consent of his mother's parents to marry until he proved that he could support her "as a white woman, in a good home." Jones was raised traditionally by his Fox grandmother before enrolling in Hampton after a brief stint as a cowboy. After entering Hampton in 1889 when he was eighteen years old, Jones at first refused to convert to Christianity. Later, when he did so, he reportedly took it very seriously, believing that it meant giving up a traditional life in the West. He declined the honor of giving the valedictory speech when he graduated in 1892, arguing that he was more white than Native American. Jones went on to Phillips College at Andover, earned his baccalaureate degree at Harvard, and then undertook postgraduate work at Columbia University, gaining his doctorate in anthropology in 1904.[8] Franz Boas believed Jones would become *"the* man whom our Government—*i.e.,* the Smithsonian Institution—will need for the study of Algonquin languages."[9] On a visit back to Hampton, probably during his doctoral candidacy, he became engaged to Caroline Andrus. Jones apparently delayed the marriage until he was more financially stable. Unfortunately, before they could be married, Jones was killed in 1909 while doing research in the Philippines.[10] Andrus remained at Hampton, unmarried, until her retirement. She then became joint owner, with another former member of Hampton's staff, Dorothy Averill, of a "delightful tea house and gift shop" called the Magnolia Tree in the township of Hampton. Cora Folsom, Andrus's predecessor in the Indian Records Office, also made her home there.[11]

In all probability, George Owl's status as a war veteran, Charles Eastman's medical degree, and William Jones's doctorate were qualifications

5. William A. Jones, "Hampton's most illustrious Indian graduate." Courtesy of Hampton University Museum Archives.

that made them acceptable marriage partners for white women. At Hampton, the toleration of these couplings demonstrates that marriages with white people could be seen as evidence that Native Americans had successfully assimilated, rather than, as might perhaps be expected, as evidence that the white spouses had somehow slipped out of acceptable white society. This is not to say that there were no anxieties about interracial relationships at Hampton. But it was not relationships between white women and successful Native American students that concerned Hampton's staff. Instead, white anxieties at Hampton appear to have centered more on sexual relationships between African Americans and Native Americans than on those between white people and other races. Thus it is impossible to understand how marriages of white women and Native American men were understood at Hampton without paying attention to the particular racial makeup of the students and faculty.

Late Victorian attitudes toward active sexuality before marriage would have caused intense anxiety at any coeducational institution operating during this period, but at a school where different races boarded togeth-er, the prospect of miscegenation was bound to cause particular conster-nation. Armstrong was constantly forced to defend his coeducational policy from the numerous attacks of various philanthropic groups and government bodies upset about the proximity of young men and wom-en of different ethnicities at the school. He had been aware of the poten-tial problems caused by mixing races and sexes from the beginning of the Native American program, and he advised Pratt not to "go in strong about girls" when he wrote to the commissioner of Indian affairs about the proposed "Hampton scheme" in 1878.[12] In 1888 the school under-went an investigation by the Board of Indian Commissioners to examine allegations of cruelty, poor health among students, and negative conse-quences of the inclusion of both African and Native Americans on cam-pus.[13] Hampton again faced criticism in 1899 over the latter issue, and H. B. Frissell, the principal after Armstrong's death in 1893, begged the Board of Indian Commissioners for support.[14]

Despite Hampton's efforts to deny the accusations, Congress failed to include funding for Hampton in the 1912 bill dividing up the gov-ernment appropriation for Native American education.[15] Although this decision was made in the context of an increasing lack of faith in the boarding school system, the *Southern Workman* suggested that the close proximity of the races was "perhaps the chief reason" for the loss of the appropriation. The magazine described the decision as based on a "view [that] loses sight of the benefits which come to both races from mingling together upon terms that secure both a better mutual understanding and mutual regard."[16] The school administration argued in vain that "so far as [is] known no interracial marriage has ever resulted from the bring-ing together of these races at Hampton, and an important demonstration has been made of the possibility of harmonious co-operation between them."[17] The government's contribution of $167 for each student cov-ered board, tuition, and some incidental costs. Scholarships from phil-anthropic individuals and the students' own labor made up the differ-ence.[18] The loss of the appropriation meant that the numbers of Native American students declined slowly but significantly until the last of them graduated in 1923.

Although it is difficult to make assumptions about their prevalence, some sexualized expressions of interest across racial lines occurred among the students at Hampton despite the school's frequent protestations to the contrary. Early on in the experiment of educating both racial groups on one campus, anxieties were not so intense, as is evidenced by the light-hearted treatment of interracial sexual contact in the school newspaper. In 1879 the *Southern Workman* recorded that "the Indian boys are look-ing favorably upon the colored girls of the school. . . . When asked if he would take an educated squaw or one of the Indian women at home to [be his] wife, [one boy] replied, 'No; I marry a colored girl; she will teach me good English.'" Another boy reportedly planned to ask his father for six horses to trade for an African American wife.[19] In 1888 Hampton published its self-congratulatory *Ten Years' Work for Indians at Hampton Institute*, in which Armstrong claimed that there had not been "a single case of immorality, between the students of both races and of both sex-es."[20] That same year, however, the discipline books and faculty minutes recorded the dismissal or reprimand of three Native American girls and three African American boys for meeting late at night and writing each other letters. A faculty meeting held on August 13, 1888, ordered further investigation of allegations that a Native American girl had left her dor-mitory at night in the company of an African American boy. An exten-sive, two-day examination revealed that the "midnight strolls" involved three couples. All were either reprimanded or expelled.[21] Historian Joseph Tingey has described one instance in which the school wrote to an Afri-can American male student in 1911 suggesting that he not return to the school after the administration had discovered his relationship with a female Native American student. Tingey also details a number of other relationships recounted by alumni many years later in interviews.[22]

In 1919 Caroline Andrus reported that the declining number of Native American students was in part due to "knowledge of the . . . flirtations, and three marriages between the two races, [which] has spread far and wide, preventing some parents from sending their children here."[23] In 1923 she hinted in a letter that part of her reason for leaving the school was the possibility of relationships between Native American girls and Afri-can American men, and she mentioned gossip caused by three interracial marriages of Hampton students.[24] Files on former students record that at least two Native American women married African American men after they left the school.[25] Remarkably, Richard Pratt claimed in a letter to SAI president Arthur C. Parker that in the time he spent at Hampton (presumably in the late 1870s) he had had many "warm discussions" with Armstrong, who was "in favor of amalgamating the negroes and Indians and letting the Indians of this country be lost in the negro race."[26] Unkindly, Pratt intimated that Armstrong held such views as a means to "perpetuate [his] business"—that is, to make his biracial school more acceptable, or perhaps even to create more students for his school. If Armstrong did have this opinion, he was careful to keep it out of the public record.

Although Hampton staff certainly did not encourage relationships (licit or illicit) between students of different races, they did not discourage relationships between students of the same racial background. One of the main fears of the administration was that Native American students who returned to the reservation would slough off "civilization" and resume their traditional lifestyle. The staff at Hampton felt that this was especially likely to occur when students returned home and married partners who had not been similarly educated. In 1878, the year in which the first Native American students arrived at Hampton, Armstrong argued that the "co-education of the sexes . . . is indispensable to . . . true civilizing work."[27] Cora Folsom wrote in 1893 that the "first, and generally the severest test of character the returned student has to meet is in regard to marriage and the public sentiment of the less advanced Indians in regard to it."[28] Armstrong put it more strongly, highlighting the school's need to recruit more young women "to offset the young men, for relapse was inevitable whilst they return home to mate themselves with savages."[29] An equally difficult problem, according to the annual report of 1884, was that of former female students being "burdened with a savage and cruel husband, [causing the] further development of the educated Indian girl in Christian and civilized ways . . . [to] be painfully slow, if not impossible."[30] In one of Armstrong's many defenses of his coeducational policy, he argued that, for his African American students, "Mingling in recitations, at meals, in social intercourse, always under reasonable direction and restraint is good for both [sexes] . . . the freedom we have allowed . . . has resulted in many well and wisely mated pairs."[31]

Hampton gave effect to its founder's feelings that the family was the most important "unit of Christian civilization" by instituting a special program for married couples in 1882. Two years later, Richard Pratt, who had left Hampton to establish his own school in 1879, told the annual Lake Mohonk gathering of white reformers interested in the plight of Native Americans that the program for married couples had been started because "the eternal 'go-back' is the calamity. . . . If a boy wants to marry he must take a savage girl, or an educated girl has to mate with a savage boy."[32] Small numbers of specially selected married couples received cottages on Hampton's campus, where they combined family life, academic classes, and manual training. After both husband and wife had been "advanced," the couples were meant to return to the reservation to become exemplars to their community. Hampton ran the scheme on a small scale, but it was widely discussed by reformers. The experiment ended in 1894 when Congress prohibited Native Americans over eighteen years from attending eastern schools, presumably because they no longer wished to give financial support to students who were old enough to earn their own living.[33]

Government officials and reformers shared these concerns about the marriage partners of educated and at least partially acculturated students. In 1886 the commissioner of Indian affairs, John D. C. Atkins, recommended that Congress should offer financial incentives to boarding school graduates who married one another.[34] In the same year, Byron M. Cutcheon, a member of the U.S. House of Representatives, wrote to Pratt to suggest that "marriage between the educated Indians . . . should be encouraged, but they should be grouped into little communities where they could help each other."[35] In 1885, the well-known reformer and president of the Lake Mohonk conference, Dr. Lyman Abbott, used the issue to argue against the reservation system. If, Abbott argued, "you educate an Indian boy and send him back to the Indian Territory," then he is doomed to bachelorhood. Racial prejudice meant that "he must not find a wife [in the East], because that would be 'intermingling' with the American population," but he was no longer a suitable husband for an uneducated Indian woman, who would "look with as natural disgust upon a beaver hat as he would upon a squaw's blanket."[36] Even the conservative Indian Rights Association argued in its annual report for 1888 that "much of the work which the Government is doing educating the boys will be necessarily undone by their subsequent marriages with wild, untrained Indian girls."[37]

While Hampton was defending itself against accusations of immoral episodes caused by the mixing of races and sexes on its campus, it was at the same time concerned with encouraging its students to mingle and marry, albeit with guidelines. Alice M. Bacon, a teacher at Hampton, described the surprise many visitors felt when observing the "easy way" that male and female students ate, recited, studied, and socialized together. This behavior, she said, was not restrained or discouraged.[38] Bacon's account, however, published in one of the many reports designed to justify and advertise the school, should be read with a certain amount of skepticism. For example, the reports of the six students who were punished for their interracial relationship mention a guard patrolling the girls' dormitory throughout the night.[39] It seems, nevertheless, that social evenings and various other opportunities permitted boys and girls of the same racial background to become acquainted.

According to historian Donal F. Lindsey, Armstrong had been "'forced to the conclusion . . . that only by encouraging, if not arranging [Indian marriages] can we save our work for that race.'" Lindsey has argued that Hampton faculty and staff actively promoted most of the marriages among the Native American students.[40] The annual report in 1888 described "a tradition at Hampton that the first thing a new boy buys is an umbrella; not because the climate is particularly damp, but because on rainy days the boys have the privilege of escorting their especial friends to and from school."[41] The Native American student newspaper, *Talks and Thoughts*, was also not shy about hinting at the romantic life of students. The March 1887 issue gossiped that "our violinist who is lonesome is learning to play 'The Girl I Left Behind Me,'" while the July 1887 edition reported, "The girls write pleasant letters telling of the good people they are with, long descriptions of their rooms, of a new apron that looks 'too pretty for anything,' of some of the boys coming to see them."[42] In August 1888 the paper described summer evenings on which boys and girls were allowed to walk and talk together on the green usually reserved for female students in front of Virginia Hall.[43]

These social occasions were part of the program of cultural assimilation, as was nearly every activity run by the school. To the Victorian mind, a racial group's relative level of civilization could be measured by its treatment of women. This belief was largely responsible for Hampton's decision to enroll female students, as the school administrators felt that the presence of women in the student body would encourage proper behavior among male Native American pupils. Armstrong wrote in 1881 that male Native American students came to Hampton with "the traditional ideas of the inferiority and insignificance of women, but they grow to a spirit of courtesy and chivalry towards their teachers, and to some extent towards the girls of their own race."[44] In 1892, under a heading of "moral and religious work," the annual report explained that "when the Indians first came to us, in order to give the boys that respect for the girls in which they were somewhat deficient, upon their arrival . . . the girls were allowed to ride to the School while the boys walked, a reversal of their former experiences. Thus the first lesson was given them in the respect due to the weaker sex."[45] As Native American girls learned the domestic tasks of late Victorian womanhood, and Native American boys received instruction in the patronizing attitude shown to women by late Victorian men, both sexes were receiving a subtle education in Victorian gender roles and courtship rituals.[46]

Hampton painstakingly kept student records that, mainly for publicity purposes, noted in detail the successes or failures of former Native American students. Cora Folsom and Caroline Andrus collected information about former students by mail and during western trips taken by them and by members of the faculty. Folsom even developed a five-point scale by which returned students could be graded from "bad" to "excellent." The latter, Folsom wrote in 1888, were those "whose influence [was] by nature and circumstance very strongly for good." Those determined to be "good" lived "civilized, Christian lives," while those rated "fair" meant "to do well but . . . [did] not at all times exert a good influence." Those recorded as "poor" were "shiftless" and "fickle," and those designated "bad" were either sexually promiscuous or criminal.[47] Hampton used Folsom's statistics extensively in its annual reports to Congress to contradict those who argued that students of eastern boarding schools only "returned to the blanket" at the end of their education.

In their reports, Folsom and Andrus carefully recorded in many cases whether the spouse of an ex-Hampton student had also been a student of Hampton or Carlisle Indian School in Pennsylvania, whether he or she was white, or simply whether that person was, for example, an "excellent young man."[48]

Hampton Institute's interest in the romantic relationships of its students helps provide the context in which three white women teachers took the unusual step of agreeing to marry Native American men. The school created an environment that emphasized the importance of marriage to a student's later "success" in living up to white people's expectations. These three cases represent a logical if surprising progression of such thinking whereby the marriage of a Native American to a white person came to indicate advanced assimilation. It appears that, once converted to Christianity and educated in white culture, Native American men were not unthinkable marriage partners for white women, and those charged with their "civilization" could see their marriages as indications of successful acculturation.

Thus we have seen one element of cultural assimilation policy in the late nineteenth century that could lead to the marriages of white women and Native American men—the emphasis on marriage as a significant indicator of "civilization." But there was another aspect of assimilation policy crucial to explaining why *middle-class* white women like Elaine Goodale, Rebecca Pond, and Caroline Andrus would consider marrying Native Americans. This was the emphasis on education.

In the United States, the idea that Native Americans could be "saved" by the abandonment of their traditional ways of living had been espoused by Christian missionaries across the globe from their earliest ventures toward the conversion of the Mexican world. But the general public rarely shared this idea, seeing Native Americans as "savages" who would probably die out before long. After the Civil War, though, the growing popularity of abolitionist sentiment made the time right for a change in views, and in 1879 a series of events had tipped the scales firmly in favor of a more humanitarian approach to Native American affairs. A Ponca man called Standing Bear and a small band of followers escaped from Indian Territory and began the long walk back to their traditional lands in Dakota Territory in order to bury Standing Bear's only son. They were soon arrested by the army and detained at Fort Omaha, Nebraska. The editor of the *Omaha Herald*, Thomas Henry Tibbles, seized upon Standing Bear's plight and organized an immensely successful speaking tour of the East Coast. In traditional clothing, Standing Bear would slowly tell in the Ponca language of the wrongs done to his people. Two young, acculturated boarding school graduates, siblings Susette and Joseph La Flesche, translated his speech. The tour's most successful stop was in Boston, where five hundred Bostonians formed the Boston Indian Citizenship Committee, one of a number of associations established at this time to lobby the government for what they saw as "progress."[49] These reformers, familiar with the philosophies and tactics of the abolitionist movement, believed that the answer to the "Indian problem" lay in Native American citizenship, education, and assimilation and an end to the reservation system.

The establishment of Native American reform organizations such as the Boston Indian Citizenship Committee, the Indian Rights Association, and the Women's National Indian Association heralded a new phase in the development of ideas about the future of the indigenous peoples of North America. As the organizations grew in numbers, they became powerful enough to influence not only popular opinion but also government policy. These reformers found a way of forcing even those Americans dismissive of humanitarianism to come to terms with the disturbing fact that Native Americans were showing no signs of perishing. They began to espouse policies based on the ideology of assimilation, by which Native American people would be firmly encouraged to become self-supporting, arguing that the government had made a mistake when it created reservations on which Native Americans lived segregated from the white population, often continuing their traditional ways of life. Instead, they began to advocate the breaking up of the reservations into personal allotments and the "mingling" of Native Americans with the white population. This, they argued, would cause them to begin acting like white farmers, prevent them from sharing communal resources, and stop them from being such a troublesome financial burden to the government. Politicians were convinced by these arguments. In

1887 Congress passed the General Allotment Act, or Dawes Act, which divided the reservations into individual allotments of land.

The idea of assimilation espoused by these groups and embodied in the Dawes Act had three aspects. First, Native Americans were to be Christianized: the numerous missionaries who had worked among Native Americans since North America was first colonized had begun this process. Second, they were to be educated in the language and culture of the colonizers. Attempts to begin this mammoth task had begun in the early 1870s and were now given solid governmental support. Finally, assimilation had a political and economic foundation. The Dawes Act attempted to dissolve tribal authority by introducing the concept of private property to Native Americans. The act divided reservation lands into individually owned blocks, 160 acres for the heads of families and smaller blocks for other individuals. The land was held in trust by the government for twenty-five years, and the recipients of allotments were granted American citizenship. Land that was left over from this process became available for purchase by white settlers.

Of all the many aspects of the assimilation project, in the minds of humanitarian reformers and government officials, education was to play a crucial role. Not only would education hasten the cultural evolution of Native Americans, allowing them to leap from "savagery" to "civilization" in a single generation, but it also made economic sense. As Samuel Chapman Armstrong argued bluntly at a meeting of the American Missionary Association in 1881: "The Indian question is this: education . . . or extermination. But at least one white man must fall for every Indian who is shot, and it takes as much money to kill one red man as it would to train a hundred of their children in civilized ways. To educate is at least economy."[50] Only through education and cultural assimilation could Native Americans, many believed, be inculcated with the basic knowledge, the desire for material property, and the capacity for hard work necessary for their survival in mainstream American society.

The last two decades of the nineteenth century were halcyon days for Native American education, as the government provided wholehearted support for the humanitarian emphasis on cultural assimilation. Annual congressional appropriations for Native American education rose from

$75,000 in 1880 to nearly \$3 million in 1900.[51] In 1877, 3,598 Native American children attended 150 boarding and day schools; by 1900, 21,568 children attended a total of 307.[52] During this period, reformers argued that Native Americans had an equal right to exactly the same education as other Americans received, including the same curriculum and access to colleges and higher education. By the turn of the century, they were arguing something very different: that Native Americans were to be educated in schools that offered a special curriculum—one designed to fit the supposedly lower aspirations of an inferior race. This is certainly not to say that the earlier period was one in which philanthropists and government officials were somehow more inclined toward socially just policies. Rather, a number of factors combined to make this period a brief moment in which it was not impossible for a Native American man to attend college, enter a profession, and marry a white woman.

Perhaps the most important reason why educational opportunities became available to Native Americans was the philosophies of mainstream education that had come to fruition during this period. By the late nineteenth century, the United States had a well-established belief in the right of common schooling for all. Educational historians have offered many opinions as to why the United States adopted this ideal earlier than other societies, such as those of western Europe. Ira Katznelson and Margaret Weir argue that a key factor was the basic precepts on which American society had been founded—the ideologies of democracy and republicanism. In combination with increasing industrialization in the early nineteenth century, these beliefs led to the formation of a politicized working class in the northern states whose members desired, among other benefits, an education for their children. Workers rejected the idea that working-class education was the concern of charity and demanded that the government take responsibility for it. The appeal for a free public school system was a major plank in the workers' political party platform from the late 1820s. Middle-class reformers such as James G. Carter, Henry Barnard, and Horace Mann also contributed to the campaign by publishing numerous pamphlets and articles on the subject. Although it was fought slowly on a state-by-state basis, the battle had been won by the end of the Civil War. The majority of the states had free public school systems, and some in the East had even established public high schools.[53]

By the last three decades of the nineteenth century, white Americans saw access to elementary, government-funded education as a right, reflected in the enormous expansion of the public education system. During this period a ladder system was established, which meant that children could progress according to their ability from primary to secondary and (for a few) tertiary institutions. This was in contrast to the system in England, for example, where secondary and tertiary education were generally reserved for the upper classes. For African Americans, and to some extent Asian Americans, however, the system was far less egalitarian. It was not until 1954 that the Supreme Court ruled that segregated schools were unconstitutional in the famous case *Brown v. Board of Education*, which finally reversed the "separate but equal" doctrine that had oppressed African Americans since the 1890s. For immigrants, however, the common school system was seen as a means of assimilation right from the beginning. Indeed, the large number of European immigrants arriving in American cities in the mid-nineteenth century was used as one of the early arguments for the necessity of having a common school system.

Once reformers had decided that Native Americans required education, therefore, the idea that education was both a right and a tool of assimilation could readily be seized upon in arguing the Native American case. Thomas Morgan, the commissioner of Indian affairs, reasoned in just this way in 1889: "A high school education at public expense is now offered to the great mass of youth of every race and condition except the Indian. The foreigner has the same privilege as those 'native and to the manner born.' The poor man's child has an equal chance with the children of the rich. Even the negroes of the south have free entrance to these beneficent institutions."[54]

While it was widely held that Native Americans should be educated, there was some disagreement about the kind of curriculum they should be taught. At first the aims of the philanthropists were modest. The platform of the second Lake Mohonk conference in 1884 argued that the "Indian must have a knowledge of the English language, that he may associate with his white neighbors and transact business as they do. He must have practical industrial training to fit him to compete with others in the struggle for life. He must have a Christian education to enable him to perform duties of the family, the State, and the Church."[55] But this simple goal was quite rapidly taken further. In the late 1880s, reformers began to wax lyrical about the possibilities of educating Native Americans to a higher level. This idea reflected one of the few redeeming qualities of the often patronizing and culturally insensitive reformers: their inherent belief that Native Americans did have intelligence and abilities equal to white people, although they had not yet been taught to use them in ways the reformers were prepared to recognize.

In 1884 the Indian Rights Association stated that one of their three objectives was the education of Native Americans, "signifying by this broad term the developing for their highest use physical, intellectual and moral powers."[56] Commissioner Morgan, who assumed office in 1889, advocated higher education for Native Americans and was later credited with "establishing education as a fundamental principle underlying the Government's whole Indian policy."[57] At the Lake Mohonk conference in 1889, Morgan made it clear that education could create more than competent farmers, explaining that education was the medium through which Native Americans would gain many of the trappings of a middle-class lifestyle. Educated Native Americans would enjoy "the sweets of refined homes, the delight of social intercourse, the emoluments of commerce . . . the advantages of travel, together with the pleasures that come from literature, science and philosophy, and the solace and stimulus afforded by a true religion." Morgan argued that "while for the present special stress should be laid upon that kind of industrial training which will fit the Indians to earn an honest living in the various occupations which may be open to them, ample provision should also be made for that general literary culture which the experience of the white race has shown to be the very essence of education." He also argued that higher education should be provided for all those who had a "special capacity" to become leaders or teachers.[58] These ideas dominated the Lake Mohonk conference long after they had begun to lose favor elsewhere. As late as 1913 the conference's platform asserted that the "great principle that for thirty years has controlled the action of these conferences is that humanity is one." The conference committed itself to racial equality and its legal and social implications, arguing that "no one race or rank of culture has the right to look with contempt on another as . . . unworthy." Thus every ethnic group ought "to be given equal opportunities to reach its highest limit of training in the arts of civilization, and to share with the best of us the rights of self-government."[59]

All over the country a three-tiered system of Native American education was established. Small day schools situated on the reservations taught the lowest grades. Students could then progress to boarding schools, also situated on the reservations, which taught the middle grades as well as practical industrial and domestic subjects. The upper grades, which could lead to a higher education, were mostly taught at the growing number of off-reservation boarding schools, such as Hampton Institute, Carlisle in Pennsylvania, Chilocco in Oklahoma, and Phoenix in Arizona. There were twenty-six of these in 1902.[60]

It is important to emphasize that the majority of Native Americans, especially those who remained on the reservations, never received the higher education that was granted to a few. According to David Wallace Adams, "The Indian school system never did come to approximate Morgan's ideal. In 1913, Commissioner of Indian Affairs Cato Sells admitted to the fact that even the better off-reservation schools only provided academic education equivalent to the eighth or ninth grades." There were some exceptions to this general rule: big boarding schools such as Carlisle, Haskell, and Santa Fe, which after 1894 offered courses of study beyond the basic eight-year program. Even so, Adams argues, it was not "until the late 1920s that several off-reservation institutions attained the status of full-fledged high schools."[61] At their fullest capacity, off-reservation boarding schools only educated one-third of the total number of school-aged Native American children.[62] Similarly, for a variety of reasons only a very small number of boarding school students graduated. In its forty years of operation, only 761 students successfully completed the ten grades of study at Carlisle Indian School.[63]

Instead, the day and boarding schools on reservations, where the majority of Native American children were sent, were small and inconsistently funded. Although the situation varied, in some areas they were too small to offer more than a tiny minority of the children a chance at an education. In 1881, for example, 100 day schools were overseen by the Cherokee Agency in Indian Territory, serving 2,808 students, while at the Crow Agency in Montana one school educated only 35 of the 715 school-age children on the reservation.[64] As the twentieth century progressed, the Bureau of Indian Affairs put greater emphasis on placing Native American children in mainstream public schools, offering less and less support for schools catering exclusively to Native American students. Given teachers who were often incompetent or racist and a chronic shortage of funds, the education of most Native American children during this period was of an unrelentingly industrial kind. Anthropologist Alice Littlefield has argued that the low standard of education and emphasis on manual skills in most federal "Indian" schools means that the word *proletarianization* rather than *assimilation* better characterizes their objective, which was to incorporate Native American students into the "wage labor force."[65]

Nor should we forget that the education received by Native Americans at any institution during this period was based predominantly on the idea of removing all traces of the children's culture. As Ward Churchill argues, although nonreservation boarding schools offered a more thorough academic curriculum than other Native American schools, they also "systematically 'deculturated'" their pupils, subjecting them to a "grueling regimen of indoctrination in Christian morality, mainly the 'virtues' of private property, sexual repression, and patriarchy."[66] These practices and the verbal, physical, and sexual abuse that many students experienced led to widely documented emotional scars.[67] Such stories have prompted many scholars and activists to label the kind of assimilation practiced in boarding schools during this period "ethnocide" or "cultural genocide." "The intent to offer instruction or education," José Barreiro has argued, "would not be so offensive, per se, but the attitude was one of emptying a vessel before filling it."[68]

The social climate that gave Native American students the opportunity to pursue higher education was not to last, however. During the mid- to late 1890s the government slowly changed the emphasis of its educational policy. Due to a combination of budgetary concerns, doubts about the efficacy of boarding schools, and a growing disillusionment with the idea that education was all that was required to effect the assimilation of Native Americans, the Bureau of Indian Affairs began advocating segregated, and therefore by definition inferior, schools in Native American communities.[69]

The relationships of the three white teachers at Hampton with Native American students are better understood, therefore, when placed within the wider context of a particular style of Native American educational policy that briefly existed in the United States in the second half of the nineteenth century. Unlike many schools that came after it, Hampton was an instrument of a policy that gave some Native American men the opportunity to reach high levels of education. It was the perception among reformers that this education was a civilizing influence that played such an important part in assisting these men to "win" the hand of an educated white woman and made their marriages more acceptable to the Hampton community and society at large. In an environment where relationships between black and Native American students were a real possibility, such marriages, despite their involvement of a white woman, were more acceptable because they fitted with the project of cultural assimilation. It should also be noted that they were in harmony with ideas of biological absorption, although this aspect was never publicly discussed at Hampton.

As an uncompromising agent of cultural assimilation, Hampton provided a context in which marriages between white women and Native American men were possible despite the prejudices of the day. The school was one of the few locations in the country where white women and Native American men could meet regularly in a setting conducive to sympathy between the races. It attracted white women who were educated and of a humanitarian inclination and gave Native American men the opportunity to reach high levels of education, in some cases far beyond that which many white American men could expect. Administrators' concerns for the welfare of their former charges and for the school's reputation were so great that they encouraged marriages among Native American students that they believed would reinforce the lessons learned at

Hampton. With Native Americans, at least, the level of assimilation of a potential spouse was seen as more important than his or her ethnicity. It was an atmosphere in which the choice of marriage partner was deeply connected to the ideology of assimilation and all the cultural shifts that occurred during this period of American history. The doctrine of cultural assimilation did not just influence the public life of every Native American student who attended Hampton. It also had implications for all aspects of their private lives, especially their choice of a partner with whom to build their future. How a different set of boarding school students, those who attended Carlisle Indian School, coped with these interactions between assimilation and interracial marriage is explored in the next chapter.

2. Interracial Marriages of Male Carlisle Indian School Alumni

When John Walker Labatte, a Lakota man, married a white girl from Minneapolis in 1910, it was unusual enough an event for it to be reported in a local newspaper. The author of the brief article entitled "Indian and Caucasian Wed" refused, however, to sensationalize the story. "Reporters," he or she wrote, "are wont to make up a very romantic story of such incidents and long paragraphs in the newspaper naturally ensue." Instead, this level-headed reporter chose to differentiate between the "natural sex attractions" which led to interracial mixing in the "early pioneer days" and marriages such as the Labattes'—a relationship between two "highly educated people [who] came into contact socially in the ordinary way, learned to esteem one another, grew into the closer relations of love by reason of a common possession of culture and mutual affinity, and the result has been wedding bells and the promise of future happiness."[1] This newspaper clipping was proudly included in Labatte's student file at Carlisle Indian School, one of the many pieces of evidence the school collected which demonstrated the "success" of their policies of education, assimilation, and immersion into white culture. Indeed, the school itself could have written the story, so perfectly did it demonstrate what the humanitarian reformers who supported the Native American school system thought about the interracial marriages of its male students.

Carlisle was established in 1879 after Richard Pratt had convinced Congress that his experiment of having Native American students at Hampton had worked well enough to deserve the funding for his own school where he might fully develop his ideas about Native American education. Pratt's school, housed in an army barracks in Carlisle, Pennsylvania, was the first non-reservation boarding school established exclusively for Native American students, and it quickly became a very public example of assimilation policy. As the last chapter demonstrated, assimilationists' ideas about interracial marriage affected the way Native American boarding school students were treated while at schools like Hampton and Carlisle. But their concerns did not end once students had left their grounds and returned to their homes. Indeed, "returned" students were almost an obsession with those interested in the "Indian problem" during this period. The lives of ex-students were the subject of constant discussions in which they were upheld by reformers as examples of the possibilities of assimilation or by their opponents as failures who quickly went "back to the blanket." In other words, as David Wallace Adams has put it, returned students became a public and contested issue in the debate over whether reformers had "promised too much"—both to students left to sink or swim in a society often not ready to accept them on equal terms, and to mainstream America who had little idea of the complexity of changing someone's identity nor of the resilience of indigenous culture.[2] This chapter explores the role of interracial relationships in the lives of male students after they left Carlisle Indian School, which was perhaps the best known boarding school for Native American students operating in the assimilationist period.

Carlisle Indian School and Hampton Institute staff made significant efforts to collect information about what happened to returned students. Both published newsletters, kept up correspondence, collected statistics, and even sent staff west on fact-finding missions to discover how their ex-students were faring in the real world. In the 1910s Carlisle sent out questionnaires to their alumni, asking open-ended questions about property, employment, and lifestyle. The forms that were filled out and sent back to the school survive, and although they give information only about a brief period in the assimilationist era, they contain more than simply the students' own voices, achievements that were celebrated by the school, and tragedies that still have the power to move nearly one hundred years later. They are also documents in which worlds can be seen colliding, as ex-students attempted to describe their complex and conflicted lives to an institution that represented a clear and unforgiving ideology, one which often could not assist them in making sense of the confusion that many had felt since leaving the school grounds. The myriad ways in which they answered the questions within, against, or in uneasy acknowledgment of the school's philosophy reveals how clearly they knew what was expected of them. Their answers also indicate that interracial marriage formed a significant part of white thinking about the assimilationist ideology of the period.

The school's reaction to interracial relationships of Carlisle students reveals that the issue of interracial relationships played into the ideology of assimilation in specifically gendered ways. Indigenous women, for good reason, have traditionally been seen as the focus of anxieties about interracial relationships. It was they who most often crossed racial boundaries as wives, single mothers, or rape victims, and they who embodied much of the eroticized desire of colonialism. There is a wealth of evidence in the Carlisle records of the fraught nature of interracial relationships for indigenous women. There are also surprisingly many instances where Native American men have files thick with information about their marriages to white women, and it is on these that this chapter concentrates. Indigenous men are often seen as having little to do with actual interracial relationships in colonial societies. The taboos against such relationships were strong, and indigenous men were rarely seen as acceptable sexual partners for white women, who carried the symbolic burden of keeping the white race pure.[3] In the Carlisle alumni questionnaires, however, there is evidence that male students who married white women were fulfilling an ideal version of assimilation. For humanitarian reformers who insisted, despite their often patronizing attitudes, that all races were of "one blood," acculturated Native American men were perhaps the most shining example of what assimilation could achieve. And what could demonstrate their ability to compete equally with white men more than a white woman willing to marry them? Thus John Walker Labatte, who ran away from Carlisle after four years of schooling, but without graduating, could be read by the school as a success story—a Native American man who, eight years later, was educated and civilized enough to win the hand of a white girl.[4]

Such relationships were understood by white Americans through the prism of cultural assimilation, not as a means of biological absorption. Indeed, it was only the students themselves who discussed the impact of such relationships on the identity of the next generation. Through their statements of defiance, collusion, or protest, ex-students revealed in their questionnaires that they knew their marriages could be seen as part of the assimilationist project, and the extent to which they resisted or were influenced by the ideology of assimilation and the social mores of the school allows us a valuable glimpse into the multifaceted worlds that assimilation policy had created.

The alumni questionnaires sent out by Carlisle Indian School during the 1910s placed great significance on whom students had married. It was the very first question to be answered, almost as though this was of more or even equal importance to the later questions about property acquired and positions held. The question "Are you married and if so, to whom?" was responded to in a variety of ways by ex-students, sometimes with a simple yes or no, often with a name, and sometimes with other pieces of information. Many times the ex-student added a note indicating their spouse's race: whether it be "Wife Died. Halfbreed," "a white girl," "Married a Miss Annie Williams of the Skopomish Reservation," or even "Married—Squaw."[5] Often, too, whether or not the spouse was a "Carlisle girl" or "Carlisle boy" or a student of some other "Indian school" was noted, demonstrating the students' awareness of the importance this would have to the school. Millard Hendrick noted that his wife, Jennie, was "a graduate from Tomah Ind. School," Ella Stander, an Arapaho, that her husband was "an educate [sic] Indian," Lucius Aitsan, a Kiowa, that he "married a Carlisle girl," Ned Brace, also a Kiowa, that he married an "ex-Haskell student," and Oneida John Schenandore that he chose a Carlisle student of the Class of 1905.[6] Lakota Jacob White Cow Killer wrote bluntly: "I married uneducated woman."[7]

Anthropologist Genevieve Bell contends that the school's desire for students to marry each other was one factor that resulted in a significant proportion of student weddings, and she estimates that 5 to 10 percent of Carlisle students married each other.[8] Devon Mihesuah's research into the Cherokee Female Seminary reveals similar pressures on stu-

Ithaca, N.Y.

Record of Graduates and Returned Students.

U. S. INDIAN SCHOOL, CARLISLE, PA.

April 30th 1910.

NAME Wm Moses Patterson

1. Are you married and if so to whom? Yes. Miss Sara Coleman M.D. a white lady who is a graduate of Howard University (Washington D.C.)

2. What is your present address? Lewiston, Niagara Co., N.Y.

3. Did you attend or graduate from any other schools after leaving Carlisle? No. Give names of schools and dates if possible

4. What is your present occupation? Farming

5. Tell something of your present home. I am living on my own home about ( ) acres. (10) acres, standing and beautiful grove, in which visitors are welcome.

6. What property in the way of land, stock, buildings or money do you have? I own about ( ) acres of land and have chance to farm about 52 + acres with buildings thereon.

7. Have you been in the Indian Service? In what position? How long in each? I have not

8. What other positions have you held since leaving Carlisle? Carpenter, Stationary Engineer, Boilermaker, (Pleased Painting while at Carlisle)

9. Tell me anything else of interest connected with your life:

I am ever thankful for what the school did for me and I have always regretted that I met called home and not permitted to graduate from Carlisle, and I feel that if I was there to graduate I could have received just the letter —

Since I have now passed all the early through duties much more at home —

interested in medicine —— and if my boundary education was more advanced my wife also help me to take that course.

She is a graduate now and practice in Pharmacy she registered in Pharmacy in the District of Columbia. Was public school teacher in Bryn, Pennsylvania.

My wife and I would be glad if we could get installed at your institution or any of the sub-stations connected with the records. We would like to get hospital or drug work to do.

With thankful for anything you can do to enable us to do so far we will be in your to meet any. And there is much to meet any. Yours most respectfully,

Wm Moses Patterson.

6. William Moses Patterson's completed alumni questionnaire. From Carlisle Indian Industrial School Student Records, 1879–1918, RG 75, William Moses Patterson (Tuscarora) file. Courtesy of National Archives and Records Administration, Washington DC.

dents to marry an acculturated spouse. Mihesuah found that the majority of the most successful female students—those who graduated—married "white men, or men who had a smaller amount of Cherokee blood than they had."[9] That a student's choice of a suitable spouse was seen by Carlisle as the culmination of the civilizing process is most evident in the school's reaction to the weddings of its students to each other. These weddings often took place in the superintendent's private residence on campus and were reported in the Carlisle *Arrow* or *Red Man* in glowing terms. The "quiet but pretty" wedding of John Big Fire (Winnebago) and Rose Simpson (Nez Perce), for example, took place at the school in the presence of students and staff. Rose was "tastefully attired in white chiffon over white satin and carried bride's roses." Their school friends served as bridesmaid and best man, played the "Wedding March" and selections on the violin during the reception, and then accompanied the couple to their train back west.[10] Sometimes, if they were romantic or titillating enough, the stories would also find their way to the local mainstream press, either as part of the paper's normal reporting of local weddings or as a separate news item. Although the wedding of Rosetta Pierce (Seneca) and Thomas B. Owl (Cherokee) in 1912 was reported in the local newspaper under the painfully stereotyped headline "Heap Big Injun Wedding," the subsequent article, which described the wedding feast and the six other students who attended the happy couple, could only have made the school proud.[11] Just the fact that these students had weddings that were "civilized" enough to be reported in the press was a matter of pride for the school. One wedding that appeared in a number of mainstream newspaper articles was that of students Henry E. Roberts (Pawnee), the "star end" of the Carlisle Football team in 1911, and Rose Denomie (Chippewa), who nursed him through a concussion after a game in the school hospital.[12] The wedding of "Sioux Princess" Daphne Waggoner (Lakota) to a "Lansdale businessman" who met her during a visit to the school was also reported in several newspapers.[13] Such marriages, as one newspaper report put it, provided "no better evidence of the permanent progress in civilization of the . . . Indian people under the patient and self-sacrificing guidance of unselfish American instructors." The article stressed the gap between the "primitive mating customs of the southwestern natives" and the "elaborate ceremonial" of Anna May Savilla and Jefferson Miquel (both Yuma) which included the "Wedding March" from Wagner's opera *Lohengrin*, a long tulle veil with orange blossoms, and a Catholic Mass.[14]

The civilized achievements of brides and grooms were often a feature of the descriptions of their weddings. Helen J. Kimmel (Lakota) and Lancelot C. DeCory, who married in 1913, were described as "an ex-student of the Carlisle Indian School . . . a lady of pleasing personality . . . held in high esteem by all who know her . . . [and] an ex-student of Flandreau Indian School [who] is engaged in the automobile business in Valentine, where he has many warm friends."[15] Emil Hauser, "famous [Cheyenne] Indian athlete," and "Carlisle graduate" Dollie Stone's wedding was glowingly portrayed as "one of the most notable nuptials in the history of the Umatilla Reservation."[16] Even Viena Nevongoimsie Jenkins (Hopi) and Lewis Edward Thompson (Navajo) were praised for their respective employment by the National Indian Association and the Presbyterian board, despite the fact that their wedding ceremony appeared to be a mix of at least three cultures: "The bridal party entered the room, which was decorated with Navajo blankets, to the strains of the wedding march," while the cake was served "in a Navajo wedding basket and the coffee on Hopi placques."[17]

At least one parent believed there was a subtle pressure for students to find partners at the school. Osage student Minnie Onhand's father was horrified by the news that his daughter wished to marry a fellow student. "I will object to her getting married in School," he wrote the superintendent. "It has been great talk among our people that every Osage girl goes off to school, and gets marry to some Indian boy, and that is reason that Osage Indian object sending their children . . . way off to Gov. School." The school capitulated to his request, sending Minnie home for the summer and refusing to let her get married.[18] The school might also try to prevent students from making what it saw as an undesirable marriage. In 1916, Nellie White Clay's summer holidays with her Crow family were threatened when the school found out that "a certain young Indian man of the reservation whose character and habits of industry are not of particularly high order, is anxiously awaiting the return of this young woman, with the intention of marrying her." Although Superintendent O. H. Lipps felt unable to expressly prevent Nellie's return, he suggested that perhaps a direct order from the "Washington office" might persuade her.[19]

There are many examples of cases where the school was not quick enough to promote an approved match, and these predominantly involved female students. Many scholars have suggested that assimilation policy was gendered to the extent that there was special emphasis on the importance of educating and civilizing Native American women. As Brenda Child has recently argued, the importance placed on female students had its "origin in strong negative imagery of American Indian women," who, reformers thought, needed special help to make them into "capable" and moral wives.[20] Genevieve Bell has also argued that Carlisle's concerns about marriage were aimed for the most part at female students.[21] Certainly, in terms of "approved" and "disapproved" relationships, the female students' files contain more examples of the latter. The long history of sexual exploitation by white men is evident in the numerous heartbreaking cases where a teenaged Carlisle girl got pregnant, often while working for a white family during the school's summer "outing" program.[22] By contrast to these transgressions, marriages to white men were something to be cautiously celebrated, as long as the man was not "shiftless." Eight of the eighteen Carlisle girls who wrote to the school to tell of their marriage to a white man made a point of emphasizing the worth of their husband. Grace Warren's mother wrote that her Colville daughter was married and "has a good home. Her husband is a white man and doing well." Sophia Wilkins, a Klamath, described her husband as "a young man of honor and Ambition," adding, "He is an American of German and Scottish decendent [sic]." Zenobia Barcia, a Mission Indian, also married a German American, whom she described as "a very good man." Ellen Martin, an Osage, "married white man doing well," Minnie Paul, a Seneca, described her marriage to a "white man in business," and Emma Millie Marrel, a Spokane, portrayed her husband as "a gentleman from Russia."[23] Cherokee Etta Batson described how her husband "works all the time and is making an honest living," and sent a photo that showed her unmistakable pride in her family.[24] This notice-

7. Etta Crow Batson included this photograph when she returned her questionnaire to Carlisle. It listed the names of all her family on the back. File of Etta Crow (Cherokee), Carlisle Indian Industrial School Student Records, 1879–1918, RG 75. Courtesy of National Archives and Records Administration, Washington DC.

able emphasis was no doubt because there was a history of relationships between white men and Native American women that didn't necessarily mean a step toward civilization. As Arnold Krupat has pointed out, it was more common for white men to marry Native American women for land than it was for Native American women to marry white men to be civilized.[25] It was apparently important to Carlisle "girls" that their marriages were not perceived as relationships in which they were exploited by their husbands.

The marriage of a female student to a white man did not necessarily mean to white Americans that she would lead a more "civilized" life, but marriages of male Carlisle students to white women were read quite differently. Indeed, it was much more likely for a Native American man's civilization to be assured in the minds of reformers thanks to his marriage to a white woman. It has been suggested that the male students faced a harder road than their female counterparts once back on the reservation. In his comprehensive history of Native American boarding schools, David Wallace Adams briefly argued that it was in fact more difficult for Native American men to live up to the expectations of reformers. While Native American women were expected to practice domestic arts to a high standard, this was at least an approximation of what they would have been doing anyway. For the men, trying to be economically self-sufficient on reservations with few opportunities for employment, or in mainstream America with all its racial biases, proved extremely difficult.[26] Students might suffer from the insecurities caused by their belonging to an ethnic group constantly portrayed as inferior, such as George Marks, an Ottawa, who wrote, "Although I may be brighter and more ambitious and more energetic than the average young men of my race, yet the fact that I belong to the Indian race makes me feel uneasy on entering any line of work that requires lot of preparatory study and lot of brain power." Apache Eben Beads, at the other end of his life, was confused by the racism he had encountered. "The white man used to be kind to me," he wrote on his questionnaire, "but this time I am so old man . . . I don't go nowere yet, because the white people [they bother] me to[o] much, and tesing [sic] me too, I don't know why? You know I am good man, and honest."[27]

Perhaps these difficulties were part of the reason why comparatively many "Carlisle boys" made the decision to marry outside their ethnic group. The Carlisle student records show that of the several thousand students who spent time at Carlisle, and the fifty-three feet of surviving files, at least twenty-seven male students married white women compared with eighteen marriages of female students to white men.[28] This disparity is surprising at a time when most historians have argued that relationships between white women and nonwhite men were those tabooed to the greatest degree. In their correspondence with their alma mater, several Native American men expressed the view that white women were the ultimate prizes, and Carlisle appears to have supported their view. Joe Sheehan, for example, was a well-known Alaskan Carlisle footballer who eloped in 1913 with Viola Buerchort, a young white woman from Baltimore where Joe worked as a clerk. The young couple received not only the blessings of Viola's parents but also some sympathetic news coverage in the *Baltimore American* that Joe clipped and sent to Carlisle. Superintendent Friedman replied with his best wishes and congratulations "on having won a wife in the city where you have made yourself known." Joe continued to send newspaper clippings regarding his marriage to Carlisle, often with a request for them to be republished in the *Red Man* or the *Arrow*. When the school did not oblige, he complained, prompting another letter from the chief clerk reassuring him, "You are one of the boys whom Carlisle considers their successes and I hope you will not feel hard against the school." When Joe's first child was born a year later, he sent a copy of the announcement, adding, "This will interest you as I am a former student. . . . Married a Baltimore girl—a birth of this kind here is rare."[29]

When it came time for Tuscarora William Moses Patterson to fill in an alumni questionnaire, he wrote proudly that he was married to "Miss Sara Dolan MD. A White Lady, who is a graduate of Howard University (Washington DC)." Perhaps Sara's experiences at the predominantly African American university had helped her to decide to make such an unusual marriage. After receiving William's questionnaire, the superintendent wrote to ask Patterson if he would send photographs of his home and family because "One of the strongest arguments that can be presented to the public is, to show them by means of pictures that Carlisle students can make good, and live in a same manner as their white neighbors." Patterson complied, and he also later sent the school a copy of a petition that he wished forwarded to the federal legislature lobbying for the rights of Tuscarora men married to white women. The petition reveals the problems that acculturated Native American men could be confronted with back on the reservation. Among the grievances of the five men who wrote the petition were their complaints that their children were not entitled to rights as Tuscarorans, unlike those with white fathers, that if they should die their wife and children could not inherit the family property, that different cultural ideas of property and owner-ship meant their families could not leave their homes or "we may return to find some one else in possession" or that "chiefs can come into my home . . . if they feel like doing so can beat me out of my own house and I am powerless to prevent it." The petitioners strongly believed that they should be rewarded, rather than penalized, for their white wives. "We are trying to live honorable lives," they wrote, "and want to advance in all that is desirable and necessary in a civilized life. Some of the Indian customs which have the force of a law on the reservation are a hindrance to our welfare and we feel the time has come that some of those customs should be abolished." Like the reformers, or perhaps in the knowledge that those who read the petition would think in this way, the petition-ers believed that their white wives helped them to be more assimilated. "We believe," they wrote, "that our white wives are an uplift to us, help-ing us to lead good, decent lives."[30]

Harry West (Washoe) even took the idea that acculturated Native American men deserved white wives onto the vaudeville stage. In 1914 he wrote to the school to ask permission to advertise himself as a Carl-isle student. The hero of the sketch was "Jim Cloud, a graduate of Carl-isle, once a football star, who is a guest of a prominent lady in N.Y. City, in whose house jewelry is stolen." The suspicion falls on Jim, who is in love with his hostess's niece. Her brother objects to the match. After a speech in which Jim "becomes angry [and] tells him that it is not in the past centuries but the Indians are making great progress today that his love should not be forbidden," Jim reveals that he is a detective in the Secret Service and that his hostess's nephew is the thief. He wins the niece in the final scene. The Carlisle staff member who replied to Harry's letter was hesitant about letting him use the school's name. "I will have to be careful how the name of Carlisle is used in an advertising capacity," he wrote, adding that the school did not want to encourage Harry to "give up a good position" as draftsman "for a more or less visionary career." Harry's career on the stage, for whatever reason, turned out to be limit-ed. Three years later he had been drafted to fight in the War, but found himself staying at home drafting and designing "battleship engines to submarine chaser turbines" for the Westinghouse Company.[31]

There is some evidence that mainstream America shared the idea that a white wife was convincing evidence of acculturation. Russel White Bear was described in the *Boston Advertiser* in 1910 as "gifted in tongue, in artful expression by hand and in wisdom equal to that of his elders" after he put his people's case to Congress as part of a deputation of Crows protesting the proposal to sell their reservation in Montana. The article portrayed Russel as exemplifying "what education can do for these savages . . . his diction was far superior to that heard from many a Yale or Harvard graduate," and concluded this portrait with the irrefutable evidence of Russel's civilization. Not only was "White bear . . . dressed as a pale face [but he had also] married a white woman."[32]

Although the idea that a white wife was a symbol of success seemed to be widely, if often quietly, held, the Carlisle student records reveal that it did not always work out that way in practice. Edward Fox, a Shawnee, got his wife, Mary, a local girl from the nearby town of Carlisle, pregnant while he was still a student. The school did not consider Mary a "suitable wife" for Edward, but gave consent to the marriage "to save Edward from prosecution for statutory crime, which would probably have been instituted by the father of the girl because of her age and delicate condition." Although Edward had been trained as a painter, he and Mary struggled to make a living in Carlisle and were encouraged to go west to Edward's allotment in Oklahoma. Here they were very unhappy. Mary was "homesick for her relatives and friends in Carlisle," and they made repeated requests in 1915 to be allowed to return. Three years later, they were still in Oklahoma.[33] The Foxes reveal the reality behind the assumption that a white wife equaled assimilation, a reality in which a young white woman might find herself in the strange and poverty-stricken environment of a reservation. In such matches, in the eyes of reformers, the race of the spouse was not so important as the level of civilization reached by the ex-student. His white wife did not help Henry K. Fox, for example, in his repeated requests for help from his alma mater for help getting a position at the Ford Factory in Detroit or to help pay for medical attention to his epilepsy. Instead, the school insisted repeatedly that his hard times were no responsibility of theirs.[34]

Thus it seems it was the male ex-students who were seen by reformers as the ultimate expression of assimilation policy. While educated Native American women were seen as a step in the assimilative process, their most important role being the mothers of a civilized next generation, it was educated Native American men who epitomized the reformers' most radical claim: that acculturation could occur in a single generation. That assimilation could be privileged over racial mixing of the most forbidden kind, at a time when anti-immigrant feeling and the Jim Crow South were at their height, tells us much about the complicated meanings of race and gender in the United States at the beginning of the twentieth century. Taboos against interracial mixing certainly existed, but in the context of indigenous assimilation they could be overlooked by some in favor of an emphasis on acculturation and self-support.

Thus far, this chapter has been about the beliefs, assumptions, and expectations of white humanitarian reformers. Unmistakable in the Carlisle alumni questionnaires, however, are the voices of the students themselves. Many used the forms as an opportunity to let Carlisle know just how bitter they were about their experiences there. "I really think," wrote Seneca Walter Paul, resentful about the amount of hard labor that had been required of him as a student, "that the Carlisle School is the last place I would want any of my relation to go to get an education." John Suseip, a Penobscot, was still angry about the wages he had never been paid ("some day God will pay me for the money you stole") and Maud Allen, a Seneca, still smarted years after being expelled for stealing eight dollars: "Now Mr Friedman I wish to tell you that this was not true. . . . It makes me think a good many students was served in the same way." Wilson Silas told the superintendent in no uncertain terms about the good wages he was now being paid compared with when he was employed on the outing program. "I am never going back to Carlisle anymore," the Oneida man wrote. "I am working out here at Adonah, Ws. Sawmill. . . . When I was out to Pennsylvania state, I used to get only $12.00 a month. Out here I get $12.00 per week! Now that's $48.00 a month. It is no good out there! . . . That's all I got to say about it! No more Carlisle for me!"[35]

More specifically, there was considerable resistance to the school's unspoken policy regarding interracial marriage. Some replies to the question "Are you married and if so, to whom?" seemed to proudly state the respondent's decision to marry in an unassimilated way. Clarke Asbury, a Pueblo, wrote that he was "married to an Indian-girl: My own People." Ottawa Isiah Wasaquam stated, "It has been nearly ten years since I was married to my Race." Pueblo Bruce Fisher simply got "married to my own people," and Mohawk John Thompson married "one of my own tribe." Betsy Collins, a Chippewa, seemed to perceive an inherent racism in the idea that Native Americans should intermarry with whites. "We have 5 children," she wrote, "and the 4 of them is going to school with white children. But I do not intend to have intermarriages. I hope the children will marry their own kind. I respect my own race."[36]

Other ex-students were more positive about the effects of interracial marriages on the next generation. Wyandotte Cordelia Hicks wrote Carlisle about her "three very pretty little girls. Aside from brown eyes the two have they do not show their Indian blood. I have one blue eyed little one she has the golden curls also." By contrast, the "only fault" Peter J. Powlas, an Oneida, could find in his family was that "the children all take the fair complexion and light hair of their Anglo Saxon mother but if they all turn out as good and consciencious [sic] Christian as their mother I shall forgive them without any effort."[37]

Vasha Nakootkin revealed that attitudes toward interracial marriage outside Carlisle might not be so positive. "I went to Carlisle school," the Alaskan woman wrote, "and I know that the students will not feel hard towards me and my family because my husband happens to be a white man." Vasha had recently discovered that her marriage to a white man disqualified her family from help from the local agency, despite her own ill health. Putting her "pride in her pocket for once," she wrote to Carlisle to ask for help. She outlined the reasons for her dire straits. "I am married as you know to a white man he is good and industries [sic] but can't make enough to keep as we should be. The people go up to Alaska drive the native away from what little they try to live on." On top of all this, "Living is high and coal and every thing so expenses [sic] we can't turn around." It was hardly the bright future she had been promised by the school, who replied with one of the hundreds of letters refusing financial aid contained in its records.[38]

These varied responses to the issue of interracial marriage at Carlisle

Indian School reveal a complex picture of both white and Native American ideas about interracial relationships within the different worlds of mainstream America and the more focused world of Indian reform. Depending on the circumstances, Carlisle might celebrate the interracial relationship of one of its students, bemoan them, or punish them, and these reactions are revealing of the intricacies of what assimilation meant during this period. There seems to be sufficient evidence that like Hampton, Carlisle placed some importance on whom its ex-students married and saw marriages of male students to white women as an indication of successful acculturation. Those Carlisle students who married interracially did so within an ideology that divided people into sharp categories, even as it attempted to assimilate one category into another. But these students knew, perhaps more than most, about the slipperiness of indigenous identity at this time, a subject that scholars are only beginning to explore, and they did not hesitate to try to gain the best of both worlds.[39] From most white reformers' perspective, though, the ways in which these marriages might have changed indigenous identity through biological absorption was not openly discussed. Rather, marriages of Native American students to white men and women were understood in terms of cultural assimilation, rather than through their potential as erasers of the outward signs of indigenous identity, a subject which was rarely, if ever, discussed. The next chapter explores in detail the ways in which two Native American men who married white women grappled with the ideology of cultural assimilation through which their private choices were understood by the outside world.

3. Educated Native American Men and Interracial Marriage

In 1889 Commissioner of Indian Affairs Thomas Morgan advocated a scheme that would help Native Americans who were "endowed with [a] special capacity" to undertake higher education. "There is an imperative necessity for this, if the Indians are to be assimilated," Morgan told the Lake Mohonk Conference. "There is an urgent need among them for a class of leaders of thought—lawyers, physicians, preachers, teachers, editors, statesmen, and men of letters."[1] For the humanitarian reformers who believed in assimilation, there was no better demonstration of their goals than an educated, civilized Native American who had been born into traditional society and then, through education, had acquired the trappings of middle-class America. Although many reformers were painfully outspoken about their disdain for indigenous culture, many also simultaneously and passionately believed that Native Americans were not inferior to whites in intelligence and, if given the chance, could achieve on par with whites. Alice Fletcher, a reformer and anthropologist who had a mother-son relationship with an Omaha man called Francis La Flesche, also believed that some Native American men and women were more "advanced" than others; indeed, some were so acculturated, she claimed, that it was hard to "detect [them], save by some physical traces, from the mass of our citizens."[2]

In 1892 the Board of Indian Commissioners reported to the commissioner of Indian affairs that the Mohonk conference had decided to offer some practical support for this ideal and had established a "Mohonk Fund" to help "bright and promising Indian scholars in the pursuit of a higher education than is now given in the Government and contract schools."[3] The Women's National Indian Association also provided financial support to "bright Indians" who wished to have a professional education. Funding Susette La Flesche, an Omaha woman (Francis La Flesche's sister) who became the first Native American female to graduate from medical school, was their largest and most long-lasting project, although their Special Education Committee, established in 1888, claimed to have aided several others in "medical education or train[ing] as nurses . . . preparing for teaching or some other department of work among their own people."[4] These efforts helped to create a small group of highly educated Native Americans whose lives as "leaders and examples" led to a complex position as cultural mediators. To reformers, they were living demonstrations of the possibilities of assimilation; as individuals they had complex lives in which the public and private spheres were far more blurred than those of normal Americans.

A shining example of the reformers' success in creating a group of highly educated "leaders and examples" was the formation of the Society of American Indians (SAI). In 1911 a number of Native Americans who had successfully entered middle-class professions met in Columbus, Ohio, to form an organization dedicated to "the welfare of the Indian race in particular, and humanity in general."[5] They had been gathered together by a white man, Professor Fayette A. McKenzie, who believed strongly in the utility of a "native leadership" and who had personally contacted six Native American men and women to encourage them to form the society. At the second conference of the SAI, the founding principle of the organization was formulated; the minutes recorded that the "primary aim of the organization is to develop and organize men and women of Indian blood as wise leaders of their race."[6] This shows that the SAI was very much a product of the early period of assimilationist policy, even though by the time it was formed the government had already begun to reduce its support for the assimilationist policies embodied by the Dawes Act. The SAI published a journal, ran annual conferences, and lobbied mainstream America on behalf of the Native American peoples. Active members had to have at least one-sixteenth Native American "blood." White people were "associate" members.[7]

8. "The Descent of Man." The SAI hung this painting by Powers O'Malley in its offices, interpreting it for SAI members as follows: "There is perplexity in the Indian's face— shall he go forward to a professorship and into a profession and win a banker's daughter, or shall he fly back to the plains and become the warrior-horseman, the wise man of the tribe, the free wanderer of wide stretching prairies? . . . What Indian who has conned his books within the ivied walls of 'dormatory hall' [sic] has not had a flash of appreciation for the old life and with a choked sigh turned his face forward?" *QJSAI* 4, no. 2 (April– June 1916), 174. Reproduced on the cover of *Life*, January 22, 1914.

Many of the Native American men who held high positions in the SAI were married to white women, including Carlos Montezuma and Charles Eastman, who both held medical degrees; the Reverend Sherman Coolidge, an Arapaho who had been captured by the army as a child and brought up by a white army officer; Thomas L. Sloan, an Omaha who had attended Hampton Institute, practiced as a lawyer, and later become a judge; and Chauncey Yellow Robe, a Lakota man who wrote to Montezuma in 1911 that whenever he and his white wife visited her relatives he was

9. Chauncey Yellow Robe and Lillian Springer on their wedding day, May 22, 1906. Courtesy of the Minnilusa Historical Association and Pioneer Museum at the Journey Museum, Rapid City SD, and the Beinecke Rare Book and Manuscript Library, New Haven CT.

"always entertained like a Prince and so I do not regret for my intermar-riage."[8] Arthur C. Parker, the longest serving president, was the son of a white woman and a Seneca.

Educated, articulate Native Americans such as those involved in the sai were real-life examples of education and assimilation at work and often were used as such by white reformers. Richard Pratt shamelessly promoted Apache doctor Carlos Montezuma as a living example of his philosophies. He wrote to McKenzie just after the second conference of the sai about the importance of making the Native American members well known: "I would give more for a dozen well educated Indians like several of those at the convention, who would move out into our civili-zation and take up the cudgel for their people in traveling up and down speaking to our people sanely and forcibly, demanding that the Indians have as full and fair a chance as all foreigners who come to this country, than I would for 10,000 Indians well educated, who seclude themselves on their reservation and make battle from that standpoint."[9]

The members of the sai were uncompromising in their support for the higher education of Native Americans. In 1913, the *Quarterly Journal of the Society of American Indians* argued that "a 'grammar school race' can-not compete with a college bred race."[10] While planning the third con-ference of the sai, Arthur Parker wrote to the governor of Colorado in 1913 to tell him, among other things, that:

> we are sending our citizen fellows to congress as senators and representatives, to state legislatures, putting them on the legal bench, filling county and state offices with them, gradu-ating them as doctors, lawyers, clergymen of all creeds, scien-tific men, and we are moulding the sentiment of the country by members of our race who are newspaper men and editors. We are red men still, even though we have plucked the feath-ers from our war bonnets and are using them for pens. The battle scene has shifted and the contest becomes one of brain and wit. We have the capacity and the ability when opportu-nity is afforded.[11]

The leaders of the sai saw themselves as "practical social missionaries," spreading a message of equality through their success within white society rather than by relying on ideas of the equality of all groups.[12]

Indeed, these men played an important part in the development of the ideology of assimilation. Carlos Montezuma (who married Romanian-born Marie Keller in 1913) and Charles Eastman (who married Elaine Goodale, a descendant of two old New England families in 1891) were members of a small, interconnected group of Native Americans who were seen as living examples of the possibility of assimilation.[13] To those interested in the "Indian problem," they were well-known figures. They occupied an often ambivalent position as representatives of assimilation. Hazel Hertzberg has described this particular group of "Pan-Indians" as occupying a "middle ground, marginal both to the tribe and to the dominant society." Their marginal position did not mean that they were ineffectual. Rather, they were "honest broker[s] between two cultures," a role that simultaneously brought rewards and exacted punishments and that "often involve[d] difficult inner conflicts, but [which might] also bring prestige, recognition, and the satisfaction of service to one's fellow man."[14]

This situation must have complicated their choice of marriage partner. The apprehension about whom educated, assimilated Native American men should marry, which was often expressed about the graduates of boarding schools such as Hampton and Carlisle, applied threefold to these men. Not only were they educated, but they had also often lost their familial ties to their tribes and risen to respectable positions in white society. Open-minded white wives were the answer, and their willingness to marry these men could be seen as "proof" that the assimilation of Native Americans was possible. The small size and extraordinary nature of this group does not detract from the significance of their lives. They were influenced by the ideology of assimilation, and through their public work they affected people's beliefs about it. Their compromises with its demands reveal much about the expectations of both white and Native American reformers during this period. Their existence—they had no equivalents in the Antipodes—testifies to the emphasis placed on education and cultural assimilation in the United States' particular version of assimilation policy.

An important aspect of these men's lives was their position as examples of assimilated Native Americans. Living, at least outwardly, according to white standards, their lives became, in a sense, public property. Their very existence was, to white reformers, a success story that simultaneously demonstrated the inherent equality of their people with Anglo-Americans and the superiority of the white way of life. This position dictated the direction of their careers. Both Montezuma and Eastman, who had qualified as medical doctors, had to make the choice whether to minister to Native American patients in rural areas or to white patients in urban areas. Both options had drawbacks, and each made a different decision in this respect. Lack of money dogged both men. An important aspect of their lives was their attempt to publicize the Native American plight to white audiences through speaking engagements, involvement in various organizations, and writings—books in Eastman's case, a newspaper in Montezuma's. The SAI, of which they were both members, cited their names as examples of "strong affirmative living answers" to the "Indian problem."[15] But even these facts do not exhaust the extent to which the details of their lives became common property in the public sphere, linking their private lives inextricably to a very public and political issue: the story of their assimilation into mainstream society.

The narrative of Carlos Montezuma's childhood might have been a fairy-tale or piece of propaganda written especially to demonstrate the efficacy of assimilation. It was a story that was told and retold many times during Montezuma's life and which defined his public image so ineluctably that its effect on his private self can only be guessed at. The story began with Montezuma's birth in the mid-1860s to a Yavapai (Mohave-Apache) couple in Arizona. His name, Wassaja, meant "signaling" or "beckoning." During his childhood the encroaching white population caused violent competition between the various tribes living in Arizona, as game and forage became increasingly scarce. In 1871, in one of several altercations between the Yavapai and the Pima people, Wassaja and his two sisters were captured. After only a few months, the Pimas sold Wassaja for a small cash amount to an itinerant Italian photographer named Carlos Gentile. Wassaja was separated from his sisters, and they and their parents died soon afterward. In Florence, Arizona, Carlos

Gentile had Wassaja baptized as Carlos Montezuma, the latter name a reference to a Mexican emperor who supposedly had some kind of historical connection with the surrounding area.

As he moved around the country, Gentile sent Montezuma to a number of schools where he made good progress. When Gentile's business failed, he gave responsibility for Montezuma to George Ingalls of the American Baptist Home Mission Society's Indian department. Many years later a friend sent Montezuma a letter Ingalls wrote in 1878 that described his ambitions for the young boy who had been put into his charge. This letter contained an early expression of the enthusiasm of white reformers and philanthropists for Native American "leaders" as agents of assimilation:

> I want Montezuma to become, first a *real* Christian and then to be a Physician and with a good education and love of Christ in his heart, to go back to his people and labor for their good as a Christian or missionary Physician. I want him to have a knowledge of some trade perhaps a carpenter or other useful trade [and] a knowledge of farming so he can direct such branches of industry among his people.[16]

Ingalls arranged for the Rev. William H. Steadman to give room and board to Montezuma in exchange for "his doing some few duties around his place." Montezuma enrolled at the University of Illinois and attained a bachelor of science degree. He then entered Chicago Medical College, completing his degree and, as Ingalls had hoped, becoming a physician in 1889. During his studies Montezuma became acquainted with Richard Pratt, then head of Carlisle Indian School in Pennsylvania. Their correspondence, which began in 1887, lasted for the rest of Montezuma's life.

If Pratt had personally invented a Native American "prototype" who would support his views, he or she could not have been more appropriate to his needs than Carlos Montezuma. Pratt advocated removing children from their Native American families and bringing them up in white society. "Savagery is a habit," Pratt claimed in a speech he made before some Protestant ministers in 1891. "We are not born with language, nor are we born with ideas of either civilization or savagery. Language, savagery, and civilization are forced upon us entirely by our environment after birth."[17] If Native American children could be removed from their cultures completely, they would simply not be able to resist taking on the habits of white culture. In a speech delivered at the Second Conference of the SAI at Ohio State University in 1912, Montezuma described how, as a child, he underwent exactly the experience Pratt predicted: "Very soon, unconsciously, I took on [white children's] ways. I could do nothing else. In school, in the streets and in whatever way I turned I was led to become like my schoolmates. I was carried by the current of my environment. I was lost in it and had to stick to it."[18] Despite the cruelty of his theories, Pratt's views differed from those of many white people in that he constantly defended the intelligence and capability of Native Americans. It was not inherently inferior abilities which prevented them from assimilating into white culture, but the disadvantages they received growing up among their people, who could not teach them the necessary skills to be a success on white terms.

Carlos Montezuma was the ultimate proof of this theory, and Pratt did not hesitate to utilize him as such. Among Montezuma's papers are the invitations Pratt sent every year to the Carlisle Commencement ceremony, often offering, despite the school's shaky finances, to pay his costs. Although he had not attended Carlisle, Montezuma was the perfect example of what the school tried to achieve. Pratt wanted him on the stage during the ceremonies so he could point, literally, to living proof of his theories. When, after graduating, Montezuma spent some years in the West working for the Indian Bureau as Agency physician at a number of posts, Pratt hoped that he might recruit some students for Carlisle to accompany him to the Commencement ceremony for dramatic effect:

> I want you here and I want you to take five or six minutes for remarks, sifted down, concentrated, the very quintessence of your best thought. I will pay your expenses. It may be you can bring a little party with you. I would be glad if they were brought in the rags and tatters of camp life and would be glad if they arrived just in the nick of time for you to march them in and come before the audience and make your speech.[19]

Pratt often passed on Montezuma's letters to interested people, or his opponents, in order to support his arguments. In 1892 he sent Henry Dawes, whose name was associated with the 1887 General Allotment Act which attempted to end the communal living of the reservation system, a letter in which Montezuma argued: "Captain, if the choice of my life remained with my mother, father or myself I would not be writing to you. Ignorance and at the very lowest depth of an uncivilized life of which the reservation bondage bestows would have been my fate. So, you see I believe [in] compulsory education for the Indians." Pratt explained in his covering letter: "He is thoroughly Apache, and yet I have reason to believe that he is a good deal better all around man, including medical qualities than a very large proportion of Agency physicians."[20] When speaking publicly, the "full blooded Apache Indian . . . [who] knows nothing of his native Apache language, nor . . . [harbors] a trace of Apache superstition" was one of Pratt's favorite means of supporting his arguments.[21]

If Montezuma was significant to Pratt because of the support he provided for his ideas both in his own words and as an exemplar, Pratt's significance to Montezuma's life was more complicated. In one sense, Pratt proved an important mentor for Montezuma, who often wrote to him when a difficult decision needed to be made. Indeed, Montezuma's decision not to fulfill Ingalls's wishes completely by practicing as a physician among his own people was no doubt influenced by Pratt's advice. When Montezuma was unhappily working at the Western Shoshone Agency in White Rock, Nevada, Pratt wrote to him:

> I do not want you to get lost and I want you to keep me in mind. I understand very well what you stand face to face with now. It is not, as you know, my way. I would have had you continue among the whites and become part and parcel of the civilized portion of the country, and leave to others of our own race the duties that you now perform.

Pratt went on to pressure Montezuma to be an example to the Western Shoshone community, a position which cannot have been easy to endure. "I trust," he wrote, "that in all respects you will be what the Indians call you, a white man, not only white in conduct outside but white in the inside. You will understand me."[22]

Soon afterwards, Montezuma decided to become what he called "a missionary to the whites," rather than an example to other Native Americans. He wrote to the Indian Bureau in 1893 to ask for time off from his position as Agency physician to find a location in the East in which to practice medicine, arguing, "I ask this not for a selfish purpose—a living example of what the Indians can be among the whites is better than returning them to camp life to disgrace their nation."[23] Previously he had written to Pratt:

> I have come to the conclusion that I would do more for the Indians in the east than on the bondage system of a reservation. The white people can appreciate the Indian question more to see the *real living proof* that the ignorant and superstitious Indians [can be educated]. . . . Not only this, but if one of them can be educated to the highest standard, why send him on a reservation to be stunted in his progress with the environment of a reservation life?[24]

There is no doubt that, on a philosophical level, the relationship between Pratt and Montezuma benefited both men. Quite apart from the fact that Pratt and Montezuma were in complete agreement on the "Indian question," often writing at length about their support for each other's ideas and their shared disagreement with the philosophies of others, Pratt's theories allowed Montezuma to see both his history and his lifestyle in positive terms, and this must have been a valuable gift to a man who occupied such an uneasy position between two cultures.

Another, darker side to this position and the public life it entailed were the occasions when Montezuma experienced obvious prejudice. Montezuma confronted racist views that were both similar to and different from the racism experienced by Native Americans who were living a more traditional lifestyle. These included instances of overt racism such as the unspecified accusations made against him by the superintendent of a school at Fort Stevenson, North Dakota, early in his career as an Agency physician. Montezuma put these accusations down to *"prejudiced, distrustful feeling"* and recorded hearing the matron of the school repeating to the other employees that she would "not trust the doctor alone with my seven [year] old daughter."[25]

A more subtle form of racism was the patronage of well-meaning white people, such as the gushing prose of the woman from Webster City, Iowa, who wrote to Montezuma to ask for a picture of himself to adorn her library. "All my friends are getting pictures of Indians and I thought to have yours would be best of all," she wrote. "An *educated* Indian Dr!! I will have your picture *framed* and hang it up."[26] Montezuma was often treated as a "representative" Native American, although surely it should have been obvious to all that he was no such thing. In 1900 a student at Cornell College wrote to him for information to assist his entry into an oratorical contest:

> Feeling that you are a representative Indian, I now write to get some of your views and opinions on the subject. I desire to write the composition in the first person, thus taking the part of the Indian myself, and taking up the Indian's view of the matter as I think he sees it.[27]

In 1899 a member of the Young Men's Christian Association at the University of Chicago wrote to Montezuma asking him to provide the entertainment at a social occasion designed to recruit new members:

> To do so, we must prove that we are really jolly fellows who can appreciate a good lively time as well as anybody else. We hope to have at this affair apples, nuts, college snaps, jokes, etc.— just what a boy likes. Now to cap the whole business, won't you dress in your Indian costume and tell the fellows, in a 20 minutes talk, how you were captured and brought up?[28]

Much later in his life Montezuma would tell Pratt of his aversion to such requests, but there is evidence that he often gave colorful talks on his upbringing to white audiences.[29] Stories of his life were also published in newspapers and in pamphlet form a number of times.[30]

A form of cultural conflict that must have been very confronting to Montezuma's philosophy was that which occurred when his advocacy of Pratt's method of education resulted in suffering by his Native American relatives. One cousin wrote to him in 1898 to complain that his eldest son "has not heard from his brother for over six months and also that he or his brother haven't been to school for a long time and that both have been at hard work and only are being paid (4) four dollars per month." This situation was far from what Montezuma had led his cousin to believe. "What you told me was that they were going East to go to school and learn to study and educate themselves," the cousin wrote. "I wish you to see at once about my children and write and let me know about them as I am very anxious about them.[31]

Despite, or perhaps because of, these frictions, Montezuma attached himself to a radical version of the doctrine of assimilation very similar to that espoused by Pratt, and this brought him into conflict with other members of the SAI and with many white reformers and government officials. Both Pratt and Montezuma believed strongly in the ability of Native Americans to live like white people. In 1916 Montezuma began his own small journal in opposition to the SAI's magazine, since, as he wrote to Pratt, he could not "rely on the Society's Magazine."[32] Montezuma introduced the very first edition of his paper, which he called *Wassaja* after his Native American name, with the promise that "this monthly . . . is to be published only so long as the Indian Bureau exists. Its sole purpose is Freedom for the Indians through the abolishment of the Indian Bureau."[33]

In the November 1916 edition of *Wassaja*, he wrote, "To promulgate the doctrine that the Indian is so different in human characteristics from the Caucasian that it is impossible to obliterate the lines which divide them . . . is to hold him not entitled to the liberty and equality of rights to which all men are born."[34] Devoted to the idea of the dominance of nurture over nature, both Montezuma and Pratt argued that the most effective way of solving the "Indian problem" was to remove Native American children from Native American society and raise them as white children. As Montezuma, borrowing one of Pratt's favorite images, maintained in a paper given to the Fortnightly Club of Chicago in February 1898:

> I wish that I could collect all the Indian children, load them in ships at San Francisco, circle them around Cape Horn, pass them through Castle Garden, put them under the same individual care that the children of foreign emigrants have in your public schools, and when they are matured and moderately

educated let them do what other men and women do—take care of themselves. This would solve the Indian question.[35]

The belief in the inherent equality of Native American people seemed to lead logically to a belief in the possibility of interracial marriage. Pratt was often vociferous in support of the intermarriage of Native Americans and white people, and he did not hesitate to advocate the marriage of white women to Native American men as well as the more common alternative. In 1913 Pratt gave an address which, after describing a number of examples of Native American men living in cities with successful careers and white wives, argued that "through all the years white men have taken Indian wives and made their homes with the Indians. Why should not Indian men take white wives and live with the whites?"[36]

Pratt often used a white wife as evidence of the successful assimilation of Native American men. In a letter to the superintendent at Carlisle Indian school some years after Pratt retired, he described a visit to the Montezumas' home in Chicago to illustrate his opposition to the methods of Indian Commissioner Cato Sells:

> As we came through Chicago, Dr. Montezuma, to whom I had written of our coming and that we would be in that city from five in the evening until ten thirty at night, met us at the station with a limousine, took us to his home and gave us a delightful dinner cooked by his wife. He had a little company, among them two old Carlislers, now residents of and engaged in business in Chicago, both married to white wifes [sic] with children attending public schools. I am willing to place these two Indians absolutely against all that Mr. Sells says to the contrary.[37]

In a 1913 speech he made in Philadelphia, Pratt described five successfully assimilated Native American men who had married white wives and who were living "scattered and individually in happy contact with our people, instead of living together in a race mass nursing and plotting prejudice to their own hurt." He pointed out that "through all the years white men have taken Indian wives and made their homes with the Indians." Why, therefore, "should not Indian men take white wives and live with the whites? Just now we have two United States Senators and one member of the National House of Representatives who are the products of these intermarriages, which ought to end all cavil."[38]

In 1912 Pratt brought up the subject in a letter to Montezuma, just after mentioning Elaine Goodale Eastman and her novel *Yellow Star*, which described the marriage of a Native American woman to a white man:

> I spoke to the Presbyterian preachers in San Francisco the day before yesterday. After I was through one of them asked me if I believed in intermarriage. I, of course, affirmed my position and instanced not only a number of happy and distinguished intermarriages (which will present themselves to you), but the grand results from the progeny of such Indian marriages. Another preacher thought he would stump me by asking: "Would you want a daughter of yours to marry an Indian?" I said that if my daughter Marion had come to me at the time of her young womanhood bringing a young Indian who had won as many medals and graduated as highly in his schools as did Mr. Stevick, who had passed through the Law School of the University of Pennsylvania with as much distinction as he had, and had been solicited to enter one of the greatest law firms in the city of Philadelphia, but declined, as he did, and who was as much of a gentleman in every way as my present son-in-law, I should certainly have quickly said "all right." That it was not a question of race, but a question of quality absolutely.[39]

This hypothetical son-in-law, Pratt's questioner might have replied, was an implausible prospect. But, as Pratt and Montezuma knew all too well, a small number of highly qualified Native American men did exist. Indeed, the unspoken implication in this passage is that Montezuma himself could well have been sufficiently qualified to become Pratt's son-in-law. It is therefore hardly surprising that Pratt felt he should have some control over Montezuma's choice of a wife.

Unexpectedly, however, Montezuma kept his marriage deliberately quiet, even from Pratt. Illinois, where the couple were married, was not one of those states which had prohibited interracial marriage between white people and Native Americans, so illegality cannot have been the reason for this reticence. The fear of a scandal, however, might have been a factor. Peter Iverson, Montezuma's biographer, argues that quite possibly Marie Keller's family did not approve of the match and were therefore kept in the dark. The only evidence for this is a letter which Montezuma wrote to his wife only a few days after their marriage. Montezuma had left immediately after the wedding on a journey west. "The rest are uneasy that I do not write any more to you," he wrote to Marie on Department of the Interior stationery, "but we know best that if the folks do not know anything about us, the less letters to you will be better. You know we know each other and these people do not know. I feel good and happy that everything turned out all right. I hope you are still safe from the others finding out what happened. . . . Your husband."[40]

Over a month after his marriage, Montezuma received a letter from Pratt explaining that he had read of the event in the *Chilocco Indian School Journal*: "As you have said nothing to me about it and have failed to ask my permission, I am not a little surprised." Despite his obvious consternation Pratt added: "At your years, I should be entirely willing to believe that you have been wise in your selection. However, I refuse entirely to believe it until I hear from you."[41] A week later he must have done so, and he wrote a letter of congratulation, informing the newlyweds that "you can both feel assured of our continued fatherhood and motherhood." Marie Keller was obviously a choice of which Pratt approved. "The fact that you have such a practical, homemaking companion is a source of the greatest possible gratification to us," Pratt added, giving a clue as to the terms in which Montezuma had described his new bride.[42] Indeed, through his marriage to a white wife, Montezuma had complied with the version of assimilation to which both he and Pratt subscribed.

Charles Eastman's public life exhibited similar tensions. After being raised by his maternal grandmother in the traditional Sioux manner, Eastman's life took an unforeseeable turn when his father, who had been presumed dead after the Minnesota Sioux uprising in 1862, returned in 1873. He had converted to Christianity, and he immediately sent Eastman to school "as if [it were his] first warpath."[43] Attending school, Eastman often felt torn between his old and new life: "At times I felt some-

10. Carlos Montezuma and his wife, Marie, ca. 1920. Courtesy of the Carlos Montezuma Collection, Arizona Collection, Arizona State University Libraries.

thing of the fascination of the new life, and again there would arise in me a dogged resistance, and a voice seemed to be saying, 'It is cowardly to depart from the old things!' "[44] After attending various Agency schools and then Santee Normal School and Dartmouth College, Eastman, as his biographer Raymond Wilson records, made his decision to pursue a medical degree with his racial background very much in mind.

When choosing between the study of law and medicine, he decided on the latter not because of any personal preference but because it would be of greater service "to his people."[45] "I wished to share with my people whatever I might attain," he wrote, and "looked about me for a distinct field of usefulness."[46] In his application to the Bureau of Indian Affairs for a position as an Agency physician, he showed himself to be aware of the possibilities of his role as a representative of assimilation. He argued that the "government physician can be the most useful civilizer among the force of government officers placed in any Indian Reservation if he

11. Charles Eastman while a student at Boston University School of Medicine. Elaine Goodale Eastman Collection, record 1385. Courtesy of Sophia Smith Collection, Smith College.

could understand the language and the habits of the people," as of course, Eastman did; few others could make this claim.[47]

Eastman was assigned a post at Pine Ridge Agency in South Dakota, where he soon confronted numerous tensions arising from his position as an assimilated Native American. It was here he met schoolteacher Elaine Goodale. The Wounded Knee massacre took place soon after their engagement. Eastman was among the first to discover the extent of the killing while searching for survivors among the frozen corpses. It was a "severe ordeal for one who had so lately put all his faith in the Christian love and lofty ideals of the white man. Yet I passed no hasty judgment, and was thankful that I might be of some service and relieve even a small part of the suffering," Eastman later wrote in his autobiography.[48] After his marriage, conflict with the Agency meant the end to this part of Eastman's career.[49] He never practiced as a doctor again, instead gaining a position with the Young Men's Christian Association and supporting himself through writing and lecturing. Indeed, for most of his life his Native American origins were more of a source of income than the medical profession. Eastman wrote eleven books and numerous articles, all on subjects related to Native Americans. He became a popular lecturer on Native American topics. In 1904 and 1905 he spoke on "A School of Savagery," "The Real Indian," "The Story of the Little Big Horn," "The True Story of Hiawatha," "Wild Animals and Indian Hunters," and "Indian Wit, Music, Poetry, and Eloquence."[50] A few months after the first SAI conference, Fayette A. McKenzie, a white man who was instrumental in forming the organization, wrote to Arthur C. Parker, who would eventually become its most influential leader, to encourage him to lobby for Eastman's support for the SAI:

> The more I think over the Conference, the more convinced I am ... that Dr. Eastman was the statesman of the movement. This without any reflection upon the equally honest and earnest efforts of others. Moreover, whether rightly or wrongly, Dr. Eastman is the best known Indian in the country and his cordial co-operation is a matter of great significance.[51]

Eastman's writings have been seen as the output of an assimilated Native American. However, as Raymond Wilson has pointed out, Charles Eastman was "acculturated" rather than "assimilated," meaning that his character was modified rather than transformed by his contact with white people.[52] Eastman concluded his autobiography with a statement about his complex identity:

> I am an Indian; and while I have learned much from civilization, for which I am grateful, I have never lost my Indian sense of right and justice. I am for development and progress along social and spiritual lines, rather than those of commerce, nationalism, or material efficiency. Nevertheless, so long as I live, I am an American.[53]

Charles Eastman's opinion of assimilation was based on an enduring faith in the nature of white Americans. He told the first SAI conference in 1911 that "no prejudice has existed so far as the American Indian is concerned" as long as they lived up to certain standards. "I have found that it lies within us to show the paleface what we can do. . . . You must be honorable and moral, and in this way move up and be of service to your neighbor, for it is only the ignorant, the worldly of the worst kind that turn up their noses at our people."[54] Eastman firmly believed in the qualities of both cultures. Although he thought that Native Americans would have to submit to the economic growth on which white American culture was based, he also felt that their spiritual qualities and ideas should be influential in the other direction. "We are not going to live in teepees all our lives" he told the 1919 SAI conference. "We are not going to continue our hunting. The white man's hunting is business. We must conform to this life, this new life, and we have." But, referring to the popular belief that many of the sentiments in the Constitution were inspired by contact with Eastern tribes, he argued that Native Americans also had something to offer American society. "[The Indian] will save this country," he wrote. "We must keep our heads and our hearts together. Keep our . . . characteristics that we have contributed to the country—those characteristics that have been put into the Constitution of the United States itself.[55]

As Phillip Deloria has argued, Eastman endeavored to "carve out a positive role for native people in twentieth-century America" through his emphasis on the qualities of Native American culture.[56] In a speech given to the New York City Indian Association in 1914, Eastman described his happiness with the formal declaration of the Universal Races Conference held the previous year (which Eastman attended) that the "original North American Indian represented the highest type of pagan thought." He supported this line of thought with "various amusing and interesting incidents showing the mental acumen and intellectual perceptions of Indians." Eventually he convinced his audience more "than ever that as a race the Indians form splendid material out of which can be made not only Christians of fine character and attainments, but also capable and energetic ministers, missionaries and administrators."[57] In 1915 he published a book entitled *The Indian Today*, the stated aim of which was

> to set forth the present status and outlook of the North American Indian. In one sense his is a "vanishing race." In another

and an equally true sense it is a thoroughly progressive one, increasing in numbers and vitality, and awakening to the demands of a new life. It is time to ask: What is his national asset? What position does he fill in the body politic? What does he contribute, if anything, to the essential resources of the American nation? In order to answer these questions, we ought, first, to consider fairly his native environment, temperament, training, and ability in his own lines, before he resigned himself to the inevitable and made up his mind to enter fully into membership in this great and composite nation. If we can see him as he was, we shall be the better able to see him as he is, and by the worth of his native excellence measure his contribution to the common stock.[58]

Despite these views, Eastman participated in government assimilation projects such as the lengthy process of renaming Sioux people under the 1887 General Allotment Act, a task which engaged him for seven years.[59] Eastman drew a firm distinction between the idea of Christian civilization, which he supported and believed to be compatible with his Native American beliefs, and the reality of mainstream American society. After the Wounded Knee massacre in 1890, he admitted that he "had been bitterly disappointed in the character of the United States army and the honor of Government officials. Still, I had seen the better side of civilization, and I determined that the good men and women who had helped me should not be betrayed. The Christ ideal might be radical, visionary, even impractical, as judged in the light of my later experiences; it still seemed to me logical, and in line with most of my Indian training. My heart was still strong."[60] It was his personal belief, he wrote, "after thirty-five years' experience of it that there is no such thing as 'Christian civilization.' I believe that Christianity and modern civilization are opposed and irreconcilable, and that the spirit of Christianity and of our ancient religion is essentially the same."[61]

Eastman's views on assimilation and interracial marriage are clearly based on his own experiences. For example, he argued in 1915 that all a Native American needed in order to be "popular, and indeed to be lionized if he so desires, is to get an education and hold up his head as a member of the oldest American aristocracy." He went on to claim that "many of our leading men have married into excellent families and are prominent in cultivated white communities."[62] Eastman firmly believed in the inevitability of "race mixing" through interracial marriage and saw this process as a positive development. Although he thought it "too late" to "save [their] color," young Native American men who married interracially were "rearing a healthy and promising class of children. The tendency of the mixed-bloods is toward increased fertility and beauty as well as good mentality. This cultivation and infusion of new blood has relieved and revived the depressed spirit of the first American to a noticeable degree."[63] Eastman's positive view of assimilation never addressed the difficulties that most Native American men would encounter in reaching a position in white society similar to his own.

Eastman's views on interracial marriage and assimilation were similar to those held by the other members of the SAI. As other scholars have demonstrated, the SAI grappled with notions of identity and culture in a complex manner.[64] Highly acculturated, often personally involved in interracial relationships, and stubbornly engaged on behalf of their people, the members of the SAI had a unique perspective on the subject of assimilation and a considerable personal investment in the mainstream perception of it. Sherman Coolidge explicitly connected his own circumstances with the aims of the SAI when he outlined his hopes for the organization in a 1919 edition of the SAI's journal, the *American Indian Quarterly*.

> My wife is a full blooded white woman. I am a full blooded Arapaho Indian. My children are half-breeds. In a short time there will not be such a thing as an Indian, a pure-blooded Indian. . . . So I am anxious that this society . . . as it grows and becomes stronger and stronger, will be a service not only to the American Indian, but also to his brothers in the North and the South and to humanity at large the world over.[65]

There is no doubt that the SAI believed in the inevitability of assimilation, but they talked about the issue in ways which were at the same time designed to uphold and defend their status as Native Americans.[66] The SAI insisted, for example, that assimilation would not mean the disappearance of the Native American race. Sherman Coolidge assured the readers of the very first issue of the *Quarterly*: "We are not 'a vanishing people' because we have sought adjustment to environment." In fact, the Native American people had a unique contribution to make: "Some day the American Indian will be recognized as having given to the American race, as it will be found, many of the finest qualities that it possesses. The blood of the so-called 'vanished people' will have leavened the new race."[67]

Other writers insisted, as did Oliver Lamere, a Winnebago man, that assimilation "did not mean that American elements and Indian elements will have to become so mixed up and intertwined that it will be impossible to separate one from the other." Lamere believed that some elements of Native American culture could not "possibly . . . unite with the American culture of to-day . . . and these we must try to keep side by side with American characteristics, and not swallowed up by them to form a watery mixture."[68] In 1917 the *Quarterly* approvingly quoted a portion of an essay on current Indian policy written for a competition run by Stanford University. Its author acknowledged that the "opinion prevails among the body of thinkers and writers who deal with the Indian question that he will soon lose his identity in the white race." The "Indian," he or she said, quoting Commissioner Francis Leupp, "is losing his identity hour by hour, competing with white people in the labor market, mingling with white children, intermarrying with white people and rearing an offspring which combines the traits of both lines of ancestry." Although the Native American was "approaching [the] end of his pure aboriginal type," the writer predicted the "upgrowth of another which will claim the name 'American' by a double title as solid as the hills on his horizon."[69]

Using the language of the period, the SAI also attempted to emphasize the quality of Native American "blood." Sometimes this topic was broached in terms of defending the qualities of persons of mixed descent, no doubt in part a reaction to the negative stereotypes of "half-breeds" that were prevalent at the time. The *Quarterly* argued that it was not "the racial combination or the national blood of either parent that produces depraved offspring" but "the diseased and immoral white man or woman uniting with a diseased and immoral Indian man or woman. Good Indian blood and good white blood have produced some of the finest Americans who ever lived."[70]

When speaking of the quality of Native American blood, contributors to the *Quarterly* often attempted to secure an advantageous place in the racial hierarchy that dominated American thinking at this time. Frank G. Speck of the University of Pennsylvania bemoaned the "shame" of the fact that "thoroughly deculturated Indians often lose their pride enough to mingle and marry with their social inferiors among certain classes of negroes and whites." Native Americans, Speck argued, were at least one step up from other "dark-skinned" peoples and should not "lower themselves socially to the status" of those groups. Despite his dark skin, the Native American was a member of a noble race, in fact, the "thing which holds the Indian up is his Indian-ness, so to speak."[71] An especially revealing piece entitled "Problems of Race Assimilation in America with Special Reference to the American Indian" was published in 1916. It pointed out that the relationships that produced people of mixed descent were often between respectable married people and not just casual relationships between white men and Native American women. After stressing, yet again, the qualities of such children, the article noted, "There is not the prejudice against good Indian blood that there is against some foreign bloods *because of race*. Indians so assimilated and amalgamated constitute no grave social or race problem." Compared with those of the immigrant working classes, Native Americans' "aims and methods of thought are thoroughly American."[72]

The interracial marriages of these male SAI members to white women were solidly middle-class affairs. Unlike the working-class white men who were scorned as "squaw men," reviled because it was thought they lived as freeloaders on reservations, these men fitted comfortably into ideas about what respectable members of society should spend their time doing.[73] They were doctors, lawyers, and preachers, and in their role as representatives of their people they wrote and spoke eloquently to white audiences. In mainstream American society they could play by the rules and still hold their own. Nevertheless, the SAI felt it had a necessary part to play in making public arguments which emphasized the qualities of

Native American people to the mostly racist members of the mainstream population. To these people, SAI members presented themselves as examples of assimilation "gone right" in two ways: first, as a step toward the genetic merging of two good quality races and, second, as a painless, respectable, and middle-class version of racial amalgamation.

Assimilation was not the only doctrine with which educated Native American men had to grapple. Charles Eastman and Carlos Montezuma lived at a time when the American idea of masculinity was in transition. Industrialization had changed the workforce from one primarily based on agriculture and domestic industry to one in which men left their homes every day to work at tasks defined by another. The idea of success was based on the "self-made man" (a stereotype that had been operational since America had declared its independence). New qualities such as competitiveness, strength of character, and will were required alongside more old-fashioned personal assets such as honesty, industry, sobriety, diligence, and politeness. As corporate, white-collar work required less and less a demonstration of the latter qualities, men turned to sports such as boxing and hunting, went to the gymnasium to build their muscles, and joined fraternal organizations that promoted more physical and adventurous ideas of masculinity than those required by the workplace.[74]

Eastman and Montezuma appear to have assimilated the dominant ideology of masculinity just as much as they absorbed Christianity and white culture. Their stories of completing their education against great odds, and their transformation from "savage" to "civilized," meant that they were, literally, self-made men. Their exotic pasts as members of "savage" tribes made them especially congenial to their times. White men romanticized the frontier and strove to emulate the qualities of the rough-living, physically able frontiersman. Gail Bederman has explored how Theodore Roosevelt deliberately changed his somewhat effeminate image to that of the rugged, adventurous frontiersman.[75] Eastman and Montezuma were able to live up to this idea of manhood better than most. Their Native American features reminded white Americans that, although they were successful, middle-class professionals, they were also "warriors," with physical and spiritual abilities that white men could only dream of possessing. Charles Eastman, for example, worked for many years as a spokesman for the Young Men's Christian Association, personifying just the right mixture of Christianity and physical manhood that the organization wished to encourage. Eastman and Montezuma did not ignore their indigenous backgrounds or see it as something from their distant past; rather, it was an important component of the way they portrayed themselves. "Stand up and face the foe," Montezuma wrote to Pratt during 1892, despite his strong assimilated stance, "for you have one Apache in an ambush ready at any moment to rush out and present the Indian question black and white."[76]

During the 1910s the Eastmans ran a camp for girls in the New England wilderness. The aim of the camp was to train "American girls as Indians."[77] In a newspaper article subtitled "Dr. Eastman, College-bred Brave, to Teach Pretty Palefaces from Big Cities Primitive Ways in New Hampshire Nook," the reporter included his own romanticized impressions of Eastman's position between two cultures:

> "Will you tell them," asked the reporter, "about your own father Many Lightnings, and about the Sioux Massacre in Minnesota." . . . In the Big Chief's eyes there came that imperturbable look once more. He was a thousand miles away, away from his pen and his manuscripts—back with his great, great grandfather Cloud Man, who pitched his tent on the shores of Lakes Harriet and Calhoun now in the centre of Minneapolis suburbs. There he first saw the Washechu (White man) there he heard Secoka sing in the early spring and listened to the wondrous tales of Uncheedah (his famous grandmother). Silence reigned. Then the telephone rang—and the vision was swept away.[78]

White America's fascination with Native American culture was played out, literally, in clubs like the Improved Order of Red Men, secret societies in which white people appropriated aspects of Native American culture.[79] Hazel Hertzberg has explored the close links between these societies and the members of the SAI, some of whom, like the Reverend Red Fox Francis St. James Skiuhushu, formed their own organizations, which incorporated elements of Native American culture in their rules and ceremonies.[80]

Men like Charles Eastman and Carlos Montezuma have provided a challenge for biographers and historians hoping to evaluate their lives—in the simplest terms, were they activists of or traitors to traditional Native American society? Most conclude that their lives were far too complex for such dichotomies. As Phillip Deloria points out, the "very future" of the Native American people depended heavily upon men like Eastman and Montezuma's "ability to negotiate American society." Their complex identities were the result of their "cultural quests for social power," not just for their own personal standing but also for the benefit of their people.[81] This responsibility no doubt lay heavily upon their shoulders and impacted on their private lives in ways we can only try to understand. It seems clear, however, that their position impacted on their choice of spouse. They occupied such an unstable position between two cultures that not many women existed who were suitable partners—that is, similar in terms of class, education, and ethnic background. While there were white women who had received an equivalent education and expected a middle-class future, most of these would not be willing to cross the barrier of race. Although there were a small number of highly educated Native American women, the majority were hardly likely to have received an education that would equip them for entrance to the middle class.[82] In addition, reformers had a vested interest in encouraging educated Native Americans to marry each other, restricting marriage choice from yet another direction.

When Charles Eastman met and fell in love with Elaine Goodale, he described an "inward struggle" caused not by her ethnic identity but by the fact that he "had planned to enter upon my life work unhampered by any other ties, and declared that all my love should be vested in my people and my profession." His inclusion of the phrase "my people" in the sentence hints, perhaps, that he had intended to "invest" his love in a Native American woman. Nevertheless, he found Elaine's "sincerity . . . convincing and . . . [her] ideals . . . very much like my own. Her childhood had been spent almost as much out of doors as mine." Her aims for the Native American people were also similar to his own: "She had been moved by the appeals of that wonderful man, General Armstrong, and had gone to Hampton as a young girl to teach the Indians there. After three years, she undertook pioneer work in the West as teacher of a new camp school among the wilder Sioux, and after much travel and study of their peculiar problems had been offered the appointment she now held." Finally, she was not a stranger to Dakota culture: "She spoke the Sioux language fluently and went among the people with the utmost freedom and confidence." Indeed, she had much in common with Eastman, perhaps more than the vast majority of Native American women, only a tiny number of whom had had the chance for an equivalent education. It is no wonder that Charles should speculate that an "unseen hand guided me to her side."[83] Indeed, as Walter R. Johnson and D. Michael Warren have argued, an interracial marriage can disguise the real similarities a couple might share: "A couple can be very much alike, but a culture can impose the differences it wants to see."[84] An educated Native American woman might have political views and expectations of marriage significantly different from those of a middle-class white woman.

Carlos Montezuma married Marie Keller when he was in his forties, and prior to his marriage he was certainly not inactive romantically. His papers contain many friendly letters from female acquaintances, and there is evidence to suggest that he conducted at least two serious love affairs. The first of these was with a young Dakota woman named Zitkala-Ša, or Gertrude Simmons, who was born at Yankton Agency in Dakota Territory and educated at various schools before teaching at Carlisle and studying music at the New England Conservatory of Music.[85] By the time she and Montezuma became romantically involved in early 1901, Zitkala-Ša had returned to the West to care for her aging mother. Their fiery correspondence, while incomplete (Montezuma's replies have not survived), shows that they were two people very much aware of the significance of their lives in the cultural conflict taking place between Native Americans and white people. Although Montezuma and Zitkala-Ša disagreed about this issue on many levels, both believed strongly in the caliber of the Native American people. "I consider the Indian spiritually superior to any race of savages white or black," Zitkala-Ša wrote to Montezuma. "If the Indian race adapts itself to the commodity of the times in one century it won't be because of Carlisle! but because the Indian was not a degenerate in the first place! I will never speak of the whites as elevating the Indian!" Zitkala-Ša was often skeptical about the tenets of Christianity and believed that Carlisle, with its strong work ethic, turned out "drudges" and that "to be compelled to work when you do not wish is drudgery not civilization."[86]

Both Montezuma and Zitkala-Ša were conscious of the public dimension of their lives. Zitkala-Ša was very aware of the fact that Pratt did not approve of many of her views, which she published widely in the form of short stories and articles. "Dear friend," she wrote to Montezuma early in their relationship:

> Your prophecy is correct—already I've heard that at Carlisle my story is pronounced "trash" and I am "worse than a Pagan." Certainly people are welcome to their opinions. . . . Do be cautious and do not stand too much for me. You have long kept Col. Pratt as your friend—do not now lose him on my account. He has revealed himself woefully small and bigoted for all his imposing Avoirdupois.[87]

Zitkala-Ša was not afraid to criticize Montezuma's relationship with Pratt and Carlisle. "I resent Carlisle's talking of you as it does," she wrote. "Its talk-boast of you as a savage Apache and now an honorable physician in Chicago—the result of Education!! I guess if the character was not in you—savage or otherwise—Education could not make you the man you are today."[88]

The couple's differing views became a problem once they became engaged and began to discuss the practicalities of their future life together. Zitkala-Ša felt they should make a life among their people on the reservations, arguing that "the *old folks* have a claim upon us."[89] Her feelings of responsibility ran in two opposed directions. While believing that they both owed their people the benefits of their eastern learning, Zitkala-Ša also felt a great deal of obligation toward her mother:

> I am drawn by instinctive love to my old mother. Visit her only? That is cruel and heartless. I must live with her and show her each day a practical demonstration of my love for

her. She will never realize what cost it may mean to me who has acquired so many artificial tastes that they have become my second nature. . . . You could do a vast deal of good by filling the position here of Agency physician—better than any of your precursors. But remember *I* do *not* ask you to do it. You must do it from choice. If . . . you cannot then you don't love me enough after all.[90]

Three times in April 1901 Zitkala-Ša attempted to convince Montezuma to move west, but it appears that his idea of providing a prominent example of a "civilized" Native American to white society was not to be altered, even for her. "Seriously," she wrote to him, "is there no reason that would make you think it by far a grander thing to live among the Indians, to give a little cheer to the fast dying old people than to be a missionary among the whites? Consider this well for on your reply my mind is likely to be changed. Earning more money is a fair inducement but surely not the highest."[91]

Zitkala-Ša expressed some radical opinions about the restrictive role of a wife, which may also have added to her doubts about the marriage. "I would not like *to have to obey* another—never!" she wrote.[92] A related foreboding concerned her worries about domestic responsibilities: "I know so little about keeping a house in running order that the undertaking is perfectly appalling to me. And from sheer cowardice I almost back out of the experiment."[93] When Montezuma wrote to her of his plans for an organization made up only of educated Native American men (in the end the SAI admitted both sexes from its inauguration), she replied: "I do not understand *why* your organization does not include Indian women. . . . Am I not an Indian woman as capable to think on serious matters and as thoroughly interested in the race as any one or two of your men put together[?] Why do you dare to leave us out? Why? Sometimes as I ponder the preponderous [*sic*] actions of men—which are so tremendously out of proportion with the small results—I laugh."[94]

Although the real cause of their separation is not clear from the correspondence that has survived, by the summer of 1902 Zitkala-Ša had married a Nakota (Yankton Sioux) called Raymond Bonnin. The relationship between Zitkala-Ša and Montezuma, which had once been one of both respect and strong feeling, had turned sour quickly. Many argumentative letters continued to flow between them even after Zitkala-Ša's marriage, often prompted by his anger that she had lost the engagement ring he had sent her. In later years, however, they renewed their friendship, often working together closely for the SAI.

While their conflicting beliefs about assimilation were perhaps only part of the reason for ending their relationship, they were a constant theme of their letters. At one point, Zitkala-Ša was angry enough to be sarcastic about Montezuma's efforts to gain a standing in white society. On hearing that he had purchased a house, she wrote:

> A House—with lawn and flowers surely is a splendid index of a splendid character. That is another feather in your cap! My! Your success will eventually fill your cap with so many feathers I'll have to call it a "War-Bonnet." "Montezuma's War-Bonnet!" What a striking title for your biography![95]

Nevertheless, both were aware of the problems caused by the duality of their identities and their differing ways of dealing with it. As Zitkala-Ša wrote in the midst of their romance: "Dearest Heart—It is as you say; the greater part of civilization is the complication of desires!"[96] Their failed relationship is evidence of yet another phenomenon that could limit the marriage choices of educated Native American men. While Zitkala-Ša had much in common with Montezuma—her education, her knowledge of both white and Native American culture, and, of course, her ethnic identity—their different approaches to their unique position led to conflict.[97]

Only a few years after the end of his relationship with Zitkala-Ša, Montezuma appears to have once again considered marriage. This later relationship is far less documented in his surviving papers. One letter, which appears to be a draft of one sent to the potential fiancé's father, is the only one in which the recipient is specifically identified by name. However, scraps of other letters survive that might also relate to this episode in Montezuma's life. Around May 1904 Montezuma wrote to William H. Underwood asking for permission to marry Underwood's daughter. Lillian Underwood was white. Well aware that the interracial nature of their relationship might be a reason for Underwood to withhold his blessing, Montezuma made this a principal theme of his letter:

> If you feel any hesitation because of my nativity—I do not blame you one bit. Even though I am an Indian, had I a loving daughter who was thinking of marrying an Indian, before knowing the man I would emphatically rebel against such an outrageous idea.[98]

Montezuma attempted to persuade Underwood of his suitability as a husband despite his race. He provided a long list of his achievements in white society and his adherence to the American work ethic:

> On the Indian question I am known all over the United States. My home life has been in the best of Christian families. Against all odds I worked my own way through the public school, the University of Illinois and Medical Department of the Northwestern University. During my fourteen years of practice I served seven years in the Government service as physician and surgeon. My acquaintance is among the best and most influential. I'm a member of the First Baptist church. In the literary line I am personally enumerated with the Press Club. In my medical work (specialist) I am highly recognised.[99]

Obviously Montezuma was not an average Native American man. "Remember," he continued, "today there are Indians and Indians. In my case it is so different, it is an unusual exception—one out of the noble race or I would not allow myself this greatest request for my life happiness."

It is tempting to analyze Montezuma's phrase "the noble race" as evidence of an argument that Montezuma may only have wished to hint at—that at least he was not a member of more despised nonwhite groups such as African Americans. Hazel Hertzberg has noted that anti–African American sentiments were not unknown in the Pan-Indian movement of which Montezuma was a part and mostly took the form of a fear of being "bracketed" with the African American people.[100] Whatever the case, it appears either that Montezuma's arguments were unsuccessful or that the relationship ended for some other reason. Montezuma's anguish at these developments is illustrated by an undated, unsourced drawing that is included without explanation in Montezuma's papers. Entitled "A Caricature on 'Strongheart,'" the sketch shows a white woman walking away from a Native American man with her nose and chin raised firmly in the air while the man walks dejectedly back to a teepee in the background. On the ground between them lies a broken heart. Three undated and unsigned letters may be related to the proposed union with Lillian Underwood. They appear to be from a white woman who wrote to end a romantic relationship and who added at the end of her tirade, "I must tell you Monte that the very fact that you are of another race is a barrier between you and any white woman your equal. You *must* look for a cultured and beautiful Indian." This passage epitomizes the reason for the limited marriage choices of Native American men. White women their equal in education and class were not short of other marriage prospects and so were more likely to choose elsewhere.

When Montezuma finally did marry, it was not a "cultured and beautiful" Native American woman, nor was it a white woman who was his social equal by the standards of the period. Marie Montezuma and Elaine Goodale Eastman represent two kinds of women who were willing to marry a Native American: those who were not the equal of their Native American husbands in terms of social status and education, and those with a humanitarian interest in Native Americans who had been exposed to the Christian and missionary belief that all races were inherently equal, or at least equal once they had been "civilized." In the next chapter the latter type will be examined in detail.

Women could be "unequal" compared to the class and education status of their Native American husbands for other reasons. Belle Starr, for example, who married Cherokee Sam Starr in 1880, had already broken many of the rules of refined feminine behavior, not to mention actual laws, before her marriage. Her dramatic life as a Western "outlaw" has been popularized by many authors and historians, many of whom see her marriage to a Native American man as only one of a long series of shocking actions.[101] Mabel Dodge Luhan and Carobeth Laird, who married Native American men in the 1920s, were outsiders for very different reasons. Luhan was a rich, intellectual, eccentric woman who through her contact with many of the radical thinkers of the day felt apart from the normal role expected of white women. After seeing her Native American husband's face in a dream, long before she even met him, she lived with him "in sin" for a period before their marriage. Laird had a baby out of wedlock at an early age, then married her teacher, the famous ethnologist John Peabody Harrington, when she was twenty-four and he was in his late forties. While doing research for him she had an affair with one of her Native American informants. She divorced Harrington and married her lover, and when he died she became a well-known healer in the Christian Science Church. Neither woman conformed to middle-class values.[102]

Marie Keller was a young Romanian American who, judging from her surviving letters, had not attained the same level of education as her husband (although her difficulties with prose and grammar could have been caused to a large extent by her unfamiliarity with English). As a recent immigrant she was perhaps somewhat unaware of the complexities inherent in an interracial marriage in her new country. Peter Iverson records that she was not fully aware of her husband's national importance and was happy to remain uninvolved in his career.[103] The surviving letters written by the couple indicate a close and affectionate relationship that seemed unaffected by the outside pressures which must have applied to it. Truly comprehensive correspondence exists from only one period in the Montezumas' marriage. It was written during a period of separation that occurred between June and October 1921. Montezuma traveled to Washington in June 1921 to put his case for land and water rights of the people living on the McDowell reservation. His letters from this trip, during which he met with the commissioner of Indian affairs, Cato Sells, and other powerful men show that, contrary to Iverson's portrayal of her, Montezuma assumed that Marie was very interested in hearing details of his work. He described his experience at length, outlining what went on in meetings and discussing the attitude of the Indian Bureau. "You and I know the work for the Indians is discouraging," he wrote.[104]

Before his return Marie had set out on a long trip by automobile to Arizona, where she stayed with Montezuma's friends and relatives on the McDowell reservation. Montezuma had planned to join her, but decided later that the cost did not justify his making the trip. Marie felt both like an insider and an outsider during this visit. At one point she complained:

> No one will talk English with me [unless] they are up against it and want to know about something[.] I don't know[,] I am lonesome to talk to some one in English . . . at the table when they all can talk and understand and I can't understand them . . . it is not for ever and I shall not be to[o] hard on them[.] I don't mind the old People but when the young people don't care that makes me mad.[105]

Both Maria and Montezuma were aware that Marie's whiteness gave her a certain "status" among the Native Americans at McDowell. Montezuma wrote:

> I know the Indians will be glad to see you. . . . You can tell them so many things that they do not know. The Indians will be kind to you and you can live and be at rest. . . . Tonight I can imagine you are asleep and maybe dreaming of Chicago and when you awake, you are at McDowell many miles from home. But you must think you are at home with those blood relations of mine.[106]

In one letter to her husband, Maria simultaneously acknowledged both her status and her unimportance in the McDowell community. She told her husband that the McDowell inhabitants "come to me as if I was Christ and could help and know everything in the world they have no confidence in themself." However, she explained that she was able to add to her growing knowledge of their habit of gambling because "they do not care anything about me they think I am one of them (they don't know me yet) so they hide nothing before me."[107] Montezuma often asked her to act as his agent, for example, requesting that she "find out everything about McDowell matters and tell the Indians that I have not enough money to come out there."[108] On another occasion he asked her to "watch, hear, and see everything about McDowell."[109]

These letters provide rare insights into the Montezumas' tender feelings for each other as well as their everyday home life. "I am everlastingly killing cockroaches. I take one hour every night for exercise," Montezuma told his wife.[110] On other occasions he recorded his sadness over having to kill a litter of kittens, his difficulties making jam, and, when they began to make plans for her return, his anticipation that their pet "cats will be glad to see you."[111] Both professed their love and longing for each other, Marie sending "love and kisses" with many of her letters, and Montezuma signing himself in each one "Your loving husband, Wassaja."

Montezuma died only a little over a year later, in January 1923, and Marie was clearly devastated. She wrote that "his sickness and dea[th] came so fast that I can[']t believe he is dead[.] I cannot tell you my deep sorrow of loving him at this time[,] it is hard for me to bear it."[112] She telegrammed Pratt the news, who replied, "We have all been very deeply saddened by [Montezuma's death]. He seemed so strong and well and was with it all such a heroic figure. . . . Now we are interested in your welfare. Please find time to write me a line, won't you."[113] By July 1924, Marie was married again. Significantly , there is some evidence that her second husband was also a Native American who had been bandmaster at Chilocco Indian School.[114] This fact could be understood in two ways. It could be taken as evidence that Marie had become more open-minded through her marriage to Montezuma and able to cross cultural boundaries. Alternatively, it could be that, having damaged her standing in white society with her first marriage, her choice of marriage partners had become limited. So few of her letters from this time are extant that it is impossible to make a judgment.

As Peter Iverson poignantly points out, Carlos Montezuma's life describes the proverbial circle. Despite his ambition to be a "missionary to the whites" early in his life, as he got older Montezuma spent more and more time with his relatives in Arizona. Having first returned to the country of his childhood in the autumn of 1901 and retraced the steps of his journey away from his people, Montezuma discovered a number of aunts and cousins with whom he corresponded for the rest of his life.[115] Alongside official correspondence from lawyers and doctors can be found numerous poorly spelled and affectionate letters from his cousins, often asking for medical advice or money.

Montezuma visited Arizona regularly and spent much time fighting legal battles on behalf of his people, especially those on the McDowell reservation who had many problems with threats of removal and irrigation and water rights. As early as 1915 Montezuma had begun making inquiries about applying for enrollment on Apache tribal rolls. In November 1920 he submitted the numerous documents required for the application to the Bureau of Indian Affairs. In June 1922 he received notification that his application had been refused on the grounds that the reservation at which he was attempting to enroll was "more a part of the Pima country at the time of Montezuma's capture" than that of his own tribe. The fact that he was a "citizen of the United States . . . with full rights as such" was also cited.[116] Montezuma was devastated, writing in a long letter to his good friend, lawyer Joseph W. Latimer:

> If I am not an Apache, there [are] no such Indians as Apache Indians. . . . I must confess this beats all. It is unthinkable to conceive that such honorable men as the Governmental Officials should . . . deny me to be enrolled in the land of my birth, where my father and mother died . . . there is something creeping like an invisible snake, in keeping me away from my inherited home and depriving me of my rights.[117]

Only a few months later, Montezuma began to complain about his health, and in December he traveled back to the McDowell reservation in order to die with his people and on the land where his father and mother had died. This decision was eerily similar to the journey Charles Eastman made to the unsettled region of Canada just before his death in 1939. "My dear Dovie," Montezuma wrote to his wife, "I am still fighting to keep above water. . . . All I can do is resign everything and take [what may] come with brandy and God's will. You must keep your cool. . . . Be a brave girl and get up for the best."[118] When he died on January 31, Marie had made the journey to Arizona to be with him. He was buried in a simple grave on the McDowell reservation.[119] After he died, Hazel Hertzberg reports, he was remembered on the reservations in Arizona in a variety of ways. After he had traveled around several reservations in 1918 preaching against the Indian Bureau, Hertzberg records:

> Among the Pimas . . . the older men who refused to deal with the Indian Bureau and who in general shunned white ways

became known as "Montezumas," while among the Papagos, "Montezumas" were older village headmen who came to identify Montezuma with both Jesus and a tribal deity and believed that "Montezuma would one day return and restore better times and good moral behavior."[120]

This confusion over Montezuma's philosophy reflects the complexity of his life, in which he grappled with the demands of two cultures. Although his marriage was very much part of this aspect of his life, there can be no doubt that the Montezumas' relationship was a successful one, based on true affection. It is not my intention to attribute the Montezumas' marriage entirely to his belief in assimilation. Apart from anything else, this argument would ignore Marie Montezuma's agency in the relationship. Choosing a marriage partner is not a simple decision, and while political climates and legal prohibitions no doubt have their effect, the deeper level of human feeling cannot be ignored.

The lives of men such as Charles Eastman and Carlos Montezuma were grounded in the cultural assumptions of their particular contexts and their contemporaries' expectations. As Raymond Wilson argued in his biography of Charles Eastman, "Too much emphasis can be placed on the personal problems he experienced as an Indian operating in an alien culture, but they also reveal poignantly the failures of a man whose youth was filled with promise. A man who could wear both a war bonnet and a high starched collar with equal aplomb was also quite capable of messing up his finances, having encounters with women, and generally failing to remain the symbolic figure so many others wanted him to be."[121] Historians should not repeat the mistake of viewing these men as anything more than individuals struggling to find freedom and happiness in a period in which, for people of their racial background, such ambitions were not easily fulfilled.

In 1999 Devon A. Mihesuah cited Frantz Fanon's contentious statement about nonwhite men who have relationships with white women. They do so, Fanon intimated, in order to "be acknowledged not as Black but as white . . . who but a white woman can do this for me? By loving me she proves that I am worthy of white love."[122] Mihesuah believes that Fanon might be partially right in the cases of some Native American men who married white women, but warns that such conclusions require "further, sensitive inquiry."[123] In this chapter such inquiry has revealed that men such as Montezuma and Eastman do not conform to Fanon's ideas. Instead, their decision to marry white women was linked to their position as exemplars of the success of assimilation ideology, but in complex ways. Although the doctrine of assimilation and nineteenth-century ideas of masculinity impacted on the way they lived their lives, they had not abandoned their indigenous identity in any way. Instead, as symbolic figures, they struggled hard to synthesize aspects of their public and private lives. Their marriages, although often made public in various ways, belonged for the most part to their private lives, and for that reason the historian, in the end, can know only a little about the personal and emotional reasons for them. The following chapter explores the other side of the equation, delving into the motivations and feelings of the white woman married to Charles Eastman, one of the educated, acculturated Native American men vaunted by American assimilation policy.

4. A Middle-Class White Woman Philanthropist and Interracial Marriage

During the nineteenth century, when the industrialization of American society meant that white men were spending more and more time away from their homes and families, a new image of American womanhood was born. White women were seen as purer, more pious, and gentler than their husbands, and they were expected to safeguard the morality of the nation using a very powerful tool—domesticity. Set apart from the masculine world of business and politics, the home was the feminine sphere of influence, and it was woman's responsibility to make it a moral, caring, and nurturing place. American scholars have explored this image of womanhood under many names, but they have agreed that it emerged and was popularized, thanks in part to books, sermons, and magazines, by the middle of the century. Barbara Welter called it the "cult of true womanhood," Aileen Kraditor the "cult of domesticity," and Nancy Cott the "doctrine of woman's sphere."[1]

White women were told in no uncertain terms that if they wished to contribute more widely to society, they should use the qualities of the domestic sphere to improve the world as teachers, nurses, missionary workers, or other similarly nurturing professionals. As Valerie Sherer Mathes has pointed out, it is not surprising that this doctrine led, almost simultaneously, to women taking tentative steps into the public sphere as moral reformers.[2] In the antebellum period, numbers of white middle-class women had joined and formed benevolent societies and organizations directed at reforming many areas of American society, perhaps most seriously in the abolitionist and temperance movements. These organizations increased in number and secularity in later decades, and the "Indian Problem" was one of the areas at which women directed their energies, claiming a special role for themselves in uplifting and civilizing Native American people.

Peggy Pascoe has labeled the power derived from the idea that purity, piety, and morality were essentially feminine values "female moral authority" and has examined its important implications for cross-cultural relations between women.[3] It also had undeniable ramifications for relationships between white women and men of different races. Not only could white women influence the world by civilizing their husbands and children in the privacy of their homes; they also could exert influence across racial lines in order to civilize and Christianize those whom society often felt were most in need of it.

White women found careers as missionaries, teachers, writers, or activists in female-run organizations such as the Women's National Indian Association, formed in 1883, who saw themselves as having a special and separate role in the work of assimilating Native Americans. When, during their fourth annual meeting, the leaders of the Association were asked if they contemplated combining their efforts with the male-dominated Indian Rights Association, the general secretary "thought not." Such a union had been mentioned, she said, but "she had found in conversation with officers of the gentleman's Association that their lines of work absorb their attention, as do our own lines our attention, and that the present relation of the two societies was thought to be best for both."[4]

These women were part of the group of people in the late nineteenth and early twentieth centuries who believed in humanitarian notions of equality. Not only did this lead them into professions such as teaching or missionary work which brought them into contact with Native Americans, but it imbued them with a belief in the ability of Native Americans to acquire completely the trappings of white society, once properly educated. Thus their philosophies were grounded in the idea that Native Americans were inherently equal to white people in ability, if not in education. Margaret Jacobs has argued that these views, in combination with the ideology in which women were seen as having a special role in the civilizing of Native Americans, could be construed to encompass interracial marriages. After all, what more could a "civilizing angel" do than combine her influence in both the public and private sphere by marrying a Native American man—especially if that man was already a promising candidate for assimilation?[5] In 1891 President Seelye of Smith College told the Lake Mohonk conference of the importance of "induc[ing] Christian men and women to make their homes among these Indians." Seelye hinted that he meant more than missionaries living in proximity to Native American communities by his reference to Elaine Goodale Eastman, who had married Charles Eastman that year: "We know what Miss Goodale did before she was married and what she will do as a married woman among them."[6] In the Carlisle student newspaper, the Eastmans' marriage was simply portrayed as a "Solution to the Indian Problem" in which Charles, "having gained high qualities by long association with Massachusetts civilization, has wisely concluded to continue permanently in that environment. That Indian's problem is solved."[7]

In the last few decades, scholars have provided many interpretations of white women who interacted with Native Americans, particularly those women who lived in the West. In the 1980s women's historians grappled with the image of women as angels who transformed the frontier from a rough and uncivilized place as just one of the many stereotypes of white western women that needed dismantling. Historians have worked hard to expose the fact that many white women were also invaders and oppressors of Native Americans. Still, as Patricia Carter has argued in her study of white women who taught Native American children during this period, even more complex overviews are required of the lives of white women who worked with Native Americans, taking into account both the racist ideologies within which they worked and their often sympathetic and humane views.[8] In this chapter, the examination of one extraordinary white woman who married a Native American illuminates the ways in which interracial marriages between educated Native American men and white women of a humanitarian bent could fit the prevailing ideology of womanhood as moralizing and civilizing agents. Such marriages had no equivalents in Australia, where, to my knowledge, almost no educated, middle-class women married Aboriginal men. The existence of educated couples like the Eastmans in the United States is further evidence of the niche of acceptance created for such marriages in mainstream society in the brief period during which cultural assimilation and education were strongly emphasized by reformers. When this ideology was dramatically replaced by the "New Deal," Elaine Goodale Eastman's consternation is revealing. As she saw it, the principles by which she had lived much of her life were ripped from under her, calling her vocation as domestic reformer and "angel of civilization" into doubt.

The coupling of the "cult of true womanhood" with Native American reform is perhaps one explanation for the unusual numbers of liaisons between white female teachers at Hampton Institute and Native American men. Caroline Andrus, Rebecca Pond, and Elaine Goodale, all teachers at Hampton Institute, are excellent examples of white women who combined their public sphere efforts to assist Native Americans to assimilate with more personal relationships with individuals. There are other examples of missionary women who married Native American men during this period. Anna Heersma, who married Jason Betzinez (Apache) when both were middle-aged, was also of a Christian missionary background. She was a Dutch missionary who met Betzinez in Oklahoma after he had returned from his years at Carlisle. In 1907 she had left Chicago, where she lived with her parents, to work in a mission for Apache children. Despite being well known for having fought with the famous warrior Geronimo (before his time at school), Betzinez became involved with organizations such as the Apache Mission Christian Endeavour, while he worked as a blacksmith and farmer. He wrote to Pratt in 1901 to reassure him that he had not "throw[n] himself away into a 'blanket Indian' as some returned students do when they returned to their people, instead of to show them what they have learned from school, they go back in to camp as useless men when they have [the] chance to do some things but they wouldn't do it. But I am more than thankful for what I have learned at school and shop at Carlisle, for I have been doing some work ever since I came back to my people."

For eleven years, Betzinez hesitated to declare his feelings for Anna because he had "no house, nothing to offer a wife." In his 1959 autobiography, published when he was in his nineties, he and his wife were described as "devout Christians and active church workers."[9]

White women married to Native Americans who lived on reservations could be seen as a welcome civilizing influence to traveling reformers. Both Herbert Welsh and J. B. Harrison spoke highly of the white wife of the Reverend Luke C. Walker, a Presbyterian missionary, after visiting the couple at the Lower Brulé reservation in South Dakota. Welsh thought Mrs. Walker was "well fitted by kind heart and courteous manner to aid her husband in his work among their dark-skinned brethren," and Harrison was impressed by her "ideas and perceptions relating to Indian interests, conditions and needs [which] appeared to be, in an unusual degree, the result of direct and in-telligent observation of facts, without much interference from prepossessions of any kind."[10] Grace Coolidge's writings also demonstrate the empathetic perspective that the white wife of a Native American might gain while living on the reservation, where one could be "overpowered suddenly and strangely by the sense of being an outsider in one's own land."[11] Theodore Roosevelt was also impressed with the insights of a "bohemian" white woman married to a man of presumably Lakota origin and living on the Pine Ridge reservation. Mrs. Crocer impressed Roosevelt "as being one of the most intelligent, capable, and genuinely philanthropic women I have ever met . . . and is doing all in her power to elevate the Indians round about, devoting herself especially to the women, striving to raise their home life." It would be impossible, Roosevelt thought, "to get a woman better qualified for the duties of field matron among these Indians. It was a great pleasure to listen to her conversation. She was the most sincere and devoted friend of the Indians, and yet . . . she had not become a mere silly enthusiast about them."[12]

Alice Robertson, who was also interested in Christianizing and civilizing Native Americans, did not marry a Native American. Her speeches at the Lake Mohonk conference, however, are remarkable for the numerous mentions of marriages of white women, many of whom were members of her family, and Native American men. In 1886, while running a school for Native American girls in Oklahoma, Robertson told the Lake Mohonk conference, "I have known a great many missionary families brought up among the Indians, and I have yet to know one in which at least one member had [not] intermingled with the Indians. I have one sister whose husband is an Indian and an aunt whose husband is an Indian. This shows that there is nothing inferior in the Indian. I don't know any such general rule of marrying among the negroes."[13] In Robertson's world, it appears that the marriage of a missionary-minded woman and a Native American man was far from unusual and indeed made sense in terms of the ideology of assimilation she espoused.

Just like those of their husbands, the lives of women such as Caroline Andrus, Rebecca Pond, Anna Heersma, and Elaine Goodale Eastman were complicated by overlaps between public and private realms. Although missionary work and teaching were two of the very few occupations open to women during this period, the former, and the latter when applied to nonwhite pupils, required at least some sense of vocation. In a sense their vocation to "help" Native Americans led these women, in one way or another, to their marriages. Elaine Goodale Eastman's decision to marry a Native American man, for example, was seen by many as connected to her vocation of civilizing Native Americans. One newspaper saw her marriage as an "interesting sequel to [her] work as a teacher among the Indians," while the school's newspaper, the *Southern Workman*, explained that the school's community felt a "special and deep interest" in the marriage because it was part of a "chronicle, which of course is not new to . . . Miss Goodale's friends and former associates in Hampton Institute where her work and enthusiasm for the Indian race began." She herself saw the marriage as stemming from her career. "The gift of myself to a Sioux," Eastman wrote in her memoirs in the late 1930s, "followed almost inevitably upon my passionate preoccupation with the welfare of those whom I already looked upon as my adopted people." In 1896 Eastman explicitly linked her career and marriage in the journal of the Women's National Indian Association when she noted that "my friends sometimes ask me whether I am still in the Indian work. I believe in marriage as a vocation and I am now in the Indian work as I was for seven years, but only as a wife may help her husband." Eastman's most revealing recollection is that of her feelings when she resolved to marry Charles Eastman. She remembered that she did so "with a thrilling sense of two-fold consecration." Her love for Charles and her desire to be his wife and mother to his children were combined with "the conception of life-long service to my husband's people."[14] Others saw it differently. Lamenting what they saw as the inevitable end to her career in Native American reform, Carlisle's weekly newspaper, the *Indian Helper*, saw her marriage to a Sioux (Dakota) man as "Another brilliant career end[ing] in Sioux-i-cide."[15]

The social status of their Native American husbands was crucial to these women's decision. Elaine Goodale Eastman made this explicit in her frivolous description of a marriage proposal she received from another Native American man:

> On one occasion he told me, by way of showing his gratitude for the interest I took in his character, that he had three wives, all of whom he would give up if I would "leave Eastman, and come and live with him." I received his proposition, however, with Indian indifference, merely replying that I did not fancy having my head split open every few days with a stick of wood. He laughed heartily, after his fashion, conscious that the cap fitted, for he was in the habit of expending all his surplus bad temper upon his wives.

Eastman's suitor obviously lacked the attitude toward women proper to a "civilized" people; his aspirations for a white wife, therefore, were ridiculous.[16]

Elaine Goodale Eastman's plentiful writings offer a rare opportunity to explore assimilationist ideas held by a white woman who married a Native American during a period in which she, in a sense, was their personification. For what better exemplified the ideas of indigenous education and equality and speedy acculturation than a white, middle-class reformer who married a Native American man? Moreover, her life spanned a period in which government attitudes toward Native American people in the United States underwent two major shifts. Eastman was a young woman when the Dawes Act was passed in 1887; she was nearing the end of her long life when "New Deal" Indian commissioner John Collier reversed the Dawes ideology in the Wheeler-Howard Act of 1934, paving the way for recognition and support of Native American culture.

Eastman was a journalist, an author, and an active member of the reform movement dedicated to the rights of Native Americans that sprang up in the last decades of the nineteenth century. Studies of Eastman have presented her as one of many white women who took up the cause of Native American reform in the late nineteenth century and have described her struggles to combine this concern with her ambitions as a writer and her responsibilities as a wife and mother. Her writings have also been analyzed as part of the tradition of white women writing about the American West. Like many other white women involved in the reform movement, Eastman wrote numerous articles, taught Native American children in both eastern boarding and western reservation schools, and attended the influential gatherings of Native American reformers at the Lake Mohonk conferences of the Friends of the Indian. Her marriage to a Native American man, however, distinguished Eastman from the majority of white women reformers. Aspects of Eastman's private life, specifically cultural issues relating to her husband and children, affected the viewpoints she expressed publicly in her later years. In her writings she situated herself as having an uncommon perspective on the policy of assimilation—the "stand-point of a woman whose knowledge is immediate and personal."[17] It was a unique point of view of a person affected by assimilation both personally and politically.

According to the memoirs that she wrote in the late 1930s, Elaine Goodale was born in 1863, the daughter of two educated members of well-known New England families. She grew up on an isolated farm in Massachusetts, experiencing a childhood that she would always remember with satisfaction. Educated at home by her mother, Elaine and her younger sister, Dora, became well-known poets, publishing their first book when Elaine was thirteen. Subsequent changes in family circumstances made it necessary for her to earn a living despite her ambitions for a literary career. At the age of twenty she took up an offer of employment as a teacher at Hampton Institute made by a friend of the family, Gen. Samuel Chapman Armstrong. Later in life she would think of this decision as "largely determin[ing] my destiny."[18]

Perhaps in response to the school's need for constant public justification of its methods, during her several years at Hampton she began a casual journalistic career that would last for the rest of her life. Journals such as the *Christian Union* and the *Independent* began publishing her articles written in support of Hampton and its agenda, which were, as she later described, "animated by the zeal of a recent convert." In her second year at Hampton she undertook a tour of the Sioux agencies in Dakota Territory with a party that included Herbert Welsh, cofounder of the Indian Rights Association, and Bishop William Hare, a well-known Episcopal missionary to the Dakota. It was on this trip that Goodale hit upon her own particular method of what was by then an established process of inculcating the Native American population with the values and standards of white culture. Unlike most reformers, she rejected removing Native American children from their families and sending them to boarding schools as the most efficient means of assimilation; instead, she suggested strengthening day schools on reservations, in which the influence of single white teachers could reach into the homes of the Native Americans living nearby.[19]

In 1886 Goodale opened her own day school with a colleague from Hampton at the Lower Brulé reservation in what was to become South Dakota. She remained in the West for another five years. She became fluent in the Dakota language and spent her summer holidays traveling around the Great Sioux reservation with Dakota rather than white companions, often sleeping in a "well-filled" teepee. She ignored the advice of "solicitous white friends" to carry a weapon: "A revolver in my baggage would only have served to advertise lack of trust . . . and in the fact that I did trust them completely lay my sole and sufficient guarantee of safety."[20]

In 1889 Elaine Goodale was made the supervisor of education of North and South Dakota. Equipped with a horse and wagon and a "Dakota lodge" (a kind of teepee), and accompanied by a Dakota couple as driver and cook, she traveled around her jurisdiction inspecting the variety of schools that existed on the reservation, taking pride in her method of arriving unannounced in the middle of a lesson. When white authorities became aware of the unrest caused by the growing popularity of the Ghost Dance religious movement among the Dakota in 1890, Eastman was ordered to return to Pine Ridge agency for safety. It was there that she met Charles Eastman. As Ruth Alexander has pointed out, the attraction

12. Elaine Goodale shortly before her marriage to Charles Eastman in 1891. Elaine Goodale Eastman Collection, record 1385. Courtesy of Sophia Smith Collection, Smith College.

between the young Dakota who had made his way in white society and the white woman who spoke the Dakota language and who, while strongly believing in assimilationist policy, was not afraid to be outspoken in her appreciation of Dakota culture, was almost inevitable.[21]

Elaine and Charles Eastman were married at a well-publicized ceremony on June 18, 1891, at the Church of the Ascension in New York. Their wedding was treated as a curiosity by the press, and two sensationally titled articles appeared in the *New York Times*: "She Will Wed an Indian" and "The Bride of an Indian."[22] Six children were born to the couple, and the family was often short of money. Elaine kept up her writing but concentrated more on assisting Charles with his many publications. While only one of his eleven books acknowledged her assistance, Raymond Wilson argues that she collaborated with him on them all. Later

Elaine would insist that Charles "was . . . the *author*—altho' he wrote very carelessly and would not even try to correct or revise, therefore I did *all* the drudgery."[23] The couple remained involved in the Native American reform movement, and both spoke briefly at the Lake Mohonk conference in 1895. In 1921, when Elaine was in her late fifties, and after thirty years of marriage, they separated. Both kept private the reasons for the disintegration of their marriage, but it seems safe to assume that Charles's extramarital affairs were a contributing factor. Charles moved to a log cabin in an unsettled portion of Canada, dying there in 1939, and Elaine returned to New England, where she lived until her death in 1953.

In later life, in private letters to her family, Eastman remembered with some bitterness the sacrifices she had made for her marriage. She herself admitted that Charles's infidelities (which resulted in at least one illegitimate child) had "poisoned not only the present and future but all my memories of married life." During the marriage, she complained, his lack of assistance with domestic matters was grossly unfair when she herself had taken on so much of the responsibility for earning money for the family:

> where a wife carried much of the financial load supposed to be borne by the husband alone, it is only fair that he assist with domestic burdens . . . even after I was doing three-fourths of "his" work, he reluctantly and ungraciously, if at all, vouchsafed the least help with "mine." That one "partner" should sit around smoking and playing solitaire, most of the day, while the other worked somewhat beyond her strength and without relief at tasks which he could quite well "spell" her at, surely can't seem to you right.

These faults, rather than any issues relating to Charles's racial identity, caused Elaine to rethink her decision to marry him. "If I had had the prophetic vision you speak of," she told her sister Dora in 1930, "I am quite sure I should have refused to marry Dr. Eastman—his tragic failure of character outweighs all the blessings of children and grandchildren."[24]

Despite her bitter feelings about her marriage, she continued her journalistic interest in the affairs of Native Americans during the 1930s and

1940s, while living in the university town of Northampton, Massachusetts. As well as publishing numerous articles and book reviews in newspapers and journals, she kept up an impressive correspondence with many of the important figures of the day. Perhaps to gather information for her articles as much as for anything else, Eastman wrote to and received replies from such prominent reformers as Vine Deloria, J. C. McCaskill, Louis Valandra, Bishop William Hare, and G. E. Lindquist. It is illuminating to put her public comments on the "Indian problem" alongside what we know of her private life. It is in her writings particularly that the unique way in which the ideology of assimilation could be interpreted and utilized by such an individual, and the struggles of that individual to come to terms with the conflicting views both of wider society and those in power, can be discerned. This conflict was especially apparent in a vehement exchange of views between Eastman and the commissioner of Indian affairs, John Collier, which occurred in the mid-1930s, a time when official solutions to the "Indian problem" were changing on a national scale. Eastman's reactions to these shifts are most revealing of her position as an assimilationist.

By the time the exchange between Collier and Eastman took place, Collier was ushering in a new era of Native American policy, completely transforming the previous attitude of the government toward the Native American people. As early as 1929, Eastman had noted in print the new direction in which the government's Native American policy was proceeding. The radical "Indian New Deal" of the 1930s was about to cause much distress and anxiety to those whom Eastman saw as her peers in Native American reform, and perhaps even more so to herself, but in 1929 she was able to comment on the situation with a detachment that is surprising in light of her later writings. Taking full advantage of her almost seventy years, Eastman was able to take a distanced view of the situation. "After all," she wrote in an article published in the *Christian Century*:

> to each generation appears the age-old Sphinx in slightly different dress, since life is new only to the young who never lived it before! And for us who thrilled to the "new hope for the Indian" as far back as the eighties and nineties of the last century, who, as youthful converts, spread the all but revolu-

tionary doctrine of his inborn right and ability to share free-
ly in our gains, who marched under the banner of General
Pratt, of General Armstrong, Senator Dawes, Bishop Whip-
ple, or Bishop Hare, there is more than a suspicion of irony in
the sound of "a new Indian policy" in 1929.

In sharp contrast to the views she would express five or six years later, Eastman was prepared to admit her sympathy with the eccentric
author Mary Austin, who believed in a policy of noninterference with
native culture, as well as with Capt. Richard Pratt's extreme assimilationist views. Indeed, as she pointed out, the experiences of her youth
placed her in a perfect position to appreciate both viewpoints: "I am in
a measure sympathetic to both, having enjoyed an experience similar
to that of Mrs. Austin [living among Native American people], . . . at the
same time working under the greatest Indian educators [such as Samuel Chapman Armstrong]."[25]

Eastman probably first wrote to John Collier, the mastermind behind
these radical changes to government policy, a short time after he was
appointed commissioner of Indian affairs by President Franklin Dela-
no Roosevelt in 1933. After a few benign exchanges in which Eastman
sent some of her work to Collier and offered to write some articles that
"might help to gain timely and intelligent support" for Collier's policies, their friendly correspondence ceased by May 1934, when Harold L.
Ickes, the secretary of the interior and Collier's superior, received a letter from the editor of the *Christian Century*. The letter was prompted by
Eastman's accusation that Collier had dismissed the Rev. Floyd O. Bur-
nett from his position as director of religious education at a nonreservation Native American school in California because of his opposition to
the Wheeler-Howard Bill. This bill, which embodied most of Collier's
new policy, abrogated the law that had allotted land to Native Americans
individually in 1887 and idealistically paved the way for Native American self-government. Greeted with strong opposition from missionaries and others who still believed that assimilation was the solution to
America's "Indian problem," the bill had been introduced in February
and received with hostility both in Congress and from the general public. While the *Christian Century* promised Collier editorial support for the

Wheeler-Howard Bill, he also expressed concern about Eastman's allegations, noting that she had submitted an article about Collier's policies not as a supporter but as a "determined opponent to the Wheeler-Howard Bill," and inviting Collier to compose a reply. Both pieces were published in the August 1934 issue of the *Christian Century*.[26]

Eastman's article, entitled "Does Uncle Sam Foster Paganism?" addressed that part of Collier's policies which assimilationists found most threatening: his recognition of the constitutional right of Native Americans to practice their religion without interference. After expressing her concern that a "Bastard" religion might be formed by joining "paganism" with Christianity, Eastman clearly revealed her belief in the cultural inferiority of Native American religion: "It is to be clearly understood that the native religions thus affirmatively sanctioned . . . have no sacred books or formal theology which may be taught by word of mouth. Their priests, if any, are medicine-men or shamans, dispensing wisdom and healing through the medium of songs and incantations." In his reply Collier pointed out that she had expressed "that peculiar presumption which the discriminations of past years have been based upon," and argued that even after the damage suffered by Native American religions since white colonization, they "are not any farther departed and diminished from their full historical meaning than are many of the fractionated and conventionalized expressions of the Christian religions." However, it was not this extreme statement that antagonized Eastman so much as his positioning her with those who advocated the now outdated policy of assimilation. "This will shock or amuse all who know what my position has always been with respect to native culture and religious freedom," she wrote in a private letter to Collier seven days after the articles appeared.[27]

Collier replied in an equally passionate tone. He stated that "rereading your article in 'The Christian Century,' I do not find one word that is appreciative of Indian religions old or new, but on the contrary, from start to finish of the article, a depreciation of them and a denial that they ought to be given the constitutional protections. . . . Indeed, as I reread your article my own rejoinder impresses me as being excessively mild." Eastman thereupon published another letter in the *Christian Century*, reiterating many of the points of her private letter to Collier. Nor was this the end of the exchange. A draft of an untitled article in Collier's files written around July 1935 appears to be a reply to something written by Eastman, and Eastman's scrapbooks contain numerous articles and letters to the editor that openly criticize Collier and his policies, continuing many of the themes of their original interaction. And although a relatively polite letter from Collier dated February 27, 1941, answering Eastman's query about the right of Native Americans to vote, exists in her papers, the two clashed in print again in the November 1942 edition of the *Atlantic*.[28]

This interchange of views between Eastman and Collier might be characterized as an inevitable disagreement between a woman clinging stubbornly and blindly to the teachings received and opinions formed in her youth and a man passionate about reversing an outdated and now admittedly racist government policy. At least one historian, Francis Paul Prucha, has treated it in this way.[29] However, Eastman's position is much more complex than this viewpoint acknowledges. Her reluctance to be included with those whom Collier labeled as not sufficiently appreciative of Native American culture needs further explanation. Even though her writings consistently reveal her assimilationist ideology, Eastman clearly did not see herself as one of those whom Collier was attacking. Indeed, her articles and letters often exhibit this tension. Eastman's writings previous to this mid-1930s exchange provide an explanation of her position on the assimilation policy she found herself defending to Collier.

Eastman, like many women of her time, owed much of her public standing to her position as a white, Christian, civilizing woman. As Louise Newman has argued, many of the gains made by the feminist movement in the nineteenth century were premised on racialized arguments about the special qualities of white women. It is no surprise, therefore, to find that Eastman accepted the general assumptions of her time. She obviously believed, for example, in the underlying rationale of the ideology of assimilation, stating clearly in 1929 that "for a harmonious blend, whether biological or merely cultural, obviously there must be general acceptance by a numerically insignificant and politically bankrupt people of the language, customs, and ideals of the dominant race." Eastman was certainly not unaware of the damage which this policy could cause, admitting that it "may, indeed must, result in certain losses—of picturesqueness, of individuality, possibly of self-respect. . . . Nevertheless, these things must certainly strike the fair-minded observer as necessary stages in a kind of progress that cannot well be avoided, if there is to be progress instead of degeneracy."[30]

Despite these matter-of-fact cruelties, Eastman also possessed, as Kay Graber has noted, "an ability, particularly remarkable in the late 1800s, to see her Indian friends sympathetically as complex human beings and to adopt aspects of their lifestyle that she found admirable." In her memoirs Eastman recounted that she was once "taken to task by a good missionary of my acquaintance for habitually wearing moccasins in the house and about the camp. I am sure the same clergyman—if he had ever heard of it—would have rebuked me even more severely for taking part in an inter-camp game of 'shinny' with a hundred or more yelling and excited men and women!"[31]

Eastman often consciously set herself apart from those she portrayed as the original and extreme holders of the assimilationist viewpoint. Almost from the very beginning of her career as an "Indian reformer," Eastman had publicly and privately distanced her ideas of education reform from those of leading assimilationists Samuel Chapman Armstrong and Richard Pratt by advocating reservation day schools at the Lake Mohonk conference in 1886 in place of the boarding school system that they favored. In July 1890 she personally wrote to Pratt to protest the detention of a student against his family's wishes, adding, "I admire [your school] greatly . . . but I am . . . opposed to *your theory*, at least as I understand it." Eastman's biography of Pratt was not overtly critical of her subject, but it clearly showed her wish to dissociate herself from his more extreme views. She called her biography of Pratt, published in 1935, "a story of which, in a sense, not even Pratt but the American Indian is the hero," adding, "That Pratt, the blunt soldier and self-made American, though on some counts a radical, was influenced by the dominant social and political philosophy of his time, may be taken for granted. That he spoke the last word on our intricate and many-sided Indian problem is too much to claim." A striking expression of Eastman's position was published in an article in the *Christian Union*:

> There is a quarrel among my papers! In the middle of a big, businesslike desk lies the "Congressional Record," crammed with debates on the Indian Appropriation bill, bristling with theories upon Indian character and an "Indian policy." Its crisp, half-open leaves fairly elbow aside a thick packet of letters—personal letters from Indians East and West. . . . On the right lies another pile from Indian missionaries, missionaries' wives, school teachers, and agents. What wonder that these letters refuse to be quietly snubbed by their official neighbors— that they stare me in the face and demand to be put under evidence? The very photographs on my desk—photographs of my Indian pupils and friends—their bright, pathetic, hopeful faces seem to look reproachfully at me.[32]

Clearly Eastman saw herself as holding a unique position in her relations with Native Americans. And indeed, as an assimilationist who had taken her ideology into her personal life, she did. Far from living the life of a middle-class woman on the East Coast, like many of the early white women reformers, Eastman had taken the ideology of assimilation literally. She had gone to South Dakota, met and married a Native American man, and given birth to six children of mixed white and Dakota descent.

Eastman's memoirs, as Brigitte Georgi-Findlay has pointed out, treat interracial marriage as unremarkable. During Eastman's narrative "one gradually becomes accustomed to these frequent marriages between well-educated Indian men and white women, foreshadowing her own marriage to a Santee Sioux." When Eastman arrived in Dakota Territory in 1886, she found "two distinct worlds existing side by side, now in dramatic opposition, now intimately mixed. There were already a few Dakotas at home in the white man's world and superior in most respects to the frontier white men. There were also a good many of both races who belonged about as much to one as to the other." Eastman played down the atypical nature of her decision by describing two such marriages in memoirs, adding, "Though I had not consciously considered marriage with a Dakota, I had closely observed several such marriages which appeared successful. The idea certainly did not repel me in any way."[33]

It is probable that this rather unusual vision of the frontier reflected Eastman's individual beliefs about the future of the Native American people. Interracial sexuality would not be the unmentionable and almost-out-of-control characteristic of frontier life referred to by most assimilationists in which white men sexually exploited indigenous women. Rather, Eastman envisaged that white women would join with assimilated and educated Native American men in socially acceptable, consecrated marriages. In a short story published in 1889, a year before she had even met Charles Eastman, one of her characters, a white doctor, says to a young Native American man struggling with the problems of assimilation: "Lots of white men marry squaws—I don't know why a white girl shouldn't marry an Indian if he was a good fellow. . . . Try and make yourself worthy of some nice girl, Steve, white or red."[34]

Eastman's personal decision to marry a Native American man was made in the context of her belief in assimilation through interracial marriage. Her contribution to the project of assimilation would be twofold: not only was she advancing the project of eliminating Native American physical characteristics by marrying Charles and bearing his children but, as Ruth Alexander has argued, her family would become a "model of the assimilationist ideal."[35] Eastman must have been surprised and disappointed that so few marriages of white women to assimilated Native American men followed her own. In an article published in 1937 she quoted a Dutch scientist's pronouncement that interracial marriage was "'America's greatest contribution' to the solution of the Indian problem," and then added dispiritedly, "The inevitable transition is not far advanced."[36]

Many years after her decision to marry, however, Eastman showed herself to be less certain of her beliefs about assimilation, as is evident in her exchange with Collier. Eastman's personal situation and beliefs explain many of the themes and concerns conspicuous in her writings published during the 1930s and 1940s. Indeed, Eastman's political position as an upholder of the ideology of assimilation was in conflict with her private role as mother and wife to people of mixed Native American and white descent.

Elaine and Charles's six children had all been educated in eastern schools and were also on tribal rolls. As they had reached or were nearing adulthood in the 1920s, the position of people of mixed parentage was still uncertain in American law and society. As Brian Dippie has explained, white Americans had a variety of attitudes toward people of mixed descent, many disdaining them, others perceiving them as tragic figures or marginal people "caught between two cultures and often rejected by both," and still others seeing them as "the harbinger[s] of an integrated society." Needless to say, Eastman was a passionate proponent of the latter view. Although seldom referring to her own close relationship with people of mixed parentage, Eastman's writings reiterated examples of successfully assimilated, biologically superior people descended from both races. Devoting one chapter of her 1935 biography of Richard Pratt to the topic "Pratt on Native Culture and Racial Blends," Eastman allotted a significant portion of it to a discussion of "the young person of mixed ancestry." As well as quoting a number of instances in which such people had gone on to successful careers within white culture, Eastman described Pratt as resenting having "parties of fair-haired and blue-eyed children forced upon him at Carlisle [Indian School], upon the assertion of the agent that 'each and every one is a legally enrolled Indian.' Logically, he maintained, all who are half white or more should be classed as white Americans and dropped from the rolls." Eastman was to echo this sentiment a number of times in the pieces she sent to newspapers and journals. In 1942 she wrote, "Of our third of a million 'Indians,' probably half are in point of fact persons of mixed descent, many predominantly French or English, and inheritors of European culture rather than that of the aboriginal. . . . As normal human beings, with proper pride, we may be certain that they do not want to be subsidized, protected, and governed as a permanent minority group."[37]

In both her journalistic writings and personal correspondence, Eastman often referred to the large number of people of mixed descent who belonged to the Native American population in both her journalistic writings and personal correspondence. Her amateur estimates varied. She claimed, for example, that "about two-thirds of our so-called Indians are persons of mixed ancestry, French, English, Negro, and many other non-Indian strains. Many thousands of them are predominantly 'white' by blood, and many more are fully Europeanized in culture." A few years later she asserted that "more than half of the persons enumerated by the Indian Bureau are by no means American aborigines of the pre-Columbian era, but merely twentieth-century Americans with one or more aboriginal grandparents or great-grandparents."[38]

Eastman's pronouncements on people of mixed descent were sometimes clarified, and in a sense legitimized, if they are read with her children in mind. For example, a theme which Eastman took up in her work on Pratt was the genetic superiority of mixed-descent children, a topic in which a mother's natural pride in her children can be discerned although she was speaking in a pseudo-scientific voice: "The facts are admittedly incomplete," she wrote, "but do suggest for the 'first cross' a definite increase in beauty, vigor, and fertility." In the same vein, Eastman reiterated Pratt's belief in the greater influence of environment over biology, quoting Pratt's argument that civilization is a habit that can be taught to any child. Eastman repeated these sentiments throughout her life, for example, at a meeting of the "Altrurian Club," where she announced that "she would not talk of the 'odd picturesque trappings' that are usually associated with Indians, but [would] remind [them] that the Indians are people like other Americans." The individual, she said, "does not inherit the culture, but just absorbs that of the people with whom they are brought up."[39]

References to Native Americans who were comfortable with the trappings of white culture were common in Eastman's later journalistic writings. In 1941, for example, she mentioned "intelligent Indians of the new generation [who] will promptly desert all segregated areas, and individually find or make their place—as many have already done—in our common American life." In 1943 she asked: "Isn't it about time to write about modern Americans of more or less aboriginal descent without dressing them up in beads and feathers, or describing them as 'chiefs' and 'squaw[s]'? The fact is that these present-day youth have for the most part been bred up in ordinary homes and schools." Connecting these public pronouncements with Eastman's private life and history also brings her spirited reply to Collier's articles in the 1942 editions of the *Atlantic* into sharper focus, revealing just how much her position as a mother of children of mixed descent animated her opposition to Collier's theories:

> The truth is that Mr. Collier's mystical theories are out of harmony with the deepest desires and aspirations of the contem-

porary young man or woman possessed of one or more aboriginal ancestors. These normal young folks are plain American
citizens, and wish to be treated as such, they crave a thoroughly modern education and training. They care little for our
opinion, as foreigners, of their largely forgotten ancestral cultures, but they do demand full political, economic, and social
equality, as competent fellow Americans. The position of an
artificially protected, patronized, and isolated racial minority is hardly tolerable to their self-respect, and it is one which
the developments of the past fifty years have clearly shown
to be unnecessary.[40]

The foundation of Eastman's misgivings with the "Indian New Deal"
of the 1930s is revealed in a letter to the editor written in 1936. "The basic
objection to Mr. Collier's summing up of 'the present policy,'" Eastman
stated, "is that it assumes 'Indians' and 'whites' to be two permanently
distinct and separate groups of Americans." Although Eastman returns
to her theme of the large numbers of Native Americans who were "predominantly 'white' by blood," she does not mention that her own family would be symbolically divided by Collier's policies.

Elaine Goodale Eastman can be seen as adhering to an unusual version of the assimilationist ideology that characterized Native American reform work for more than fifty years. While deciding personally
and physically to take part in the process, she was also able to combine
it with a sympathy for its objects that was extraordinary for a person
of her generation. This is never more clearly seen than in an article she
wrote in 1934, which contains one of the few passages in which she mentions her own family:

> As a young, unmarried woman, I journeyed and camped for
> weeks at a time alone with conservative Sioux families, liv-
> ing in the traditional fashion. My children and grandchildren,
> enjoying all the standard advantages and knowing nothing
> of native culture except from books, are still "legal Indians."
> I have championed their rights and proclaimed their abili-
> ties, in season and out of season, for the best part of a life time,

and the whole of my experience can be condensed into three words: Indians are people.[41]

By calling into question the ideology of assimilation in the mid-1930s, John Collier touched a raw nerve in Eastman. Unlike most reformers, she had a personal and emotional, as well as intellectual, investment in the policies of the nineteenth century. Her life demonstrates that a social and political ideology could find expression in one of the most personal aspects of an individual's life: the choice of a spouse. A decade after her marriage had ended, the belief structures within which she had acted were being torn down, and her children were living reminders of the complexity of the fate of racially mixed people to whom assimilationists had promised an uncontested place in the dominant culture. It is too simplistic to suggest that Eastman was simply an old-fashioned reformer who clung stubbornly to the policies of her youth. Nor can her sometimes narrow and bigoted views be ignored. Her life shows the complex relationship of public standpoints to the private lives of those who hold them.

While public standpoints are one element of Eastman's story, emotional and physical attraction is another. Histories of interracial marriage rarely speak of physical attraction. This is so partly because this element is often completely missing from the surviving records and partly because it seems intrusive to speculate on such matters. However, there is no doubt that such attractions existed across the races, and they are evident in Elaine Goodale Eastman's reference to her decision to marry as "thrilling" and "passionate." Sherry Smith has pointed out the implicit sexual undertones of many army wives' writings about the Native American men they encountered while living with their husbands on the frontier. In particular, Martha Summerhayes, who lived in Arizona, wrote of the "supple muscles" and "clean-cut thighs" of her house servant Charley. When a shocked visitor asked why Charley wore so little around the house, Martha replied that she should "cultivate her aesthetic sense, and in a short time she would be able to admire these copper-colored creatures of Nature as much as I did."[42]

Gladys H. Brown expressed similar sentiments in a letter written to Marie Keller after Carlos Montezuma's death. While it is not clear how

Gladys and Maria knew each other, it is apparent from the tone and style of Gladys's letter that she was younger—indeed, she exhibits many of the characteristics that we today would recognize as adolescent. After expressing surprise that Maria had married already, Gladys exclaimed, "Another Indian! How could it be otherwise? You had such a wonderful Indian in Montezuma how could you marry a plain White man, of course not. (I hope my father never sees that line)." The reason for Gladys's concern about her father's opinions is soon made clear. "Now I am going to tell you a secret," she warned, "and I don't want you ever to tell anyone for it is . . . [a] secret only my mother knows. . . . This is it, sometime when you find a real honest to goodness Indian who *is good* capture him for me. Will I ever be so lucky." Gladys admitted that she cut "all the Indian's [*sic*] pictures out of papers and magazines" and pasted them up on the walls of her bedroom—"every inch of wall covered"—and memorized "Indian and outdoor poems." She also worried that Native Americans would not find her red hair attractive.

Gladys's letter reveals the popular fascination with Native Americans and their culture at the time, expressed most fully in the theatrical shows organized by "Buffalo Bill" Cody, transforming them into a kind of teenage fantasy. While aware of the general disapproval felt for interracial unions (as indicated by her worries about her father's knowledge), this does not deter Gladys from dreaming about having a Native American husband of her own. Gladys was clearly thrilled to have a friend like Marie who might introduce her to Native Americans and with whom she could sympathetically discuss books and poems about Native American subjects: "You write that the author of 'On the Indian Trail' is a lady[.] I kept thinking it was a man. . . . I think I should like her because she is different from most folks being interested in the Indians and wanting to help them." Their relationship opens up the possibility that some white women could consciously acknowledge their desire for men of other races, even if they had to be careful to whom they did so.[43]

Physical attraction and marriage, however, are two different matters. While physical attraction could be kept private, the subject of silent thoughts or intimate secrets, marriage had implications for the wife's social standing in the public sphere. Although the Eastmans and the

Montezumas worked hard to justify their lives in terms of the ideologies of womanhood, manhood, and assimilation that existed in this period, their private choices impacted gravely on most aspects of their lives. Elaine Goodale Eastman is a fitting subject with which to end the American section of this book. She epitomizes the ideas explored in the first half of the study, ideas that led to the marriages of a few educated, middle-class Native American men and white women in the brief moment when cultural assimilation captivated reformers most intensely. With the proper education, it was believed that Native Americans were capable of assimilating into the American middle classes within one generation. The interracial marriage of these few professional men was not just a contribution to the assimilation of Native Americans; it was testimony to the inherent equality of indigenous and white people. For the majority of Native Americans, however, such equality was hardly in evidence as they eked out a poverty-stricken existence on reservations far from the centers of reform in the East. Nevertheless, as the next chapters demonstrate, few Australian Aboriginal men would receive similar opportunities for professional advancement won by men like Charles Eastman, nor would they find a wife with a social status equal to that of Elaine Goodale Eastman.

5. The Broken Promise of Aboriginal Education in Australia

During a period similar to the one discussed in the previous chapters in the United States, from the 1880s to the 1930s white Australian settlers also attempted to find a solution to the problem of the presence of the original owners of the land. Despite the fact that their settlement was younger and until 1901 was still a British colony, a similar environment of scientific and religious ideas influenced white Australian ideas about indigenous peoples. Nevertheless, white Australians came up with a very different solution, a version of assimilation that focused on biological absorption, the loss of indigenous physical characteristics through interracial sexual relationships, rather than cultural assimilation or the "whitening" of indigenous people's lifestyle and culture. This chapter begins the Australian section of the book by describing white Australians' comparatively halfhearted efforts to culturally assimilate Aboriginal peoples implemented while America enjoyed what Siobhan Senier has called its "monolithic" assimilation period.[1] Unlike the solution epitomized by eastern boarding schools like Hampton and Carlisle described in chapters 1 and 2, it was a solution that entailed a lackluster education policy and few opportunities for social mobility.

In 1877 John Green testified to the Victorian Royal Commission on Aborigines about several cases in which Aboriginal children of both mixed and full descent had been raised in white households and educated "the same as one of the family." This happy arrangement, he said, remained trouble-free until the Aboriginal child "came to an age that they would like to make love." At this point, worried about the possibility of their sons or daughters becoming involved in an interracial sexual relationship, the white parents would tell their children "that they must not make so free with the darky; they must remember that, although he or she has been educated in the family, it would be degrading to make love with them." No longer treated as a member of the family, and with the "cold shoulder" turned toward them, Green reported, they returned to Aboriginal communities as soon as "they [could] find a chance." This series of events, Green argued, led to cynicism among Victorian colonists about the worth of offering Aboriginal children an education:

> Now, say the wise ones, "Did I not tell you what would be the end of all your kindness to these darkies? There is that J—— R——, who was sent to college, he is gone back to the camp and has married an aboriginal." These wise ones forgetting that it was mainly themselves that was the cause of the poor fellow's downfall by raising him too high and not providing those supports that are so beneficial to keep young men from falling, viz., the prospect of getting married with some one they love.[2]

John Green's testimony makes it clear that an education was not seen as a path to social equality for Aborigines in the minds of nineteenth-century white Australians. The few Aboriginal people who had been educated to a level where they might expect to be rewarded with equal treatment were held back by a lack of suitable marriage partners. It was not that white Australians were hesitant to engage in sexual relationships with Aborigines: on the contrary, casual exploitative relationships between white men and Aboriginal women were common. But white Australians hesitated to bestow the equal status implicit in the institution of marriage upon people they had decided were racially inferior (even if they had been raised as "one of the family"), and there was little opportunity for Aboriginal people to prove themselves so through education.

This is because the attempt to promote cultural assimilation in Australia through the educational system set up for Aboriginal people in the late nineteenth and early twentieth centuries was rudimentary at best. It was not that white Australians were uninterested in cultural assimilation of Aboriginal people; on the contrary, the need to "civilize" Aboriginal people was a common refrain in the speeches and articles of those interested in the "Aboriginal problem." However, these sentiments were rarely translated into efforts to help them in this respect. In a sense, what Australian historian Henry Reynolds has called a "promise" of assimilation was made to Aboriginal people: that by acculturating they would improve their status, live more comfortably, and be treated with greater respect.[3] This promise was not kept.

There was no group of educated, middle-class indigenous men in Australia married to white women, as there was in the United States. White policy makers had trouble imagining Aboriginal people contributing to the development of the nation. Scholars are only just beginning to document how Aboriginal people played an extensive role in the nation's economy. As Henry Reynolds has pointed out, one of the most important myths about the origins of white Australia is that the hard work of settlers and pioneers was responsible for the development of the nation. Aboriginal people are seen to have had little to do with this process; in fact, the stereotype of indigenous "laziness" has often enabled white Australians to justify their oppression and dispossession. The truth is that of all the points of contact between white and Aboriginal people, the exchange of labor was by far the most important.[4] Aboriginal people worked at a variety of occupations in settler society—indeed, the pastoral industry almost completely relied on their unpaid labor for most of the nineteenth and twentieth centuries—and took on the hardest, most unpleasant, and lowest paid work. While more than willing to let Aboriginal people take part in the white economy in this way, government officials, philanthropists, and educators who spoke about cultural assimilation were certainly not envisioning Aboriginal people as "ascending" to their own social status. As Reynolds has argued, "Despite the fine words about civilisation and Christianity the reality was that all Europeans offered to the Aborigines was the life of the poor and powerless at the bottom of the 'scale of graduated classes' with virtually no chance of social mobility or of the 'improvement' which well-meaning whites talked so much about."[5] In other words, they imagined that Aborigines would become members of the working classes.

The laboring classes, however, did not share this view. Threatened by the prospect of cheap labor, and keen to cling to their own uncertain status, poor white Australians emphasized the differences between themselves and indigenous people. Thus Australian Aborigines had little opportunity to raise themselves to working-class status, let alone contemplate making tentative steps into the middle classes. Instead, they teetered on the lowest rung of the working class, either providing sporadic, low-paid labor to white employers or belonging to a segregated group living and working on reserves and receiving minimal government support.

Where Aborigines did attempt to become socially mobile, their efforts were often quickly thwarted. Historian Barry Morris has pointed out that in New South Wales in the early decades of the twentieth century it was often those Aborigines who were outwardly "'assimilating' the most successfully—by way of industry, enterprise and smallholder farming—[who] were in fact wiped out by state interventions," literally losing the products of their labor to administrators who claimed they were the property of the government.[6] Aboriginal men who married white women were not exempt from this process. Their efforts to gain economic independence were often undermined, ignored, or denounced. Their wives were not seen as "angels of civilization," raising their husbands' status with their own higher standing. Instead, they were treated as outsiders and oddities, as women who did not submit to or understand the social hierarchy of their society.

This chapter describes how nowhere is the lowly status assigned to Aboriginal people more evident than in the substandard education offered to them by settlers. It takes the form of a national survey of Aboriginal education, in order to demonstrate how white Australians never offered the kind of opportunities hard-won by some students of Hampton Institute and Carlisle Indian School, where American assimilation policies to some extent culminated. If white Australians had been at all serious about cultural assimilation, this is where their efforts would be most evident. But Aboriginal education was a slap-dash affair that offered no opportunities for Aboriginal people as a stepping-stone to higher status within settler society.

When white settlers began to see the need for a system of education for their own children, rather than endeavoring to create something unique, they constructed one that was very much based on ideas prevalent in England at the time. Indeed, Alan Barcan has argued that the story of the early endeavors to establish formal education in Australia is the "story of attempts to establish the educational institutions of eighteenth-century England" in this new society. In eighteenth-century England, the state took no responsibility for education. The churches and philanthropists educated lower-class children, and middle-class and upper-class children's education was paid for by their parents at home or at private establishments.[7] These strategies were mirrored in the early years of the Australian colonies. It was not until 1830, when the Whigs, who valued education as a means of progress, won power in Britain that the British government began to put state money toward education, and Australia followed suit. The American education system underwent a similar transformation at around the same time. In both countries, education began to be seen as a right that should be enjoyed, to a certain extent, by all citizens.

During the same period, rising humanitarian sentiment in Britain resulted in pressure on colonial governments to provide at least some kind of assistance to indigenous people.[8] Some of this assistance was envisaged to be in the form of education in European knowledge and religion. In 1837 a British parliamentary select committee recommended that colonial governments should consider the revenue of each colony "subject to a charge for such sums as may be necessary to provide for the religious instruction and for the protection of the survivors of the tribes to which the lands comprised in that colony formerly belonged."[9] Such ideas soon resulted in attempts to establish a humane method of dealing with the owners of the land. In 1840 Governor George Gipps received a communication from Lord John Russell of the British Parliament which argued that "the best chance of preserving the unfortunate race of New Holland lies in the means employed for training their Children" for manual labor, "the boys to dig and plough, and the trades of Shoemakers, Tailors, Carpenters and Masons; the Girls to Sew and Cook, and wash linen, and keep clean the rooms and furniture."[10] Some early attempts at establishing schools for Aboriginal children in New South

Wales resulted from this pressure, all of which failed for a variety of reasons: the devastation of the Aboriginal population by disease, the understandable reluctance of parents to entrust the care of the children to the colonizers, and the opposition or indifference of the majority of white settlers and politicians.

Perhaps the most insidious reason for the failure of the white government to provide adequate schooling for Aboriginal children, however, not just in this early period but for most of the twentieth century, was the belief in the inferiority of the Aboriginal race. A Victorian select committee on Aborigines concluded in 1859 that although "the Aborigines are [endowed] with keen perceptive faculties, there is a considerable deficiency in the reflective faculties, and a certain want of steadiness of purpose in their characters, which appears the great obstacle to be overcome in reclaiming them, and bringing them within the pale of civilization and Christianity."[11] As late as 1937 A. P. Elkin, the well-known anthropologist, wrote:

> Full-black children seldom pass beyond the third standard, though occasionally go to the fourth, and very exceptionally any further. In almost all cases too, it takes them longer to reach that standard than is the case with white children . . . they need to be longer in each class, especially in the first class. Not one of my informants even suggests that aboriginal pupils are the equal of the white children in school . . . and this they maintain is also true of half-castes.[12]

In the early years of the colonies, schools were scarce for both indigenous and white children. It was not until the 1870s that the state governments in Australia began passing legislation that created a system of free, compulsory, and secular education for all.[13] Once this transformation had taken place, the differences between white and Aboriginal educational systems steadily increased. Part of the problem lay in confusion over exactly whose responsibility Aboriginal education was. At the same time as states were passing acts which made their education departments responsible for ensuring that every child attended school, they were also passing acts that established departments and protectorates principally to control the indigenous population, whose duties often specifically included the education and "civilization" of indigenous children.[14] This was a task that busy public servants interested in balancing their budget often hoped would be undertaken by the Education Department. At one school on a Victorian reserve, for example, this philosophical conflict resulted in practical problems evident in the lengthy correspondence in 1934 between the Board for the Protection of Aborigines and the Department of Public Instruction over who should pay to "erect a [water] tank and stand, repair out-offices, and provide heating facilities."[15]

Much of the responsibility for Aboriginal education was laid at the feet of missionaries, who for the most part conducted independent institutions with individual curricula that were not consistent either with each other or with those taught to white children in state schools.[16] Missionary teachers were often untrained or inferior in some respect, such as the schoolteacher appointed to the Cape Barren Island school in Tasmania in 1889 who had volunteered for the position in the vain hope that it would break his addiction to alcohol.[17] Even if the teacher was earnest and hardworking, many, especially in New South Wales, had to combine their school duties with managing the station or mission.[18] But teachers were often underqualified, even when mission schools came under the jurisdiction of the state's education department. A letter from the secretary of the Victorian Department of Public Instruction to the Victorian Aboriginal Group revealed that as late as 1933, there was "considerable difficulty" staffing the school at Lake Tyers station.[19] A few years later the Teachers' Union requested that the assistant at this school be given a "special allowance to compensate 'for the conditions under which she has to live and work,'" such as the teachers were paid at the Children's School at the Kew Asylum, the Special School for Epileptics, and at three schools "for the Feeble-Minded."[20] Teaching Aboriginal children was not a task to which the best and brightest of the teaching profession aspired. This had graver consequences than low standards of teaching. In 1879 several Aboriginal parents wrote to the Victorian Board for the Protection of Aborigines to complain that the teacher at Ebenezer station horsewhipped children and threw stones at them.[21]

In many places in Australia, once Aboriginal students were admitted into state schools, the almost immediate reaction was for white parents to protest against their presence. In New South Wales the newly established Board for the Protection of Aborigines reported in 1885 that the Department of Public Instruction had agreed that there would be no objection to Aboriginal children attending public schools "provided they are habitually clean, decently clad, and that they conduct themselves with propriety both in and out of school."[22] White parents across the state quickly protested that Aboriginal children were not, as historian J. J. Fletcher expressed it, sufficiently "clean, clad, or courteous" to attend school with their children.[23] The members of the Board for the Protection of Aborigines quickly saw through the "clean, clad, and courteous" postulate. In 1892 they reported that they were continuing "their efforts to secure the attendance at public schools of children of aborigines. . . . A large number do so attend, but in a few places it has been found necessary to withdraw them, owing to objections taken by the parents of European children, not that they were not clean or decently clad, but simply because they were aboriginal children."[24] In 1901 and 1902 the board complained that the "dark children are as clean in their habits and as well behaved as the white children," adding that where parental objections were raised the board endeavored to have a separate school established, "but as a rule without success."[25] Despite the inclusion of a provision in the 1909 Aborigines Protection Act which required that every child under the age of fourteen should attend the nearest school "to which aborigines will be admitted," segregated schooling and expulsion on the basis of hygiene continued in New South Wales until after the Second World War.[26]

Hygiene was also used as a pretext in Western Australia where, during the first few decades of the twentieth century, Aboriginal children were almost completely excluded from white schools. In 1928 this practice was sanctioned in a regulation under the Education Act, which allowed Aboriginal children to be excluded from schools simply "if objection is raised by parents of other children."[27] This state of affairs continued until after the Second World War, although the department wavered on occasions, for example, when it countermanded an order to expel Aboriginal children from Wagin State School in 1933.[28] Indeed, the expulsions were so widespread that A. O. Neville, the chief protector in Western Australia for most of the 1920s and 1930s, admitted that during his period of service "a whole generation of children has grown up who have missed being educated."[29] One important exception to the general apathy was Mary Montgomery Bennett, a middle-class white woman who lobbied for the rights of Aboriginal people during the 1930s. As well as writing and speaking, Bennett worked as a teacher on missions in northwestern Western Australia. In 1935 she published *Teaching the Aborigines: Data from Mt. Margaret Mission,* in which she deplored the fact that "in Western Australian to-day thousands of intelligent Aboriginal and half-caste children are growing up without any teaching whatever," and went on to describe the successful methods Bennett had formulated in her own schools. The pamphlet finished with a plea:

> Teachers! Will you come into the arena, and learn what "grace and truth" there are in our Aboriginal people, and what frightful, unnecessary, artificial bars are keeping their spirits in prison? WHO WILL COME?[30]

Unfortunately, voices like Bennett's were few and far between and were mostly ignored by the mainstream population.

There are also reports of white parents' protests occurring in Victoria, as for example when white children from Hopkins Falls State School were withdrawn because of the presence of children from nearby Framlingham station.[31] In the Northern Territory, debates continued about whether or not it was worth educating Aboriginal children at all until at least 1917.[32] Although a few mission schools were established, and the government ran a "half-caste" home in Darwin which offered some education, the standard of education was generally very low. Pastoralists who owned properties employing large numbers of Aboriginal people often refused to provide education for the children because they believed that it was superfluous and made the indigenous people less obedient to white authority.[33] John W. Bleakley, the chief protector of Aborigines in Queensland who wrote a report for the Commonwealth government in 1928, recorded that "few employers display any sympathy or interest in the question. . . . It is argued that education spoils them, making them cunning and cheeky."[34] No attempt was made by the federal government (which administered the Northern Territory from 1911) to develop an educational system for Aboriginal children.[35] Bleakley reported that "until the Territory is further developed and facilities for the education of white children are provided," compulsory general education of Aboriginal children in the Northern Territory was "out of the question."[36]

In Tasmania the problem of segregated or integrated schooling barely existed, the small surviving Aboriginal population having been moved to a few islands in the distant north in the mid-nineteenth century, far from the main centers of population. Nevertheless, there are reports of white and Aboriginal children attending school together on the Furneaux islands during the early part of the nineteenth century, although it is not difficult to imagine why white parents in this area might have a different attitude toward their counterparts in other states.[37] The area had been set aside specifically for Aboriginal people for many years—making whites, in a sense, the outsiders. In South Australia early attempts to set up government and mission-run boarding schools in the 1840s failed, and there were no further attempts to establish schools for Aboriginal children, except by missionaries, until after a Royal Commission held in 1913–15.[38] In 1923 one politician reported meeting with white parents from Maree who complained about the lack of cleanliness of children of Aboriginal and Afghan descent and asked for separate schools, demonstrating that at least some South Australian Aborigines faced problems in attending public schools similar to those of other states.[39] Queensland, like the other states, relied on a combination of mission schools and state schools. As late as 1946 children on reserves were still being taught only to the fifth primary school grade.[40]

Where Aboriginal children were educated separately from white children in segregated reserves, station schools, or missions during this period, the standard to which they were educated was most often abysmal and fitted them only for the very lowest of occupations. There are countless items of evidence of the low standard of Aboriginal education in all Australian states at many points in the late nineteenth and early twentieth centuries. In the Northern Territory the mission schools "used a syllabus which aimed to teach Aborigines by the age of fourteen what state school pupils learned by the age of eight."[41] In Queensland, as late as 1936, the government was only willing to plan "technical training on rural lines" for "half-castes" with the "right ambition."[42] In Tasmania a 1924 select committee concluded that the "school curriculum should be carefully revised in order to ensure that subjects of practical nature are given prominence."[43] Government departments did not conceal overtly the reasons for such curricula. The Victorian Board for the Protection of Aborigines stated its intention in 1861 to teach Aboriginal children "useful occupations, so as to have them fitted for employment as servants."[44] The annual report of the New South Wales Board in 1885 stated that its members looked forward "hopefully to [Aboriginal] children being in time reclaimed from the uncivilized and degraded conditions in which they have hitherto existed, and taking their place—as they are well fitted by their natural intelligence to do—amongst the industrial classes."[45] Even the "stolen generations," removed from their parents ostensibly to get a better "start" in life, were poorly educated. The National Inquiry into the Separation of Aboriginal and Torres Strait Islander Children found that any aspirations to learning the children may have had were trampled. Witnesses described "receiving little or no education, and certainly little of any value. . . . What education was provided . . . emphasised domestic science and manual training, thus preparing the children for a future as menial workers within the government or mission communities or as cheap labor in the wider community.[46] It was a syllabus remarkably similar to the "new education policy" of the 1920s in the United States, where the innate inferiority of Native Americans was seen as a reason to curb their chance to learn.

This attitude severely limited the opportunities for Aboriginal people. As Aboriginal activist William Ferguson wrote in 1937:

> Occasionally one of our people becomes famous. There are thousands of others who could show just as much intelligence and culture if they were given the chance. Yet they educate us only to the third standard in the native schools. We are not given a chance to be anything except laborers. Nobody offered to give me anything but an elementary education.[47]

There were exceptions, as Ferguson said. A small number of young men, like Charles Eastman and Carlos Montezuma, were identified by individual whites as showing "promise" and offered more than the normal substandard education.[48] In each case, however, a variety of factors intervened to prevent them from reaching the goals set for them by their sponsors. In some tragic cases, this was a European-introduced disease. In other cases, prejudice pure and simple aborted their careers. In 1860 the Victorian Board for the Protection of Aborigines became interested in a fourteen-year-old boy called Thomas Bungalene, who was working in the survey office. The BPA decided that he should be sent to St Kilda Grammar School in order that he would "receive a good education and become fitted for some profession." When the principal of St. Kilda Grammar refused to admit him, Scotch College was approached; again he was turned away. Bungalene was placed in the charge of a schoolmaster, Robert Doig, who was paid an annual fee to look after the boy's education and board. After six months the arrangement faltered, and the board decided Bungalene should go to sea. He died only a few years later.[49]

The teaching profession was one of the few to which Aboriginal men might aspire, although there are almost no examples of successful candidates. In 1887 W. Dunstan, the head teacher at Lake Condah Primary School, was told that an Aboriginal boy might apply for the position of pupil teacher at the school along with any other eligible candidates.[50] A school inspector wrote to the BPA in 1899 to ask if an "exceptionally promising" student named Joseph Wandin might be allowed to stay on at school in order to apply for a pupil teachership "and begin an honourable career."[51] It is not known what became of the former candidate, but Joseph Wandin became a pupil teacher in 1901 and was employed by the education department at West Brunswick State School. In 1908 he was employed at a state school in Mordialloc and was described as "a credit to the station" by the acting manager of Coranderrk, John Mackie.[52] In New South Wales an Aboriginal man named John Lewis was given a position at the public school at Moonahcullah. Not much is known about this man, apart from some very unflattering reports from government inspectors, who did not hesitate to incorporate some local gossip about Lewis's family in their reports, including the information that Lewis was married to a white woman.[53] If this was the same Lewis, he is perhaps the only equivalent to men like Charles Eastman and Carlos Montezuma, who became socially mobile enough to marry a white woman.

A Ngarrindjeri man, David Unaipon, did manage to reach a high level of education, although it was certainly not thanks to any broad-minded institution. Largely self-taught, "Australia's Leonardo" left the mission school at the Point McLeay mission in South Australia in 1885 when he was thirteen and worked as a servant, a storeman, and a bookkeeper. After his marriage to a Tangani woman he wrote a number of booklets about Aboriginal mythology and legends and patented ten inventions, including a shearer's handpiece and a centrifugal motor. All these patents lapsed. A devout Christian, Unaipon became a spokesperson for his people, and like Eastman and Montezuma, he was held up as an example of Aboriginal "advancement," although it is apparent that he received little white assistance (except perhaps from individuals) in his remarkable career.[54] In general, it appears that even if Aboriginal men could receive training and education above and beyond what was normally offered, they encountered insurmountable obstacles. The Queensland chief protector realized this problem in 1924, although he placed the blame firmly on the Aborigines: "The question of the future of the superior [Aborigines] is one always calling for anxious thought. . . . [B]lood is always an obstacle, and no matter how well educated or trained, he rarely is able to successfully combat the influences against him."[55]

A concern about whom potential well-educated Aborigines would marry is evident in Australia just as it was at Hampton and Carlisle. For example, Paddy Cahill, the superintendent of the Oenpelli reserve in the Northern Territory, wrote to Baldwin Spencer in 1916 to advise him that it would be "an injustice" to teach young Aboriginal women to "read and write, cook and clean," and then allow them to marry an uneducated man.[56] In Queensland in 1904 the Reverend Hey, manager of the mission at Mapoon, was also anxious about the marriage prospects of educated Aboriginal women. He wondered in his annual report to the chief protector, "What shall become of those educated girls when arrived at a marriageable age?" His expectations were lower for those of unmixed descent, who "as a rule, [could] be married to intelligent young men of their own race," but Hey did not think it was "fair to marry the half-caste girls to blacks, which might mean in many cases a return to the camp life, with its abuses, privations, and depravities."[57] Cecil Cook, chief protector in the Northern Territory, also recognized the link between marriage and education in the case of Aboriginal girls. He set up a system in which children of mixed descent were removed from their family's care and placed in institutions "where they are . . . taught domestic arts and dress and clothing making to fit them for a higher station as the wives of higher grade half-caste males or whites."[58]

The concern that educated Aboriginal people would either find no suitable marriage partners or else lose the benefit of their education by marrying someone not similarly educated was pragmatically, if unsuccessfully, addressed by the protector of Aborigines in Adelaide. He described in 1849 how at the Native School they "attempted to marry the boys and girls as they arrived at puberty and intended to assign each couple a separate room in the establishment. . . . We failed however in the marriage affair, the Colonial Chaplain could not do it as they were not baptized and the Deputy Registrar could not do it, without the consent of the parents as they were all minors."[59] From the outset this was an issue for mission educators. As early as 1814 William Shelley, who instigated and operated the first educational institution for Aboriginal children in the colony of New South Wales, wrote to Governor Macquarie to point out that the problem was particularly bad in the case of educated Aboriginal men. While Aboriginal women had always been seen as acceptable sexual partners (and sometimes even wives) for white men, the reverse was not true. These men, according to Shelley, could not:

> make themselves respectable in their new Society. They were generally despised, especially by *European females*; thus all attachment to their new Society was precluded. . . . Young Men live in a prospect of Marriage, and have ambition and pride to be respectable in their own Society. No European Woman would marry a *Native*, unless some abandoned profligate. . . . A Solitary individual, either Woman or Man, educated from infancy, even well, among Europeans, would in general, when they grew up, be rejected by the other Sex of Europeans, and must go into the Bush for a Companion.

Shelley proposed an institution in which both sexes were educated and then married to each other at a suitable age, but this suggestion (which is strikingly similar to ideas of the staff at Hampton Institute and to some extent Carlisle Indian School) was never acted upon.[60] Instead, the unwillingness of white people to intermarry with Aborigines was put forward as a reason for not providing them with the education they would need to assimilate.

For example, when around the turn of the century white and Aboriginal students studied together in public schools in New South Wales, one of the main reasons that white parents gave for excluding Aboriginal children was their apprehension that familiarity between children of different races would lead to romantic attachments. Thus a petition drawn up by a Presbyterian minister in the town of Gulargambone in 1919 gave as one of the reasons for the parents' protest against Aboriginal children attending the local school that "cases of marriage or living together between Blacks and whites is very undesirable and yet a common school fosters this."[61] White parents were well aware that sympathetic ties were forged between children, and that the closer Aboriginal people got to the social standards of whites, the more likely it was that intermarriage would result. The equality implicit in interracial marriage and identical standards of education was not something the majority of white Australians were willing to grant to Aboriginal people.

White Australians envisioned a different solution to the "Aboriginal problem" than that enacted in the United States. Creating avenues of cultural assimilation was not high on their list of priorities, and an equivalent to the group of educated, acculturated Native American "leaders and examples" discussed in the first half of the book never existed. Instead, white Australians concentrated on a different form of assimilation. In the next chapter, I begin outlining how their solution, one based on ideas of biological absorption through interracial relationships, impacted on the marriages of white women and indigenous men that took place in the colony, and then state, of Victoria.

6. Regulating Aboriginal Marriages in Victoria

In many ways, this book is about how the concept of assimilation was unstable and how it could shift meaning according to time, place, and individual. In this chapter I examine, at a local level, the ways in which some white Australians tried to solve their "Aboriginal problem" and the impact of that solution on attitudes toward interracial marriages of white women and Aboriginal men. As will be discussed in more detail in chapter 9, every Australian state and colony had slightly different and separately administered policies directed at the Aboriginal population. This chapter focuses on just one of those administrations, that which watched over the indigenous population of the colony (and after 1901 the state) of Victoria. Just as Hampton Institute and Carlisle Indian School were two of the most evolved instruments of assimilation in the United States, so was Victoria the scene of one of the earliest and most thorough-going attempts to assimilate Aboriginal people. But there was little effort to seriously attempt cultural assimilation, as occurred in the American institutions. Instead, like many Australian states and colonies, the Victorian government created between 1886 and 1910 a scheme based predominantly on the idea of biological absorption, which was intended to provide a speedy and dramatic solution to the state's "Aboriginal problem." It was a program in which interracial marriage played an important part, but as means of absorption, not as evidence of assimilation as it was often seen in the United States. Rather, interracial marriage was part of a solution that attempted to engineer the demise of the entire Aboriginal population, so that, as the administrative body in charge of the "Aboriginal problem" in Victoria envisioned in 1884, "all responsibility of the Government . . . would cease—*finality* being thus attained."[1]

Victoria was the first Australian state to create legislation to control the indigenous people living within its borders. In 1869 an Act to Provide for the Protection and Maintenance of the Aboriginal Natives of Victoria gave legal power over the individual lives and finances of Aboriginal people to the Board for the Protection of Aborigines (BPA), a body which had been formed nine years earlier. During the 1870s and early 1880s BPA members gradually developed a strategy that they believed would solve the Victorian "Aboriginal problem." By this time most Aboriginal people had been removed to one of six stations, run by managers (most of them missionaries) who were supervised by the BPA. The BPA's plan was that those of mixed descent would be removed from the stations and missions, denied financial support, and encouraged to "merge" with the mainstream population. Those of full descent would be allowed to remain on the missions and stations and continue to receive government support. It was assumed that the latter group would simply die out. Interracial relationships had been the means by which the former group had been created, and it would also be the mechanism of its disappearance. This scheme was authorized by law in an act passed in 1886.

White women married to Aboriginal men in Victoria were therefore part of a biological absorptionist rather than a cultural assimilationist solution to the "Aboriginal problem." For this reason, unlike Native American men in the United States, who received assistance from philanthropists, moral support and acclaim from reformers, and education opportunities and even employment from the government, Victorian Aborigines who showed a willingness to take steps toward cultural assimilation were discouraged or ignored. Without a vociferous humanitarian group to provide an ideological context of assimilation in which these couples could be understood as assimilative "success stories," the four couples discussed in this chapter were greeted with little enthusiasm. Instead of being welcomed as "leaders" and "examples," as some American couples were, they were seen as oddities to be ignored or merely tolerated. In part, then, this chapter corresponds to chapter 3, which described the lives of an acculturated class of Native American "leaders" who were lauded as examples of what a cultural assimilationist policy could achieve. But it also begins an argument about how ideas of biological absorption underlay the assimilation policies enacted by white Australia.

Crucial to an investigation of Victorian policy and its attempts to both regulate and take advantage of interracial marriage are the changing and diverse definitions of Aboriginal identity of the period. The 1869 act had inclusively defined "Aboriginal" to mean "every Aboriginal native of Australia and every Aboriginal half-caste or child habitually associating and living with Aboriginals."[2] The 1886 act introduced a far lengthier and more complicated definition. "Aboriginals" were defined as "Every Aboriginal native of Victoria" who was not of mixed descent. "Half-castes" became a separate category that included anyone at all of mixed descent but excluded "such half-castes as under the provisions of this Act are to be deemed Aboriginals." These included those of mixed descent over thirty-four years of age who habitually associated and lived with an "Aboriginal"; female "half-castes" who had been married to an "Aboriginal" before the act became law; children (under fourteen) unable to earn their own living; and individuals who had been given a license awarding them special "Aboriginal" status. In other words, whatever their ancestry, those who were not expected to earn their own living were designated as "Aboriginal." A simple plan underlay these complicated definitions. When the act came into operation, those designated "half-castes" (that is, anyone of mixed descent between fourteen and thirty-four) were to receive no further support from the government, thereby forcing their economic assimilation into the mainstream Victorian population.

As well as the obvious absorptionist connotations of the oft-expressed aim of "merging" the Aboriginal population into the white one, the policy was based on the logic that people of mixed descent, because of their "white blood," were better able to look after themselves in the mainstream community than those of full descent. Part of the impetus for the policy had been the resentment felt by white people that "able-bodied," lighter-skinned people were receiving full government support. "It seemed to the Board unreasonable that the State should continue to support able-bodied men who were well able to earn their own living," read the BPA's annual report for 1887. "They were supplied at the public expense with houses, food, and clothing, with all the necessities and many of the comforts of life."[3] In keeping with this logic, people of mixed descent who were in some way physically unable to work were granted exemption. The 1886 act granted the BPA all the powers over the Aboriginal population it required to carry out its assimilationist policy. It allowed the governor to create regulations prescribing the conditions under which people might be allowed to remain on the stations and in receipt of rations from the government. The governor was also allowed to remove people from the stations, apprentice children to white employers, and transfer "orphans" to institutions.[4]

From 1887 onward, the manager's reports contained accounts of the numbers of mixed-descent people who had left the stations and justifications for those remaining, and the BPA boasted of the decreasing numbers of Aborigines. From 1894, it began to reduce the land allotted to stations and brag of reduced costs. In 1898 the BPA proudly reported that they had been able to greatly reduce the amount spent by the government on Aborigines by "merging the half-castes, and the constant decrease of the pure Aborigines."[5] In Aboriginal communities families were divided as those between the years of fourteen and thirty-four left the stations, only to be confronted with an economic depression that made employment scarce even to those not hindered by racism.

Victoria did not, like some states and territories in Australia and the United States, pass a law regulating interracial marriages. Nevertheless, the BPA was able to control marriages through the ability to remove people from missions and stations and to deny them rations. An unofficial, unstated policy existed about the BPA's powers in this respect. Managers of the various stations and missions often wrote to the BPA asking permission for particular marriages to take place. By 1910 it had become the "custom of the Managers to inform the Board when aborigines intend to be married, and to ask whether it will consent, as well as allow the couple to live at the station."[6] Although the BPA had no legal powers to prevent marriages, a simple refusal appeared to be sufficient in many cases. Indeed, as the BPA had the power to remove people from their families and homes and force them out into a racist community without any financial support, legal power to prevent marriages was hardly necessary.

Interracial marriages were viewed in an entirely pragmatic way by the BPA. No objections based on religious or scientific grounds were raised in committee meetings, and the BPA had no obviously consistent policy for or against such marriages. Instead, the BPA's approval or disapproval was given largely on a financial basis, depending on who the protagonists were and what degree of Aboriginality the BPA had decided they possessed. The arbitrary definitions of "Aboriginal" and "half-caste"— the age of a spouse and the date of a marriage could define a person's race, and no doubt many decisions were based on the uncertain basis of skin color—are crucial to an understanding of the fluidity of the concept of an interracial marriage during this period in Victoria. According to the BPA, interracial marriages were not just between Aborigines and non-Aborigines. They were also between those designated as "half-castes" and "Aborigines."

The BPA was most concerned about the kind of marriage that would have the greatest financial cost. This was the marriage of someone designated "half-caste," who was ineligible for BPA support, with someone designated "Aboriginal," who was eligible. There are many examples in the records of the BPA raising no objection to some interracial marriage, but when the potential spouses were of mixed and full descent, they were always turned down.[7] As well as financial concerns, the logic of biological absorption dictated these biases. The children of people of full descent and mixed descent were undesirable. They still had a majority of Aboriginal "blood," and therefore they did not advance the project of the absorption of indigenous identity into the white population. During the 1882 inquiry into Coranderrk, the Rev. Alexander Mackie discussed a case in which he refused to marry a man to his underage fiancée. "Is it advisable to allow them to get married to whites?" Mackie was asked after telling his story. "Not for the whites," he replied. "If she had been nearly white I would have had a different opinion. . . . If you marry a half-caste to a white the succeeding race will approach nearer to the whites. If you marry a full black to a white you increase the number [of] aboriginals."[8] Such absorptionist logic underlay the 1886 act.

The BPA strictly adhered to the regulations of the 1886 act, even to the point of basing decisions on whether or not marriages had taken place before or after the date on which the act had come into operation. For example, Jessie Mullett's marriage to a mixed-descent man, Albert White, disqualified her from receiving support from the government. When the manager of the Lake Condah station, the Rev. John Heinrich Stähle, wrote to the secretary of the BPA asking for leniency, he received this testy reply: "Had she married before the 1st of January 1887 she would be deemed an Aboriginal, not having done so she has to be treated as a halfcaste. I sent you a copy of the Act some time ago. Please read subsection 3 of Section 4."[9]

When Tocas Johnson, a man of full descent, wrote to the BPA in 1897 to inform it that he wished to marry a woman of mixed descent named Ina Lancaster, the secretary wrote to Johnson to inform him of the seriousness of his decision, warning that "if you marry Ina Lancaster neither she nor you can reside on this or any other Reserve and that by so doing you cannot receive any more rations or clothes etc. but are considered by law as white people according to Act of Parliament no. MLIX Section IV. It will be well if you consider these important points before you take the proposed step."[10] He also wrote to J. Akeroyd, the local police constable and protector, to ensure the engaged couple would get the message. He asked Akeroyd to inform Johnson "that if a black man marries a halfcaste woman, *who is in the eyes of the Law, as a white woman* the same must leave the reserve and cannot any longer receive Government supplies."[11] In Victoria during this period racial categories such as "white woman" took on new financially based meanings.

The importance of the implications of the racial status of a potential spouse was emphasized by the Rev. Friedrich A. Hagenauer in a letter filled with paternal advice for a young woman at Cummeragunja, a station in New South Wales. "My dear friend," he wrote:

> Regarding the wish you have to get married to the nice young man for whom you have taken such a fancy, I am sorry to say, that I can form no idea, as I do not know the young gentleman and you said nothing about him, neither if he is white or black or halfcaste. In all such questions you have to be very careful as otherwise you would have to suffer all your life long afterwards.[12]

Nineteenth-century assumptions about women staying at home did not play a part in the BPA's decision. It was not assumed that the man would be the main breadwinner of the family, and therefore a man of full descent who wished to marry a woman of mixed descent was denied financial support once married as though it were now his wife's responsibility to support him. In one case the BPA specifically mentioned the wage-earning capacity of the mixed-descent wife in a memo:

> Woodford Robinson is an aboriginal and Matilda Hammond is a half caste. This couple if married should not according to the law be allowed to settle on a station. The girl is able to earn her own living and there is no circumstance as far as I'm aware, justifying the breaking of the will of Parliament.[13]

For some, the BPA's mandate went further than simply revoking the privileges of those who married outside their racial group. During the 1880s the BPA often debated the idea of preventing marriages between people of mixed descent and full descent altogether. In 1886, while manager of Ramahyuck (he was shortly to become the secretary and "general inspector of Aborigines"), Hagenauer had suggested that a "specified provision [be] made for future intermarriages between any full black and any halfcaste" in the new act that the BPA was then in the process of drafting.[14] In its 1888 report the BPA noted that the:

> marrying of half-caste girls to pure blacks is a subject that has been brought under the notice of the Board. The Board are of the opinion that such marriages should be discouraged as much as possible. The "Amended Act" was framed to merge the half-caste population into the general community by *encouraging* the intermarriage of blacks and half-castes that end would not be attained. As many of these girls are almost white, and have been well brought up, they will probably find husbands among the white population.[15]

This policy was not without its critics, and the Rev. John Stähle, the manager of the Lake Condah station, was one of the most vociferous. In 1888 Stähle wrote to the BPA about his concerns that young Aboriginal

women who were removed from the stations were in moral danger from
white men and suggested that they be allowed to remain on the stations until they found husbands. The BPA disagreed with this suggestion,
recording in the minutes, "The meeting was strongly of the opinion that
intermarrying between blacks and halfcastes should be discouraged as
much as possible."[16] Indeed, the BPA often organized the employment of
young mixed-descent women as servants in white households, where
it was likely that they would meet white men. The same year, Stähle's
report on Lake Condah, which was published as part of the BPA's annual report, contained a poignant description of the drastic changes recent
policy had made in the lives of Victorian Aborigines:

> As it has since come about that we have to send in the mon-
> ey for wool and stock to the Board, and the children of these
> Aborigines are forced to leave the station by Act of Parliament,
> while the few remaining blacks are to be prevented from mar-
> rying after their own choice, they have lost all confidence, and
> are determined to leave the station and earn a living for them-
> selves and their families in the best way they can.

Stähle went on to describe the problems of controlling illicit sexual
relationships between women of mixed descent and white men, repeating his request "that all half-caste girls, and especially those of a darker
colour of the mixed blood, may be allowed to remain on those stations
where they are located, until the young men, who have to leave, and who
have left the station already, have succeeded in making homes." It would
be, he argued, "a hundred times better to see them married to people
of their own race and colour, than to force them out among whites, and
thus expose them to ruin. The fact that the race is dying out fast, and that
there are only a very few to marry, ought to make it all the more desirable to put no restriction upon them in this respect."[17] These remarks are
so obviously in conflict with the BPA's philosophy that it is little wonder
they were completely ignored.

Those of mixed or full Aboriginal descent who married white people completely disqualified themselves from the BPA's financial support.
The BPA, therefore, rarely objected when white people wished to marry

Aboriginal people. In keeping with its pragmatic and cost-cutting attitudes, it had little reason to object to marriages that removed even "half-castes" a step further from government support. Thomas Harris, a white man who was employed as a general laborer and overseer at Coranderrk station, was twice granted permission to marry Aboriginal women from the station, once in 1869 and again as a widower in 1882.[18] While Aboriginal women who married white men were more common, at least six marriages between Aboriginal men and white women took place in the second half of the nineteenth century in Victoria.[19] The stories of four of these men, Thomas Braham, Richard Sharp, John Robinson, and George Briggs are revealing of the ways in which the BPA viewed such marriages.

When asked by the Royal Commission of 1877 if he had "ever known, in [his] experience, a single instance of a young native . . . who did not relapse into his savage habits, one who continued steadily pursuing the life of a civilized European, after being taught and trained as well as any European in his station would have been," Christian Ogilvie mentioned just such an example: "I have two letters in the office from a half-caste, of the name of Barham [sic], who has married a white woman, and those letters tell me that he has heard that Mr. Goodall is going to leave Framlingham, and he is asking for the situation."[20] The same year the BPA took a census of the Aboriginal population of Victoria, which was published as part of its report. Besides straightforward lists of the numbers of adult, children, male, and female Aborigines of mixed descent and those of full descent on each station, the census table included a surprising category: "Married to European Women."[21]

Although no explanation is given in the reports for the two years in which this table was published, it can only be assumed that the census taker recorded this information for a purpose. It is possible to infer that this information was of interest as a sort of count of success stories, on the basis that only very assimilated and successful Aboriginal men would have been able to win the hand of a white woman and then obligingly produce children paler than themselves.

The BPA may have perceived Aboriginal men who were married to white women to be more assimilated, but compared with the efforts

Census Return of the Aboriginal Natives in the Colony of Victoria on the 15th day of March 1877.

Station.	Black.					Mixed Blood.					Marks of Smallpox.	Married to European Women.
	Adults.		Children.		Total.	Adults.		Children.		Total.		
	Males.	Females	Males.	Females		Males.	Females	Males.	Females			
Coranderrk	22	16	6	7	51	15	24	19	26	84	...	...
Lake Condah	23	13	6	9	51	4	7	8	11	30	...	...
Lake Hindmarsh	17	4	6	5	32	5	6	7	9	28	1[1]	...
Framlingham	29	11	4	1	45	5	8	4	7	24	...	1[2]
Lake Tyers	18	18	16	10	62	...	2	1	3	6	...	...
Lake Wellingtun	18	12	11	12	53	2	4	6	8	20	...	...
Werracknebeal	2	...	...	...	2	1	...	...	...	1	...	...
Colac	...	...	...	...	...	...	...	...	1	1	...	...
Balmoral	1	...	...	...	1	...	...	...	...	...	...	...
Wickliffe	3	1	...	...	4	1	...	...	...	1	...	...
Warnambool	2	1	...	...	3	...	...	...	...	...	...	...
Elmhurst	...	...	...	...	...	...	...	...	1	1	...	...
Banyenong	1	...	...	...	1	...	...	...	...	...	...	...
Cheltenham	...	1	...	...	1	...	...	...	...	...	...	...
Beaufort	1	1	...	...	2	...	1	...	2	3	...	...
Skipton	...	...	...	...	...	1	...	...	...	1	...	1[3]
Camperdown	2	...	...	...	2	...	...	...	...	...	...	...
Casterton	6	5	2	1	14	1	...	...	...	1	...	...
Tarndwarncoort	3	2	...	...	5	1	1	1	1	4	...	...
Little River	1	...	...	...	1	...	...	...	...	...	...	...
Dergholm	...	1	...	...	1	1	...	...	...	...	...	...
Corop	2	...	...	...	2	...	...	...	...	...	...	...
Myrtleford	1	1	3	...	5	...	...	...	...	...	...	...
Fitzroy	...	...	...	...	...	...	1	...	...	1	...	...
St. Arnaud	2	2	...	...	4	2	...	...	...	2	...	...
Portarlington	1	...	...	...	1	...	...	...	...	...	...	...
Geelong	2	...	...	...	2	...	...	...	...	...	...	...
Romsey	1	...	...	...	1	...	...	...	...	...	...	...
Apsley	1	...	...	...	1	...	...	...	...	...	...	...
Edenhope	10	2	...	...	12	...	...	...	...	...	...	...
East Charlton	5	2	...	...	7	1	1	...	...	2	...	...
Kulkyne	7	2	2	1	12	2	...	1	...	3	...	...
Ned's Corner	17	4	1	2	24	...	...	...	...	...	...	...
Wyuna	10	5	...	...	15	2	1	2	2	7	1[4]	...
Swan Hill	72	39	...	...	111	2	1	...	...	3	...	...
Avenel	1	...	...	...	1	1	...	...	...	1	...	...
Towanninie	17	5	...	1	23	...	3	3	...	6	2[5]	...
Durham Ox	1	...	...	...	1	...	...	...	...	...	...	...
Narung	...	1	...	...	1	...	...	...	...	...	...	...
Terrick Terrick	1	...	...	...	1	...	...	...	...	...	...	...
Wharparilla	1	1	...	...	2	...	...	...	...	...	...	1[6]
Kerang	6	4	4	1	15	1	...	1	...	2	...	...
Cowana	17	6	1	...	24	...	...	...	...	...	...	...
Mildura	18	7	...	...	25	...	...	...	...	...	...	...
Horsham	3	1	...	...	4	...	...	...	...	...	...	...
Coleraine	2	1	...	...	3	2	...	...	...	2	...	...
Barton	2	...	...	...	2	...	...	...	...	...	...	...
Navarre	1	1	...	...	2	...	...	...	...	...	...	...
Merino	1	...	...	...	1	1	1	1	1	4	...	...
Cavendish	6	3	...	2	11	...	1	...	...	1	...	...
Hamilton	1	...	...	...	1	...	...	...	...	...	...	...
Portland	2	...	...	...	2	...	...	...	...	...	...	...
Castlemaine	...	...	...	...	...	...	...	...	...	...	...	...
Heywood	...	2	...	...	2	1	1	1	1	4	...	...
Nareen	1	...	...	...	1	...	...	...	...	...	...	...
Belfast	2	...	...	...	2	1	...	...	...	1	...	...
Dunkeld	2	...	...	...	2	...	...	...	...	...	...	...
Hexham	1	...	...	...	1	...	...	...	...	...	...	...
Carr's Plain	4	1	1	...	6	1	2	4	...	7	...	...
Wangarratta	10	5	...	1	16	...	1	...	1	2	...	...
Bairnsdale	14	9	8	9	40	...	...	...	...	...	...	...
Toongabbie	...	...	...	...	...	1	...	...	...	1	...	...
Livingstone	2	...	...	...	2	1	1	6	6	14	...	1[7]
Alexandra	3	6	...	...	9	...	...	...	...	...	...	...
Sale	2	2	...	...	4	...	...	...	...	...	...	...
Bendock	5	...	...	...	5	2	1	2	1	6	...	...
Ulupna	19	13	...	5	37	5	1	5	5	16	...	...
Total	425	211	71	67	774	64	70	73	86	293	5	3

[1] Aged 65 years.—[2] Braham.—[3] John Robertson.—[4] Mukey.—[5] Hamilton and Eliza.—[6] Cocky.—[7] George Youle.

A. M. A. PAGE, General Inspector.

13. Census Return of the Aboriginal Natives in the Colony of Victoria on the 15th Day of March, 1877. The column on the far right, titled "Married to European Women," was included without comment in this appendix from the bpa's annual report for 1877. The men's names were given at the bottom as "Braham," "John Robertson," and "George Youle." From "Thirteenth Report of the bpa," vpp 3 (1877–78): 12.

made by American reformers on behalf of acculturated Native American men, it hardly lifted a finger to assist them. Aboriginal men who married white women were disqualified from receiving government support and were therefore required to live away from the stations. Although the BPA perceived them as more assimilated than other Aboriginal men, it continued to treat them with its customary dismissiveness and disdain on account of their race. Similarly, the BPA did not display either outrage at or moral judgment of the white women who had made such a marriage. They merely exhibited a complete lack of willingness to assist them or their families when times were tough.

Thomas Braham, for example, who married Agnes Smith in Warrnambool in 1876, was aware of and attempted unsuccessfully to rely on the BPA's ideas about cultural assimilation. Braham was of mixed descent. His father, also called Thomas Braham, was most probably a white laborer, and his mother was Aboriginal, recorded only as "Christian . . . names unknown." Agnes had been born at Newcastle-upon-Tyne in England; she was the daughter of a blacksmith. A Church of England clergyman in the church at Mortlake married the couple when they were in their midtwenties. Thomas Braham was closely connected with the community at Framlingham, and shortly after the wedding he wrote to J. Dwyer, a member of the Legislative Assembly, to ask whether he could be granted some of the land belonging to the station. "I know I can go there and live," he wrote (this was before the 1886 act that removed people of mixed descent from the stations), "but can I take up a portion of land, fence it off & cultivate for myself[?] There are . . . from three to four thousand acres of land laying there waste. . . . I am lately married to a European woman and as I have a birth right I would like to have a piece of land granted to me that I might make for myself a comfortable home and also be an example to my fellow brethren." Thomas Braham was making his claim for land on two grounds. First, as an Aborigine born in the area, he had a right to a portion of Framlingham land. Second, revealing himself to be well versed in the expectations of the government officials who had the power to grant him his request, he presented himself as a promising candidate for cultural assimilation. He had married a white woman, and he had the means and knowledge to cultivate land and to be an example to the other Aboriginal people living on the reserve (something also encouraged among, for example, the graduates of Hampton and Carlisle in the United States). He revealed himself to be familiar with the codes of late nineteenth-century letter writing, "trusting to the gentlemanly kindness" of J. Dwyer and closing his letter, "I have the honour to be, Sir, Yours Humbly, Thomas Braham."[22] And to some extent he was successful. Dwyer referred the matter to the Lands Department, asking, "Can anything be done in reference to the enclosed?" Unfortunately for Thomas and Agnes Braham, the request was referred to the vice chairman of the BPA, who refused it.[23] The cultural assimilation of individual Victorian Aborigines, it seems, was not of enough importance to prompt genuine support and certainly not the relinquishment of any of the land white people had colonized only a few decades earlier.

This request does not appear to be the only one that Braham made during this period. At some point the possibility of his becoming an overseer at Framlingham (a position usually held by a white man, like Thomas Harris), and his wife the schoolmistress there (indicating that she had some education), was put to the BPA, to the white manager of Framlingham, William Goodall, and to the residents themselves, apparently through a misunderstanding. This set into motion a remarkable sequence of events. On July 4, 1877, the BPA received two letters. The first was from Goodall. He reported that earlier that evening about fifty men and women had presented him, "in a great state of excitement," with a letter for the secretary of the BPA, Captain A. M. A. Page, protesting against Braham's possible appointment as overseer. Goodall did not immediately dismiss the possibility of such an appointment, instead calming the delegation by "informing them that I would write you and inform you of their opinion in the matter." Goodall then proceeded to give his own feelings about the matter, describing Braham as "a man who is universally disliked by almost every aboriginal on the station," and expressing his doubt that the Aboriginal residents would accept authority from another Aboriginal person. Goodall continued:

> He is more frequently drunk than sober and when in that condition he is very quarrelsome and gives expression to the most filthy language conceivable. He has been several times in gaol

for committing a breach of the peace, and when he was living on the station I had to remain out till three o'clock in the morning on more occasions than one to prevent him from breaking into the huts of peaceable men and fighting when drunk; [a]nd on one occasion I had to send for the police to assist me to do so, a measure which I never had to resort to before.[24]

The residents argued in their letter, which Goodall enclosed, that they were against the appointment because "we do not like any of our own countrymen to rule over us and we are quite contented and happy to live under the care of Mr. and Mrs. Goodall and do what they ask us to do without any overseer at all."[25] Another reason for their opposition, according to Goodall, may have been that Braham had "acted entirely without their authority or consulting them any way in the matter."

Only a few days later, however, Goodall's wife, writing because Goodall had injured his hand, informed the BPA that Thomas Braham had called on the Goodalls to explain that another man, Livingstone, had asked for his appointment as overseer. Braham explained that he had asked Livingstone to obtain the permission of the BPA to reside on the station only because he "believed himself disqualified through marrying a white woman." Mrs. Goodall wrote that if "the Board did not object Mr. Goodall would be glad to have him on the station being a good worker when he is kept from the drink."[26]

The result of these letters appears to have been an invitation to Braham to appear before the members of the BPA. The minutes for July 20, 1879, recorded that "some of the members of the Board having expressed [a] wish to hear what he had to say in support of his application for a piece of land . . . and also for an appointment for his wife, a European, on the Station." Braham "expatiated at some length on the advantages to accrue to the blacks if his requests were granted," but to no avail. The BPA informed him that he was entitled to select land like any other settler, but that the Framlingham land was not open for that purpose. They also "declined the service of his wife" because the "Board were of the opinion that it would be undesirable to have a European woman married to a half-caste living on the Station."[27] The reason why this was so unattractive to the BPA was most probably the ambiguous position that would have been held by Agnes Braham had the request been granted. In any case, the reluctance of the BPA to reward acculturation is transparently obvious.

A week after Braham's visit to the BPA, the residents of Framlingham sent another letter to the BPA, this time stating that "we would like Thos. Braham living with us on this station to assist us in our work and act as ploughman as we have no ploughman amongst us & because he is a good workman & would help us a good deal." This letter had far more signatures than the previous letter.[28] Apparently Braham had cleared up any misunderstanding he might have had with the Framlingham community.

The success of Braham's original portrayal of himself as a potential candidate for assimilation is indicated by the fact that Christian Ogilvie raised him as an example during the 1877 Royal Commission into the treatment and future of Victorian Aborigines. A white wife and ambitions for a position or a piece of land were seen as indicators of acculturation, both by Ogilvie and by Braham himself, although Braham's manipulation of this particular colonial logic did not necessarily mean that he believed in it. In any case, his attempts were completely unsuccessful; while the BPA could recognize his efforts, it was singularly uninterested in his case, having absolute faith in their policy of "merging" to solve the "problem."

Richard Sharp is another example of an Aboriginal man married to a white woman who was recognized by the BPA as being on the path to assimilation. Instead of assisting him in his efforts to be self-supporting, however, it stuck firmly to the terms of the act, denying Sharp and his family support on the grounds of his interracial marriage rather than rewarding him for what it represented. Sharp married Catherine McLaughlin, an Irish woman, at Colac, a small Victorian town near Geelong, in March 1874. Richard was of mixed descent: his father, John Sharp, was most probably white and his mother, whose name was recorded on the marriage certificate as "unknown—native of country," was Aboriginal. On their wedding certificate Richard's profession was given as "labourer" and Catherine's as "domestic"; both were twenty-seven years of age. The Sharps, who stayed in Colac for the remainder of their lives, nev-

er lived on a station or mission. Instead, they occupied a dubious position in the Colac community, somewhere between Aboriginal and working-class white. Two years after their marriage, which took place in the
local Anglican church, the Sharps rented the forty acres that had been
reserved for the Aboriginal population of Colac in 1872, paying £17 per
year. According to the local guardian, the small local Aboriginal community (only thirteen members) apparently still used the land, sleeping in a
couple of houses built by the guardian, and the Sharps' rent was supposedly spent for their benefit. That the Sharps paid rent to live on land that
was reserved for the use of the Aboriginal population, despite Richard's
Aboriginality, shows that his marriage to a white woman had removed
him from the category of an Aboriginal person who was entitled to government support, even though this was well before the 1886 act.

On June 10, 1879, the *Colac Herald* pointed out this irregularity in an
editorial that accused the local guardian, Alexander Dennis, of charging
Sharp rent for land that he was entitled to use rent-free as an Aborigine.
The *Herald* reported that Richard Sharp had recently "awakened to the
fact that he was being acted unjustly with" and had refused to pay any
more rent. The paper accused Dennis of extortion, arguing first that the
other local Aboriginal people no longer used the reserve and that therefore "we consider the only industrious one of their number was justly
entitled to make use of it"; and second, that "very little of the £40 that
Sharp paid away, we think, went towards benefiting his fellows." Dennis wrote an indignant letter of explanation to the BPA, claiming that he
spent all the rent on the local Aboriginal community and enclosing a list
of incomings and outgoings "on account of the Colac Aborigines" as evidence.[29] Dennis displayed an obvious lack of faith in the capacity of the
Sharps, and particularly Richard, to undertake financial dealings with
the white community, first claiming that it was Catherine Sharp who
was the "principle [*sic*] manager" (race proving more important than
nineteenth-century gender roles in this instance), and then claiming
that the Sharps were under the influence of "evil advisers." This controversy demonstrates several assumptions that white people made about
Richard Sharp. As an Aboriginal man of mixed descent who had married a white woman, he was seen as slightly superior to other members

of the Colac Aboriginal community who were still receiving government support, yet his race emasculated him in the eyes of Dennis, who
saw Catherine as the business mind of the couple. When Dennis took
Sharp to court to retrieve the unpaid rent, the court decided in Sharp's
favor, obviously holding the view that Sharp's Aboriginal identity entitled him to government support despite his marriage.

That was certainly not the opinion of the BPA. In 1879 the reservation
was canceled, and twenty acres were temporarily reserved for the Aborigines and twenty acres for public purposes. The Sharps rented the former twenty acres from the Lands Department until Richard's death in
1919, when their grazing lease was taken over by their son, Henry.[30] They
certainly had five, and possibly eight, children during these years.[31] The
Crough family, who were of mixed descent, officially occupied the other twenty acres in 1889 or 1890 (although there is evidence that they had
been attempting to live at Colac since 1879 at least).[32] The two families
lived mostly contentedly side by side for two decades, unofficially agreeing to divide the land differently from the way it had been surveyed.

Although both families were of mixed descent and were neighbors,
they were treated very differently by the BPA, especially during the period in which the 1886 act operated. Both families did, however, enjoy the
favor of Friedrich Hagenauer, especially during his period as secretary,
because they were self-supporting. Hagenauer reported to the BPA in 1890
that "he had visited the people on the reserve near Colac and was greatly pleased with the progress they had made both in clearing the ground,
in the erection of fences, and in planting a small cultivation paddock."[33]
Hagenauer wrote in 1902, "It would be a very hard thing to remove these
families from their homes and where they do so well."[34] This sympathetic comment should certainly be read with a certain amount of skepticism. Hagenauer found it an easy thing to remove countless Aboriginal
people from their homes and families when it suited the BPA financially. It was only because the arrangement suited the finances of the BPA
that the families were allowed to remain and even to receive some support during the economic hard times that characterized the last decade
of the century.

The Croughs were often absent from their land visiting relatives at

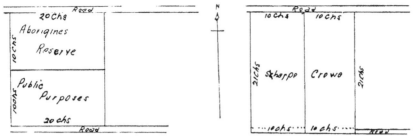

14. Concerned government officials drew this diagram to record the way the Sharps and the Croughs had divided the land with, as they saw it, little respect for the way it had been surveyed. From "(Eliminyt) Colac Inspection, 1922," item 227A, B313/1. From the collection of the National Archives of Australia.

Framlingham or Coranderrk, and they were the recipients of several letters from Hagenauer ordering them to return and reminding them that they remained there only at the pleasure of the BPA. In August 1892 Hagenauer wrote, "I was very sorry to find at Colac that you had not carried out the conditions under which you got permission to live on the reserve. You have misappropriated the land. . . . If you and yours at once return to it, the Board will not go further. . . . I think that you could get again employment at the factory if you apply for it, and if I can give you . . . some assistance in it, I will gladly do it."[35] In return for following Hagenauer's advice, the Croughs received rations and financial help with improving the buildings on the reserve, most unusual occurrences during the 1890s when the BPA was generally refusing to support the mixed-descent people whom it had expelled from the stations under the 1886 act. In March 1893 Joseph Crough received a letter from the new secretary of the BPA, William Dickenwood, warning that although some tea and flour had been sent, "An exception has been made in this instance, in granting your request, but as there is no provisions in the law for such cases, this must be *absolutely the last time* that supplies can be granted."[36] In June of the same year, however, Hagenauer wrote to Mrs. Crough to say that he had once again sent supplies, after which "nothing can be sent any more."[37] The Croughs were still receiving rations (although not on a regular basis), along with BPA interference in their lives, as late as 1910.[38]

Soon after the Croughs were granted rations in mid-1893, Richard Sharp wrote the BPA asking for similar support. The Sharps had also received financial assistance from the BPA in improving the buildings in which they lived, but they had never received rations of food or clothing.[39] Hagenauer replied: "The simple thing is that it is against the law to support you and yours, and if you wish to appear before the Board you may hear the same thing. Besides this you should be thankful that the Board allows you to reside on the Board reserve etc."[40] It was not the first time Richard Sharp had applied for assistance. The BPA's minutes noted briefly in June 1890 that "Mr. J. Miller of Colac applied for some assistance for the Half Caste man Sharp who is married to a white woman. The Board could not entertain this application."[41] At the very same meeting the BPA agreed that it "would be a very graceful act" to contribute £3 toward the wedding festivities of King William Barak, demonstrating that some marriages, at least, were approved of by the BPA. William Barak's marriage, as he was well past middle age, was hardly likely to result in any financially troublesome Aboriginal offspring. The Sharps' marriage was a very different proposition. Similarly, Eliza Warren's marriage to a man the BPA thought was African American disqualified her from BPA support, although she was a relation of the Croughs (possibly Mrs. Crough's mother). The BPA was later willing to assist in building a room in which she could stay on the Colac reserve.[42]

Richard Sharp appears to have had a very different kind of relationship with Hagenauer than his neighbor. In 1896 Hagenauer asked for Sharp's assistance in organizing contractors to build this extra room on Crough's house. He had called at the Sharps' home the previous day and spoken to Catherine Sharp, who had promised to "make due inquiry about it, but I think I had [better] write to you and to give you all the particulars in the case." Obviously in this case, Catherine Sharp's whiteness did not override Hagenauer's perception of her as a woman with little business sense. Hagenauer wrote that he did "not wish that you shall do this favour for nothing and I will ask the Board to make you some kind of allowance for your work and trouble."[43] Accordingly, Hagenauer wrote to Catherine Sharp later that year to inform her that she should pick up from Colac "one paper parcel, containing two pair of blankets in acknowledgment of Mr. Sharp's attention to the erection of Mrs. Eliza Warren's home."[44] Despite the derisively small payment, this had been a business arrangement. Richard Sharp had been entrusted with the hiring of contractors rather than Joseph Crough, despite the fact that it was Crough's home that was to be improved.

Although Sharp's marriage to a white woman seemed to have earned some measure of Hagenauer's respect, it was the object of opprobrium when relations between the neighbors turned sour. Sometime in 1897 Joseph Crough complained about the Sharps to the BPA, accusing Catherine Sharp of having land elsewhere. Hagenauer replied that both families "ought to be thankful to be allowed to have a home there. I have to direct all of you to live a peaceable and happy neighborly life and not to quarrel one with the other if you want to remain in possession of your nice home. If Mrs. Sharp has another piece of land elsewhere it is very good and I would advise you that through good work you will do your best to purchase a piece in the town of Colac yourself for your children."[45] In 1919 Joseph Crough wrote to the BPA again to complain that "Richard Sharp is dead about 2 month or more and his wife is a white woman. I am told she has no right with the 20 acres of land I am told by my gentleman friend to see about it soon and try to . . . get it for my boys they have been away to the war 4 years."[46] The BPA had by then given up all responsibility or claim to the land, and the Lands Department was of the opinion "that if Sharp has left any relatives they should be allowed to remain."[47] By then, Sharp's Aboriginality and his wife's whiteness were of little moment. Earlier in their lives, on the other hand, their racial identities caused the BPA to treat them with slightly more respect, but at the same time provided a reason for denying their requests for assistance when times were tough.

After the 1886 act commenced operation, the experiences of interracial couples on the stations became increasingly unpleasant. Nonetheless, John Robinson, an Aboriginal man, and Margaret Matthews, a white woman, who were married in December 1869, battled hard for the right to live at Framlingham. Robinson's family had strong ties to Framlingham, but as he was of mixed descent he was not welcome on the station after 1886, and his marriage to a white woman disbarred him doubly. It seems that the couple nevertheless often visited the station and lived mostly on it or in the local area with at least one of their children.[48] In January

1892 Hagenauer wrote to a Mr. Robinson at Framlingham to warn him to leave the station at once or he would be arrested for trespassing.[49] In August 1894 the BPA received reports that a white woman was trespassing on Framlingham station. Although no names were mentioned, it seems likely that the reports referred to Margaret Matthews. On August 1, the BPA recorded in its minutes that it had ordered the local agent to remove the white woman trespassing at Framlingham.[50] Ironically, one of the reports appears to have come from Mrs. Eliza Saunders (nee Warren) who lived sometimes at Framlingham and sometimes with her daughter, Mrs. Crough, at Colac, next door to Catherine Sharp. Eliza had herself been denied BPA support because the BPA said she was married to an African American.[51] On August 2, 1894, Hagenauer wrote to Mrs. Saunders to inform her that her letter had been "duly read and considered . . . and . . . the white woman, who is trespassing at the reserve at Framlingham will be prosecuted by law at once, for she has no right to be there." This information was only an aside, however. It is clear that Mrs. Saunders had written to the BPA to request that she receive rations and clothing from the BPA while she resided with her daughter at Colac.[52]

Another daughter, Victoria Alice, was born to the Robinsons on August 23, 1895, followed by Valentine Margaret on February 7, 1897.[53] With three children under five years to support and the worsening economic depression, the Robinsons fell on hard times and turned to the BPA for support. It appears they were living with another family at Framlingham. In July 1897 D. J. Slattery, the local guardian, petitioned the BPA for support for the family. Hagenauer replied, "In reference to your application for John Robertson [sic] (halfcaste) and his wife, I am very sorry to say that the Board has no power at all [to] grant the petition and to add that Robertson cannot be allowed to stay with anyone on the Reserve neither, as otherwise, the supplies for those who harbour them would be stopped. I asked the Vice Chairman if the matter should be brought before the BPA and he stated, 'no, there is no power to help in this case.'"[54] In September 1897, Robinson himself must have written to the BPA asking for help. Hagenauer wrote to Slattery that he had "read the inclosed letter of John Robinson regarding himself, his wife and family with much sympathy," but insisted that the BPA had no power to allow the Robinsons to live at Framlingham."[55] This time Hagenauer took the matter to the BPA's meeting in October, although there was no discussion of the decision Hagenauer had already made. The minutes merely recorded that "Mr. Slattery had forwarded an application from a halfcaste man, named Robertson [sic], who is married to a white woman, to grant rations to himself, wife and children and to be allowed to reside at Framlingham for some time. The Secretary informed Mr. Slattery that the Board could not grant the application as the compliance of such request was entirely against the law."[56]

In January 1898 two cottages became vacant at Framlingham, and both Slattery and another local guardian, Constable J. Akeroyd, applied for one of them for the Robinson family, who "were really . . . in very poor circumstances."[57] This time the BPA responded with compelling reasons for its refusal to support the suffering family. A letter to the chief secretary—which, like the majority written by Victorian Aboriginal people during this period, must have complained about the conditions on the station or perhaps the treatment of people by the BPA—was the subject of an inquiry. The investigation found that the letter, which had been signed by six "old black" men, was a forgery, and from "comparison with other letters in the Office and also from confidential information received at Warrnambool, it seems clear that the writer is said to be the white woman, who is mentioned in Mr. Slattery's application." The assumption that a white woman would have more education and greater ability to protest than the Aboriginal residents of the station was expanded into an accusation that allowed the BPA not only to withdraw any prospect of support but to act cruelly and decisively as well. The committee made four unanimous resolutions. Slattery and Akeroyd were ordered to physically remove the two vacant cottages altogether and to require the Robinsons to leave Framlingham immediately. It was resolved that the Robinsons had "no claim whatever on the Board" and that the Brown family, who had been "harboring" the Robinson family, were to be notified that if they did not eject the Robinsons at once their own supplies would be stopped.[58] While it is impossible to dismiss the possibility that Margaret Robinson did write the letter herself, or perhaps assisted the Aboriginal men in writing it, the whole matter was settled far too conveniently for the BPA's role not to come under some suspicion. In one leap of logic the BPA managed to dismiss as a forgery a letter alleging misconduct sent over its head to the vice chairman and to remove all obligation to provide for a starving family.

Even so, Akeroyd and Slattery made one more attempt on behalf of the Robinsons, this time enlisting the help of the acting president of the local Ladies' Benevolent Society. The BPA's files contain a letter signed by all three certifying that the Robinson family "are a very deserving case for charity and that the mother who is a white woman is a proper person to have [the children] boarded out to her." The letter recorded the birthdates of the three children and that the entire family were "All Church of England."[59] It is not known whether the BPA relented and gave the family support, but the fact that the local Ladies' Benevolent Society was involved indicates that the Robinsons had been forced to turn elsewhere. In 1909, Mrs. J. Crough was informed by the BPA that while it would not allow her to return to her family at Coranderrk while she was ill, the Colac Ladies' Benevolent Society would be asked to "assist . . . during the time of [her] indisposition."[60] There is no doubt that there were many deserving cases of charity among the people of mixed descent who had been removed from the stations by the 1886 act.

The most revealing phrase in the Ladies' Benevolent Society's letter to the BPA about the Robinsons is the description of Margaret as a proper person to have her own children "boarded out to her." This description negates the common assumption that a white woman in Robinson's situation would most likely not be "proper." It also ignores the close relationship between Robinson and her children. Perhaps Margaret Robinson's "whiteness" had been compromised. The Ladies' Benevolent Society was reacting to her not as a "white" woman but rather as a woman who had sunk to a position where assistance could not be refused and where withholding it in the hope of improvement was of no conceivable use. The Robinsons' case is remarkable for the lack of support given to them by the BPA. Far from being seen as a couple to be rewarded for contributing to the projects of cultural assimilation and biological absorption through their marriage, the Robinsons were not even allowed to remain on the station.

Another tragic case which demonstrates that the BPA could interfere with the lives of interracial families who did not even live on the stations concerns a branch of the large Briggs family. George Wright Briggs, a Woiworung man perhaps of mixed descent, and Charlotte Giles, who was white and born in Surrey, England, were married in 1880. They were no doubt in a relationship before their marriage, because Charlotte was over fifty in 1880 and the couple certainly had more than one child by the time they appeared in the records in 1882. George Briggs was in his late thirties when the couple married, and he had strong ties with Corand-errk station, where his mother and brother resided. In 1882 he appeared before the Royal Commission established to inquire into the conditions at Coranderrk station, testifying that he had married a white woman in Ararat, that she had left him, and that he had children in an industrial school. George told the commissioners that he had never stayed on the station and had been working upcountry as a bullock driver until he decided to take advantage of a short break to visit his mother and broth-er. During this time he worked on the station, and it was for this reason that he was asked to give evidence to the Royal Commission, which was investigating allegations by the residents that the BPA was underpay-ing and underfeeding them. George testified that his family never got enough rations and that he did not intend to stay on the station as long as he was "able to work."[61]

Because of George Briggs's decision not to stay with his extended fam-ily at Coranderrk under the surveillance of the BPA, little is known of his life apart from a very short period between 1881 and 1883. He appeared only briefly and sporadically in the records of the BPA until June 21, 1881, when his white wife, Charlotte Briggs, was declared insane and admit-ted into the Kew Lunatic Asylum. According to her case file she was brought in by the police suffering delusions. The couple's place of resi-dence was described as being in two parishes near Bendigo, not far from Ararat where they were married.[62] Her profession was given as a "labour-er's wife."[63] The police report added that the couple was "very poor."[64] George Briggs's Aboriginality was not mentioned in her case file, which recorded that she was "nervous and frightened in bad bodily health. Has a number of delusions, fancies that Dr. Dick is being murdered and

that she must go to his house to protect him &c." On June 28, it was noted that she "sleeps badly, eats fairly well," and on December 17 she was
allowed to leave on probation until January 17, 1882, probably for a visit home for Christmas.[65] This leave was extended until September, and
Charlotte returned to the asylum only briefly to be discharged into the
care of her husband on October 21, 1882.[66]

Just after Charlotte had been admitted, in July 1881, the manager of
Coranderrk mentioned that George Briggs had returned there. "I am
sorry to say George Briggs is here," Strickland wrote, adding, "he has
already commenced his invitations to dancing" (most probably in reference to Briggs's involvement in "undesirable" traditional ceremonies
such as corroborees).[67] In February 1882, however, while Charlotte was
on leave from the asylum, Strickland recorded that "I cannot find out
the whereabouts of Geo Briggs," perhaps indicating that he was back
home with his wife.[68]

In September 1882, Maria L. Beggs, a white farmer's wife from Eur-
ambeen whose husband often employed members of the Briggs family, wrote to a Mrs. Briggs at Coranderrk. The recipient of the letter was
either George Briggs's mother or his brother's wife. The letter informed
Mrs. Briggs that "little Mary Briggs is very unkindly treated and beat-
en like a dog by old Mrs. Franc who has her ever since her mother left . . .
if there is anyway you could find to get her to you at Coranderrk please
write me word; as you must have heard that poor George Briggs's wife
ran away from him and I hear she is at present in a lunatic Asylum quite
off her head."[69] Mrs. Briggs forwarded the letter to Page, who wrote to
Maria Beggs on September 9, 1882, asking her to take charge of Mary
for a few days and "then see her off in the train in charge of the guard[;]
I will have somebody to meet her at the train in Melbourne if you will
give me a day's notice of the time she will leave. I have written to the
police requesting them to inform Mrs. Franc that she is liable, under the
Act, to a penalty of £20, she having an Aboriginal in her service without
a certificate from the Board."[70] Page inquired about Mrs. Franc through
the local policeman, who reported:

> From my knowledge of Mrs. Franc and other enquiries I have
> made, the child was well treated. . . . The child was given to

Mrs. Franc by its mother, about four years ago, when no other person would take it from her, as she was leaving the district with her other children.[71]

Two days later, despite a second letter from Maria Beggs alleging that Franc had been "in jail once . . . for maltreating her own child," Page offered to place Mary back into her care. Franc refused the offer, being "very much annoyed by the false report of her treating the child cruel."[72]

Meanwhile, the people at Coranderrk awaited Mary's return eagerly, going every day to meet the coach from Melbourne. When she had not come by September 29, they "expressed a fear she would be sent elsewhere," but thanks to Franc's refusal she must have arrived some time in the first half of October.[73] Mary appeared frequently in the dormitory reports for 1884.[74] Then, some time between 1885 and 1888, Maria Beggs wrote to Page asking whether she could employ Mary Briggs on her farm, but he refused, saying, "Mary Briggs has lately been taken in charge by the Matron at Coranderrk with a view of teaching her domestic duties. She is contented where she is." He suggested that Maria Beggs consider taking one of the older girls instead.[75] Probably around the same time Mary Beggs's husband wrote to the Industrial and Reformatory Schools Department to say that he was "interested in the children of the late George Briggs of Coranderrk (George having been in his employ on the station) he understood that Mary Briggs (now about 13 or 14 years of age) is at Coranderrk and he would be glad to take her into his service."[76] This request was not granted. Mary appears to have received no special treatment as the daughter of a white woman, and Page never appeared to doubt his ability to control her place of residence.

The relationship between the Briggs and the Beggs appears to have been one of mutual goodwill. As well as working on the white stations, it is probable that the Aboriginal people had incorporated the Europeans into their kinship and exchange systems: hence the concern the Beggses had for Mary Briggs and her family. The BPA was determined to ignore this bond, refusing Mrs. Beggs's request for Mary to come and live with her and suggesting other girls instead, as if they were interchangeable.

Because of George Briggs's understandable desire to live away from the station and the BPA's surveillance, little more is known of the Briggses' marriage. There is no indication of the cause of Charlotte Briggs's period of mental illness, but it appears that her daughter Mary was not in her care after 1882. In the same year Page applied to have a three-and-a-half-year-old-boy named George Briggs admitted to the Victorian Deaf and Dumb Institution. His application was refused because the child was so young. Although the name is the only evidence, it is possible that this child was also George and Charlotte's and that Page was attempting to clear himself of the responsibility for caring for this child while Charlotte was in the asylum.[77] Despite George's success at supporting himself and his family away from the stations and Charlotte's whiteness, as in the cases of the other families discussed in this chapter, the BPA had no hesitation about applying to them the same policies of interference and control that it inflicted upon other Aborigines during this period. Nor did the BPA offer the Briggs any special treatment because they were self-supporting and had married interracially.

As the first decade of the twentieth century neared its end, the BPA realized that its policy was not working and began to relax its strict control of marriages and places of residence. When James Mulett, a man of mixed descent, requested in 1908 that he be allowed to marry Kate Johnson, probably also of mixed descent, and to live at Coranderrk, the BPA offered "no objection to the marriage, and that pending a decision on the question of assistance to half castes [in] general, Mulett and Miss Kate Johnson be permitted to stay at Coranderrk."[78] In 1910 a short "Act to extend the powers of the Board for the Protection of the Aborigines" was passed to reverse the 1886 legislation. The premier explained that it was thought when the original act was passed that "the half-castes would in time merge with the rest of the population, and that they would be able to help themselves, but our experiences have not confirmed that expectation." The responsibility of the failure of the BPA's policy was laid squarely on the shoulders of the mixed-descent population:

> The half-caste is frequently a more helpless individual than the full-blooded black. He certainly has Caucasian blood in his veins, but to all intents and purposes he is as much a blackfellow in too many cases as a full-blooded aborigine. The object of this Bill is to do by statutory law what they are now doing

as an act of charity, so as to bring those half-castes again under their control if it is desirable to do so.[79]

In the Council, members were reassured that "unfortunately, the aborigines were a diminishing number, and the expense of maintaining them was probably only about one-half of what it was a few years ago. Therefore, the additional expense of maintaining the few half-castes would not amount to a great deal."[80]

Interracial marriage had played a central role under the 1886 act. To the BPA it was a means of biological absorption for the mixed-descent people of Victoria, hence its disinterested tolerance for marriages between Aboriginal people and white people. Rather it was marriages between those of mixed and full descent which perturbed the BPA because they confused the neat categories the BPA had put in place for deciding whom it would and would not support. They also produced children with a preponderance of Aboriginal descent and therefore increased the number of Aboriginal people. It was these marriages which were subjected to the full force of the BPA's interference and control. Aboriginal men who had married white women were sometimes assumed by white people to have assimilated to a greater extent than their peers, but their marriages also disqualified them from the BPA's assistance. While this must have caused these couples economic hardship, the accompanying diminution in surveillance of their lives can only have been an advantage. Unlike their counterparts in America, they were not seen as "leaders" or "examples," nor did they receive any assistance because of their apparent attempts at cultural assimilation. Far from being seen as "angels of civilization," white women who married Victorian Aboriginal men during this period had, through their choice of spouse, precluded any chance they might have had for a middle-class life, and this destined them, in almost every case, to a hand-to-mouth existence. The next chapter explores the lives of three white women who married Aboriginal men and the way they were similarly perceived by mainstream Australia as oddities rather than as conduits of cultural assimilation.

7. White Women Married to Aboriginal Men

In 1900 an Australian book of marital advice reminded its white, middle-class readers about the importance of carefully selecting a husband. "A young woman in search of a partner in life," the author declared, "if she is the worthy, prospective wife and mother to whom these pages are specifically dedicated . . . is not likely to mate herself with a member of a lower race." In case readers were in any doubt about whom the author had in mind, he added: "A Negro, a Hindoo, and a Chinaman, although all civilised after a fashion, would no more be her husband than would an Australian black."[1] In this passage a sentiment that Australian colonial society rarely openly expressed was made explicit. Marriages between middle-class white women and Aborigines were unthinkable. Aboriginal people were not just one of many undesirable marriage partners. They were at the bottom of the scale, the extreme by which other inter-racial marriages were measured.

When an educated white woman and an acculturated Native American man married in the late nineteenth and early twentieth centuries, there was a place for them in American society. They were examples of assimilation at work, living proof that the color of a person's skin could, for some, be in some ways less important than their way of life. An ideological framework made up of humanitarian belief in equality, rhetoric of instantaneous improvement, and the transformative power of education made the couples discussed in chapters 3 and 4 unusual but not complete outsiders. By contrast, when white women and Aboriginal men married, they struggled to find a place for themselves in any strata of the

Australian class system. They were never doctors or lawyers, they had not attended a university, and they were rarely in the position to write letters, let alone create a persona based on the ideologies of the day in speeches, articles, or books. For this reason, this chapter deals with patchier evidence than the stories told in earlier chapters. Stories about poor, ill-educated white women and Aboriginal men who were not able to engage in the middle-class pastime of authorship or even letter-writing left behind little evidence of their lives, except when appearing in someone else's narrative. Their own words are few and far between, but there is much to learn about Australian ideas of assimilation from the way they were perceived. Perhaps most important, the idea of white women as "angels of civilization" was rarely applied, even to those humanitarian-minded women who fitted the image. Instead, the white community could react in one of two ways to white women married to Aboriginal men. The couple, especially the wife, could be dismissed as eccentric and harmless, or they could be seen as threatening to the status quo. Revealingly, the latter reaction was reserved for those couples who attempted to accept the "promise" of assimilation and thereby transgressed the role assigned by white Australians to Aborigines outside mainstream society.

In 1937 journalist Ernestine Hill published a collection of her journalistic writings under the title *The Great Australian Loneliness*. One chapter was devoted to the "strange case of Mrs. Witchetty," a patronizing account of Hill's visit with a white woman who had been married to an Adnyamathanha man and who, with her two sons, still resided with his people after his death. The chapter was also published as a sensationalized article on the front page of the *Sunday Guardian Sun* on December 18, 1932.

Hill presented the story as "the most amazing document in the annals of the Australian outback," but despite her condescending tone she seemed more interested in presenting the case as an oddity rather than as an unacceptable breach of social mores, still less as a story of assimilation gone "right." Much of Hill's story is substantiated by the marriage certificate of Jack Forbes and Rebecca Castledine, who were married on January 17, 1914, at the registrar's office in Bourke. The patronizing and sensationalist tone of Hill's writing, however, suggests the extent to which she

The STRANGE CASE of Mrs. WIDGETY

By ERNESTINE HILL

THE most astounding human document in the annals of the outback is the life history of Mrs. Jackie Forbes, otherwise Mrs. Widgety, the only authentic case to date of a white woman "living black" with the wandering tribes of Australia.

Very few have even glimpsed this extraordinary woman, for 18 years the wife of a full-blooded native, and the mother of his half-caste sons. To gain the story from her own lips I have travelled, by car and

"Mrs. Widgety"

15. In the newspaper version of the story, Rebecca Forbes's pseudonym was changed to "Mrs. Widgety." Perhaps the editors felt that "Mrs. Witchetty," which evoked an indigenous foodstuff known to white Australians as a witchetty grub, was too offensive. From *Sunday Guardian Sun*, December 18, 1932, National Library of Australia.

may have embellished the story. The condescendingly humorous name "Witchetty," for example, appears to be the result of either Hill's invention or her adoption of a local nickname. Rebecca Castledine was born in Bow, England, and she immigrated to Australia before the First World War. She was thirty-eight when she married and had not been married previously. Forbes was fifty-two, and his marital status is recorded as "widower." Hill records that the couple met while Castledine was working as a cook on a sheep station near the Western Darling River. According to his wife, Forbes was a "splendid worker, honest as the day and well-spoken of by all the station people in the district, when he proposed I could see no reason for rejecting him." The couple were married according to both European and Aboriginal tradition, and their two sons were raised speaking "good English, but better blackfella." Hill's account indicates that Rebecca Forbes had taken on some Aboriginal beliefs, recording her apology that she could not show Hill a photograph of her late husband: "We never keep belongings of the dead, and always shift camp, away from the haunt of their spirit. Since he died, the policeman at Beltana and the chief protector of Aborigines in Adelaide have written to me, asking if I would leave the camp and live white again. That would mean rent to pay, and the children to educate, and with living so dear I prefer to stay here."[2]

Although Hill records that Rebecca Forbes was "mentally above the average," she does not present her involvement in an interracial marriage as in any way threatening to the racial status quo. Instead her emphasis is, as historian Kate Darian-Smith has argued, on her eccentricity or even craziness, demonstrated by her decision to give up her own social status as a working-class white woman to assimilate, as it were, into the Aboriginal community.[3] In fact, it is Forbes's willingness to live a life apart from white society instead of demanding a place within it that allowed Hill to be so casual in her portrayal. Forbes's decision to remain a part of Aboriginal society rather than attempting to bring her husband and sons into white society also made her easier to overlook on any important level. Forbes's living arrangements had metaphorically "blackened her," allowing whites to read her as having none of the responsibilities or status of a white woman. "With no housework to do," Hill wrote, "she

spends all her days in reading hair-raising thrillers, blissfully uncon-
scious that she is the most hair-raising thriller of the lot."[4]

When a white woman and an Aboriginal man tested the opportunities offered to them by the rhetoric of assimilation, they took a more significant risk with mainstream opinion. Ethel Page was white, sixteen
years old, and five months pregnant when she married an Aboriginal
man of mixed descent called James "Jimmy" Governor in the rural New
South Wales town of Gulgong on December 10, 1898.[5] Jimmy could read
and write thanks to his attendance at Denison Town, Wollar, Gulgong,
and Coonabarabran primary schools. He had worked as a police tracker
and, after his marriage, supported himself and his wife through various
laboring jobs. Ethel was the daughter of a miner. A son, Sidney, was born
to Ethel and Jimmy only four months after their wedding, and a daughter, Thelma, was born in 1901 after her father's death. Ethel and Jimmy
were two poor and ill-educated people from rural New South Wales who
would normally have left behind few written records, but the details of
their marriage were made scandalously public after Jimmy, with another Aboriginal man, Jacky Underwood, brutally murdered his employer's
wife, three of their children, and the local schoolteacher in July 1900. Consequently, the Governors became the best-known interracial marriage in
Australian history. Although his accomplice was quickly caught, Jimmy
escaped into the bush with his brother Joe and went on the run. Outwit-
ting police for over three months, the Governors committed numerous
robberies and four more murders. Jimmy's lawyer argued that Jimmy's
actions had been provoked by the community's disapproval of his marriage, but it was to no avail, and Jimmy was sentenced to death in the
last days of 1900. His hanging was postponed until January 18, 1901, so
as not to mar the celebrations of Australia's Federation.

It is not difficult to fit the Governors into the story of the attempts made
by the government in New South Wales to assimilate Aboriginal people
into white culture during this period. In 1898, the year that Jimmy and
Ethel were married, the New South Wales government was beginning to
make serious efforts to rid itself of the financial burden of the Aboriginal population. A board of protectors had been appointed in 1882, and its
very first annual report made clear its aim to reduce the cost of assistance

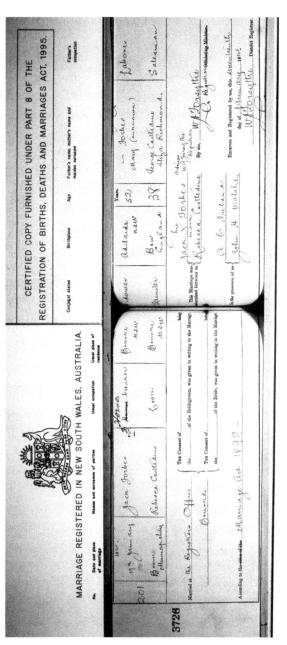

16. The marriage certificate of Jack Forbes and Rebecca Castledine. Note the correction made regarding Jack's occupation: from "house breaker" to the far more respectable trade of "horse breaker." Copy obtained from the New South Wales Registry of Births, Deaths, and Marriages.

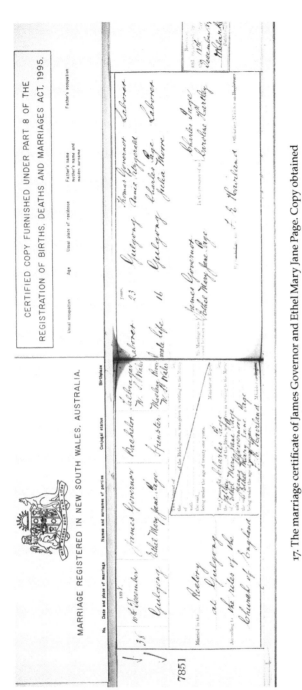

17. The marriage certificate of James Governor and Ethel Mary Jane Page. Copy obtained from the New South Wales Registry of Births, Deaths, and Marriages.

18. Ethel Governor, around the time of Jimmy's capture and trial. *Sydney Mail*, August 4, 1900, BN336. Courtesy of the State Reference Library, State Library of New South Wales.

given to Aboriginal people, especially to those whom the board viewed as capable of earning a living in the white workforce.[6] In 1898 the board issued a circular to all local boards and managers ordering them to encourage able-bodied people of mixed descent to move off the reserves and missions and to find employment in white society.[7] As Peter Read has documented, those Aboriginal people who did so suffered greatly from racial discrimination in the employment market and, in some cases, from enforced separation from their families, who remained behind on the reserves.[8]

In this context, Jimmy Governor appears to have been exactly the kind of Aboriginal man whom the board was trying to encourage. Although he associated with the Aboriginal community that lived at Wollar and was in receipt of rations, he appears to have been supporting himself through a series of jobs. On the day of his capture he told a policeman,

"I was never a loafer like some blackfellows; I always worked and paid for what I got. I reckon I'm as good as a white man."[9] His most visible attempt to join white society as an equal was, of course, his marriage to a white woman.

Jimmy was only charged with the murder of Helen Kerz, the schoolteacher who had been boarding with Jimmy's employers. As there was certainly no doubt that Jimmy had killed Kerz with a tomahawk, Jimmy's lawyer, the eminent Queen's Counsel Francis Stewart Boyce, attempted to have the charge reduced to manslaughter, arguing that Kerz had intentionally provoked Jimmy by taunting him and Ethel about their marriage. Boyce utilized the racist assumption prevalent in white society at the time that nonwhites were "savage" and "primitive." Jimmy was unable to control himself; as Boyce put it, "Could we, who had neglected, despised, and taunted the aboriginals, expect them to exercise the ordinary human control?"[10] Ethel admitted under cross-examination that she "had put up with a great many taunts because of my marriage. Some people said I ought to be shot for marrying a blackfellow. . . . Once in camp I went down on my knees and prayed, 'O Lord! take me way from here; I cannot stand what these people are saying about me."[11] Boyce reiterated this theme a number of times. He argued that Jimmy:

> was a man of sensitive nature—a better man than most blacks, because he worked when he could get work—and the taunts hurled at his wife were doubly felt by him. The jury could picture the white wife of a blackfellow kneeling in the camp and praying, "O Lord take me away from here, I cannot stand what these women are saying." The husband had seen that and there was then sown the seed of which the harvest was that terrible night.

Boyce then argued that Jimmy had gone to the Mawbeys' house only to threaten Mrs. Mawbey with legal action, and concluded that:

> it could not be supposed that he suddenly became a raging lunatic for nothing. Mrs. Mawbey and Miss Kerz wheeled round on him and laughed and sneered, and Miss Kerz said, "Pooh, you black rubbish, you ought to be shot for marrying

a white woman." That was the turning point. . . . The savage
heart, tainted with the thirst of blood, burst through reason
and one of the foulest of crimes was committed.[12]

Other commentators on this well-known case have made different
assessments of Jimmy's motivations. Thomas Kenneally's fictional account
of the story, *The Chant of Jimmy Blacksmith*, was based on a reading of contemporary newspaper articles.[13] Kenneally emphasized Jimmy's isolation from both Aboriginal and white culture. According to Kenneally,
Jimmy's efforts to conform to the expectations of white society failed
to gain him the respect he craved, and the murders were committed in
order to reestablish both power and self-respect and represent a return
to Jimmy's "savage" instincts. Kenneally portrayed Jimmy's marriage to
Ethel as an effort to raise himself up in white society. Ethel is depicted
as both lower class and unintelligent; Kenneally described the union as
one in which a "slowly descending white was wedded to a black in the
ascendant."[14] Kenneally's version has been denounced as a reiteration of
the racist assumptions of Jimmy's contemporaries.[15] Some have argued
that Jimmy's violent acts were provoked by the futility of his efforts to
assimilate into white culture.[16] Others have viewed Jimmy's actions as
a form of political protest, as a "final statement for the Aborigines," as
stemming from a "background of racial political discontent" or "as reactions to the hegemony of the dominant culture."[17]

Perhaps the most convincing explanation, however, is that the murders were caused by conflict around issues of employment. The tensions
experienced by the Governors were not caused solely by their marriage.
Ethel testified at Jimmy's trial that Jimmy did indeed have a grudge
against Mrs. Mawbey, not, as Boyce argued, because of her comments
to Ethel, but to himself:

> for a few shillings that she made him pay for rations, when she
> made up the bill about two months ago, Jimmy complained to
> me that Mrs. Mawbey made out that he [Jimmy] owed more
> than he really did. He said, "Mrs. Mawbey is a swindler."
> That's why I judge Jimmy had a grudge against her.[18]

This explanation accounts for the visit that Jimmy and Joe paid to Mr. Mawbey just before the murders. According to Jimmy, he and Ethel had had "some words" regarding the Mawbeys, perhaps prompted by a shortage of flour and sugar at their camp. Although Boyce tried to make the jury believe that these words were about the alleged insults aimed at Ethel by the Mawbey women, Jimmy reported that his wife said to him, "They rub it in; they do as they like with you," which seems a likely reference to issues of underpaid employment. Jimmy set off, as he said, to get "some flour and a bag of sugar. I went down first to Mr. Mawbey. They were in bed, so I sung out to Mr. Mawbey, 'Is Mr. Mawbey in bed?' Mr. Mawbey said, 'Yes, Jimmy, we're just about turning in.' So he came out, I said, 'Please, Mr. Mawbey, I want a bag of flour up in the morning and a bag of sugar.' He said, 'All right, Jimmy; I will send them up in the morning or some time tomorrow.' "[19]

Barry Morris's characterization of Aboriginal employment in New South Wales as "super-exploitation," in that Aborigines were paid token wages (often receiving goods rather than money) in return for performing short-term jobs on a contract basis, probably applies to Jimmy Governor's contract with the Mawbey family. Although Morris argues that this system suited the Dhan-gadi people who form the focus of his study, because it fitted in with many of their preferred ways of life, this does not remove the element of exploitation from these contracts.[20] Jimmy's work history, which in an interview published in the *Sydney Morning Herald* he described as made up of various laboring jobs in different parts of the country, was similar to that of most Aboriginal men at the time.[21] These were jobs unwanted by whites because of their low pay and because they often were located far from towns and cities.

A month after the murders took place, the police arrested all able-bodied Aboriginal men living at the Wollar camp on charges of vagrancy and jailed them for more than a month. Rumors abounded that these people had expressed sympathy for the Governor brothers, but anxieties, again, surrounded employment. A resident of Wollar wrote a letter that was eventually passed on to the chairman of the New South Wales Board for the Protection of Aborigines, urging that the Wollar community be moved away "as the white people were afraid to employ them[;]

they would be driven to do something desperate." The resident added, "The aborigines in custody worked intermittently, but appear to nearly always have had a grievance against their employers when leaving," and that "the persons threatened by the Governors are all persons for whom they worked at one time or another." Accordingly the community was placed on a train for Brewarrina where the white residents felt "considerable alarm" at their arrival. The *Mudgee Guardian* also recognized that employment contracts were central to the conflict in its somewhat philosophical discussions of the murders, reporting local conversations about the "tenacity with which the Australian aboriginal clings to the liberal terms of a bargain," prompted by the fact that this was "one of the primary causes of the Breelong tragedies, Jimmy Governor having grumbled to his wife that he had not [been] paid his full price for some work done for Mr. Mawbey, the gentleman believing that the work was not up to the contract standard."[22]

Jimmy Governor appears to fall into the category of an Aboriginal man who was punished for his attempts to take up the "promise" of cultural assimilation. In the aftermath of the affair, the Governor case provoked a number of diatribes doubting the sense of giving Aboriginal people any chance of being educated, as it only made them "cunning . . . and more dangerous." Jimmy Governor was held up, according to a teacher at the time, as "a glaring example of the evils of education."[23] Ethel was also accused of "presuming" upon the "hospitable" attitude of the Mawbeys, becoming "unpleasantly familiar," and forcing the family to express their "displeasure" by way of "one or two sharp expressions."[24] It appears that Jimmy and Ethel's most serious mistake was to attempt to live independently of the state. As Barry Morris has argued, the New South Wales government at this time operated a policy aimed at the "dependency" of the Aborigines, whose lives were supposed to be completely controlled by the state.[25] By asserting his independence (first by marrying a white woman, second by insisting on proper payment, and third by using violence to protest against his treatment), Jimmy Governor tested and then got caught in the competing demands of the ideology of assimilation that were current in New South Wales at this time.

The events of this case gave rise to some extremely vitriolic reactions to marriages of white women and Aboriginal men in the local press. Reporters for the *Mudgee Guardian* took the reporting of the murders and the resulting manhunt very seriously and evinced an extreme view of the Governors' marriage. One anonymous writer made sure that Ethel's pregnancy on her wedding day would be common knowledge, arguing that giving birth to an illegitimate child was less of a sin than marrying its Aboriginal father:

> The idea of marrying a white child, not sixteen years of age, to a brute of a half-caste, "to save her name," is really very, very funny, and might I add [be] more or less blasphemous . . . surely it would have been far better to leave her free to go and sin no more, than to perpetuate her prostitution by cementing it with the sacrament of marriage.[26]

A week later, while the Governor brothers were still at large in the district, a columnist commented that the Governors' marriage was "an extremely unpleasant topic to touch upon, for it is another terrible proof that civilization is a failure." As a woman whose social status was dependent on that of her husband, the journalist continued, Ethel had subverted racial hierarchies by consenting "to live a black gin's life."[27]

It is clear that Jimmy and Ethel were fully aware of the difficulties their marriage had caused them. While on the run Jimmy left a letter for Ethel where he knew the police would find it, along with an offer to give himself up if Ethel came for him in a horse and cart. The letter, which was published in full in a local newspaper, read in part: "My dear Ethel,—You did not suppose you was free, my dear, when you was with me. You never think you was at home, my dear. . . . I do feel sorry for you, my dear Ethel."[28] Once Jimmy was captured and incarcerated in Sydney, Ethel visited him regularly with their son as he awaited his execution. She was already pregnant with their second child, Thelma, who would not be born until after her father's death. The diary of the officer keeping watch over Jimmy records a number of times Jimmy spoke of Ethel. On December 6, the officer reported that Jimmy said "he does not care how soon the day comes but if [he] had to do life that it would soon kill him. The only thing that troubles him is he does not know how his

wife is going to get on . . . talks of his past, his wife and child." The officer also reported on December 10 that Jimmy would, understandably,
get "very downhearted at times . . . speaks harshly of his wife says she
ought to be hanged as well as him as she is guilty calls on the Lord at
times to help him."[29]

Ethel married another Aboriginal man, Francis Joseph Brown, in Wol-
longong in November 1901, in the same year that Jimmy was executed.
She bore eight more children and died in Sydney in 1945.[30] The Governor
marriage, with its undertones of assimilation and social mobility, caused
some serious consternation in the white community. In the end, though,
Ethel Governor, in her disreputable role as wife of a notorious murderer,
could also be dismissed as an oddity much like Rebecca Forbes. When a
white woman involved in an interracial marriage could not be portrayed
as an oddity, it became a matter of even greater concern to Australian
society. This is shown by an interracial marriage involving an educated, respectable, and visible bride that occurred around the same time as
the marriage of Jack and Rebecca Forbes.

In 1907 Ethel Gribble, sister to a well-known Anglican missionary, Ernest
Gribble, married an Aboriginal man whom she had met while working
on her brother's mission in North Queensland. In doing so, she became
perhaps the only Australian white woman comparable to humanitarian American women such as Elaine Goodale Eastman. Ernest had tak-
en on the responsibility of running the Yarrabah mission, situated near
Cairns in far north Queensland, when his father, J. B. Gribble, died in
June 1893.[31] Situated in Konkandji territory, the mission had been founded by J. B. only a year earlier under the auspices of the Anglican Church.
Yarrabah soon became a significant mission community. In 1897 Ethel
came to teach at Yarrabah. Four years later, after a short stint as a gov-
erness near Gympie, she was sent to teach at a mission on Fraser Island,
which was also directed by Ernest. It was here, according to oral history sources, that she met Fred Wondunna, an Aboriginal man from the
Maryborough area who earned his living as a storekeeper.[32] Ethel was
sent back to Yarrabah, where, supposedly only ten days after her arrival,
her engagement to her brother's faithful white assistant, William Reeves,
was announced.[33] Sixteen months later, in June 1903, Ethel and Reeves

were married. A daughter was born to them a year later. During this time Ethel became head teacher at the school at Yarrabah; a former student remembered her playing the piano in accompaniment to the children's marching.[34]

In August 1904, the Fraser Island Mission was abandoned, and the residents, including Fred Wondunna, took up residence at Yarrabah. In January 1906, William Reeves became ill and died. Around August 1907, Ethel and Fred must have reinstated their relationship, as Ethel became pregnant. Despite Ernest's efforts to arrange leave for her through the Australian Board of Missions, Ethel and Fred left Yarrabah without official sanction in December 1907 and were married on December 30 in Sydney in a Congregational rather than an Anglican church.[35]

The minutes of the Australian Board of Missions Executive Council meeting dated January 10, 1908, record that Ethel wrote two letters to the Council, one dated the day after her marriage and one a few days later. Although the minutes record only that she was applying for reimbursement for travel expenses, it is apparent that the letters contained information about her recent change in marital status. The board deferred consideration of her application until the next meeting, on February 11, 1908. At this meeting the Council decided that the refund for her travel expense would be paid, and a copy of her marriage certificate was read out, almost as if, Christine Halse argues in her thesis on Ernest Gribble, the Council was so incredulous that it required documented proof that the marriage had taken place.[36] It is significant that Ethel chose to write to the Council on the day after her marriage. If nothing else, it is evidence of her unwillingness for her marriage to go unnoticed, whatever the consequences. That she wrote asking for money indicates that she did not think her actions debarred her from support from the Australian Board of Missions. Ethel and Fred's son Horace, the first of their four children, was born soon after these events in April 1908.[37]

Ethel's correspondence with the Australian Board of Missions is evidence of yet another "crime." She seemed unwilling to let her marriage exclude her from the respect due to her as a missionary woman. Her request for travel expenses was perhaps more than an application for financial support. It may have been a bid to retain her position. According

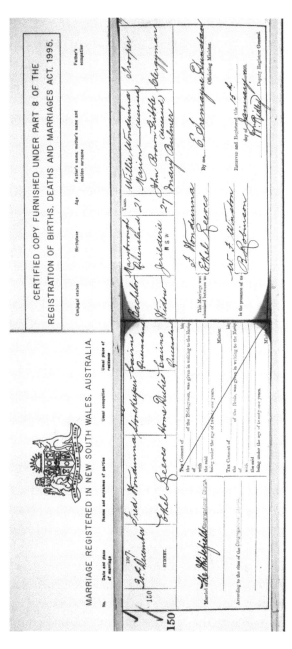

19. The marriage certificate of Fred Wondunna and Ethel Reeves. Copy obtained from the New South Wales Registry of Births, Deaths, and Marriages.

to Halse's account, the reaction of the Church of England to Ethel and Fred's marriage "reeked of bigotry and prejudice." Halse cites the Executive Council's incredulous response, the fact that Ethel and Fred apparently could not be married by a minister of their church, and the concerns of the bishop of North Queensland that the scandal would disgrace the Church. Indeed, the reaction to Ethel and Fred's marriage can be seen as the harshest of all in extant case studies of marriages of white women and Aboriginal men. As Halse argues, the "ignominy for an unmarried, white female missionary, invested by the Church with the responsibility for the moral reform of a supposedly primitive race," was greater than the disgrace meted out to working-class women such as Ethel Governor and Rebecca Forbes.[38]

The marriage may have also had an effect on the attitudes of the New South Wales government toward missionary women. In 1910 the board reported that members of the Council of the Australian Aborigines Mission had inquired about the conditions under which missionaries resided upon reserves in New South Wales. Perhaps prompted by the knowledge of the marriage of Ethel and Fred Wondunna less than two years previously, the board proclaimed that it was strongly of the opinion "that it is very undesirable for lady missionaries to reside alone and unprotected at any of the reserves, and decided not to approve of the erection of any further residences, unless they received an assurance from the Mission Council that lady missionaries would not reside alone. The board recognise the good work that is being done by the various missions, but feel that they would be held responsible should anything of an untoward nature happen."[39] The following year the board reiterated this view, extending it to include "any single person (male or female) . . . unless there is already a married couple stationed thereon in the capacity of Manager and Matron."[40] It appears that white authorities did not take kindly to the idea that white women, who were placed in an official position of power over Aboriginal people, should in any way compromise their social distance from their charges. Their middle-class status made their interracial transgressions much harder to dismiss as eccentric.

Even white women in day-to-day contact with Aborigines could be seen as dangerously subversive. In 1928 and 1929 missionary Annie Lock found herself the victim of these views when she testified to the terrible conditions suffered by Northern Territory Aborigines during a controversial trial in which white policemen were tried and acquitted of shooting thirty-one Aborigines, supposedly in "self-defense." The special government committee appointed to inquire into the massacre claimed that the bad behavior of the Aborigines had been prompted by "unattached missionaries wandering from place to place . . . and preaching a doctrine of equality." Aspersions were cast on Lock's character, the committee finding that "the presence of a woman missionary living among native blacks had lowered their respect for white people."[41] Lock was not alone; anthropologist and activist Olive M. Pink was another white woman whose criticisms of white authorities were punished with attempts to smear her character by hinting that she had sexual relationships with Aboriginal men.[42] These women, the equivalents of those in the United States who took their efforts to help Native Americans and their belief in their equality a step further by marrying interracially, were not even able to live among indigenous people without reprisal. Australia had no place for relationships based on equality and assimilation.

Australian imaginings allocated limited opportunities for Aborigines to assimilate. Aborigines had a place only in the very lowest echelons of the working class, and any attempt to breach this norm brought disapproval. An attempt to earn a working-class living led to the tragedy of the Governor murders, a missionary woman who took an Aboriginal man as a husband was rejected by the very body purporting to believe in the equality of all people under God, and Rebecca Forbes's decision to live out of harm's way in the Aboriginal community meant that she was seen at best as "odd." Eccentrics, madwomen, accessories to a crime, these women had only one place left to them by Australian ideas about their society and the place of indigenous people in it: outside.

8. Solving the "Indian Problem" in the United States

The lives of people such as Charles, Elaine, Carlos, Marie, Ethel, Jimmy, Rebecca, and Jack were unusual. In the most fundamental of ways, they allowed their hearts to lead them across the social boundaries of their time. In doing so, they left clues for the historian to follow about the society in which they lived. I turn now to the broader contexts in which marriages between white women and indigenous men took place. What did mainstream Americans and Australians, and the reformers, commentators, and politicians who influenced them, think about interracial marriage? We have already seen how differently the lives of married white women and indigenous men turned out in each country. How differently did they imagine the assimilation of Aborigines and Native Americans? In these final chapters, I argue that the unique racial landscapes of each nation influenced their ideas. And these landscapes included not just white and indigenous people but various other ethnic groups, all of whom impacted on the mainstream population's ideas about race, interracial relationships, and assimilation. In particular, this impact took the form of differing ideas about what exactly assimilation entailed: the process of cultural assimilation, teaching indigenous people to live and support themselves as white people, or biological absorption, the loss of indigenous physical characteristics through interracial relationships.

In the United States, a number of organizations, philanthropic and governmental, dictated public opinion about the issues arising from contact between white Americans and Native Americans. Established in 1824, the Bureau of Indian Affairs was an extensive government organization involved in the administration of the Indian service. An ever-changing sequence of commissioners, each with his own opinions about the current policy of the Bureau, produced annual reports that varied greatly in ambit and quality and often contained submissions from agents and other organizations that displayed quite different views from those of the commissioner. One such organization was the Board of Indian Commissioners, which President Ulysses S. Grant had formed in 1869 in recognition of the growing importance of the views of religiously motivated men and women interested in the future of Native American peoples. This group of men, selected for their eminence as well as their interest in "Indian affairs," oversaw the distribution of purchases made by the government and also acted as an advisory committee. These functions enabled the Board to exert influence over government policy.

Loosely connected with the Board of Indian Commissioners was the Lake Mohonk conference, attended by the "Friends of the Indian." It had no official status in the government hierarchy, instead acting as a gathering of those interested in the issue.[1] Hosted by Albert K. Smiley, a schoolteacher of comfortable means with an interest in Native Americans and, conveniently, the owner of a holiday resort on the shores of a lake in New York State, the conference became a focus for various reform groups and interested individuals. Government officials sometimes attended. Held annually, beginning in 1883, its sessions featured the expressions of a range of opinions from a variety of people (although the vast majority were middle-class), ranging from eastern reformers who had never experienced conditions on the frontier, to agents, teachers, or missionaries who had traveled from the West to attend.

The most influential philanthropic group weighing in on the "Indian problem" was the Indian Rights Association (IRA), which was established by two Philadelphia lawyers in 1883. David Wallace Adams believes the IRA's dominance was cemented by its many published reports and speeches, its practice of sending representatives into the field, and its maintenance of a full-time lobbyist in Washington DC.[2] By the turn of the century the organization had also fulfilled an important role as a lobbyist for the rights of individual Native Americans and nations. In 1903 the annual report noted that the work of the IRA was increasing because "the

Association has become well known all over the country, and when an Indian thinks he is being wronged, or desires advice on any points that confront him, it is quite natural for him, or some of his friends, to write to our office on the subject."[3] The Lake Mohonk conference, the Indian Rights Association, the commissioner of Indian affairs, and the Board of Indian Commissioners shaped the Dawes Act, the piece of legislation that would dictate assimilation policy until its reversal in 1934. The Dawes Act focused almost exclusively on cultural assimilation, attempting to turn Native Americans into self-supporting farmers by breaking up the reservations and allocating significant government funds to setting up a comprehensive system of Native American education.

Reformers knew about the frequent sexual contact between white people and Native Americans, but they had varied opinions about the role it was to play in assimilation. In all four forums mentioned above, it was often unclear whether the speaker or writer was referring to biological absorption or cultural assimilation when they discussed the projected eventual merging of the Native American people into the mainstream population. Commentators implied that the "delicacy" or "unpleasantness" of interracial relationships, particularly those outside wedlock, necessitated a circumspect approach to the subject. This means that a certain amount of reading between the lines is required in exploring the attitudes toward interracial marriage held by these nineteenth-century thinkers.

In the published proceedings of the Lake Mohonk conference, for example, the word *assimilation* and its many synonyms (such as *mingling, absorption, incorporation*, and *amalgamation*) were never clearly defined. In 1891 the platform of the Lake Mohonk conference commended "the policy of mingling the Indians with the white people, by seeking employment for them in Christian families and on farms, by placing them in the public schools in the States, and by encouraging their settlement together."[4] In 1893 it advocated the "breaking up of the reservations as rapidly as the interests of the Indians will allow, and the incorporation of the Indians into the mass of American citizens."[5] Neither resolution included an explanation of exactly what its creators meant by *mingling* or *incorporation*. While a general survey reveals that American reformers were far more likely to be talking about methods of cultural assimilation than the process of biological absorption, there were some instances where the latter was seriously discussed.

The minutes of the 1885 meeting of the Lake Mohonk conference recorded, for example, that one morning was devoted to discussing the meaning of the words *absorption* and *intermingling* but tantalizingly did not document what the conclusions of that discussion were. The minutes did record, however, that Gen. Samuel Chapman Armstrong, the founder of Hampton Institute, "had no prejudices against the mingling of the races. The process is going on all the time, and will ultimately result in absorption. The total number of Indians, so-called, is increasing, while the number of pure-bloods is diminishing."[6] This is perhaps the clearest indication that discussion of biological absorption as well as cultural assimilation had taken place at the conference. It was no doubt a subject that Armstrong had to confront many times in his role as principal and founder of a school where, as discussed in chapter 1, young men and women of both African American and Native American ancestry mixed with the white staff.

Certain individuals, in particular, were clear about their support for the part that biological absorption could play in assisting the assimilationist project. People from a Christian missionary background were likely to take literally, as did Philip C. Garrett, a member of the Board of Indian Commissioners, the idea of white people and Native Americans being of "one blood."[7] Alice Robertson was one of these. Her speeches were filled with stories of interracial marriages. The daughter of missionaries, Robertson was born and raised in what was then Indian Territory. After two years in an eastern college, she became a clerk in the Indian Office of the Department of the Interior and then secretary to the superintendent of Carlisle Indian School. After her father died in 1882, she returned to Oklahoma to continue his mission work and take responsibility for her aging mother. She opened the Minerva Boarding School for Girls in 1884. Speaking at Lake Mohonk in 1886, 1889, 1890, and 1904, Robertson often mentioned the prevalence of interracial marriage in Indian Territory. In 1886 she herself encouraged the marriages of Native American women from her school to white men, even going so far as to buy their trousseaux: "Some of my girls are very pretty, and some of them have a good many cows in their own right, they raise them themselves. I asked some young white men to dinner and tea one day, and asked the girls to play on the piano for them. It was really very fine, I thought; but I had three weddings in the house inside six months." In 1889, she also told the conference that the "Indian question in the Territory is going to be wiped out with blood, *white* blood by intermarriage," and she spoke approvingly of marriages between white missionary women, some of whom were her relatives, and Native American men. The latter remarks were made at the same conference at which Philip C. Garrett felt the need to assure his audience that he did not *"recommend the intermingling of the races"* after arguing that, in comparison with the African American population, "the fusion of the whole Indian population in that of the United States . . . would not be to its serious detriment." When Gen. Clinton B. Fisk, well-known abolitionist and chairman of the Board of Indian Commissioners, introduced Robertson at the 1889 meeting, he mentioned that her views were "so much more radical" than his own. In the context of these qualifying statements, it must be imagined that Robertson's assertions were somewhat outside the boundaries of majority public opinion.[8]

In private, however, some reformers expressed their support for biological absorption more openly. In a letter written in 1904, for example, Lyman Abbott made his opinion on the matter clear:

> Of course I am aware of the two policies respecting the Indians, one . . . advocating their intermixture and assimilation with the white race, and the other . . . involving the maintenance of the Indian race as a separate race in this country. You know that on this point I have heartily agreed with [the former] for many years, and have urged the policy of intermixture and assimilation by speech and pen.[9]

Similarly, once he was no longer commissioner of Indian affairs, Francis E. Leupp felt able to argue that racial fusion through intermarriage was to be the "ultimate fate" of the Indians.[10]

Other commentators, however, talked about assimilation with no allusion to biological or reproductive aspects, envisioning Native Americans becoming "Americanized" in terms of ways of living only. The Rev. A. E.

Dunning argued in 1895, for example, that "if we press forward along the line of civilization . . . some of us will live long enough to see the name 'Indian' pass into history, and we shall indeed be one people, and the difference in color even will be forgotten."[11] Dunning's vision was not one in which the clear nineteenth-century categories of "color" would be lost; but Americans would all act the same, even if they did not look the same. Senator Henry L. Dawes, whose name had been attached to the 1887 act that broke up much of Native American lands for allotment, also supported cultural assimilation, using the word *admixt*, which was more often used as a euphemism for interracial sex (hence he received an amused reaction to this phrasing), to mean:

> setting the Indian upon his feet[;] instead of telling him to "Root, hog, or die," you take him by the hand and show him how to earn his daily bread. You have got him among the fellow citizens of this body politic; you have "admixt" him. (Laughter). In a word, you have put him in a way for caring for himself."[12]

Indeed, although the issues arising from interracial sexual relationships and marriages were mentioned at the Lake Mohonk conference, they were in no way the main concern of the Lake Mohonk participants, whose central emphasis was, without doubt, on cultural assimilation. The Lake Mohonk conference reiterated over and over again the means of culturally assimilating Native Americans. Participants suggested that the laws of white America should apply equally to Native Americans, rations should be withdrawn, reservation lands should be divided up into individual allotments, and Congress should financially support various means of educating Native Americans about white ways of living.[13] If anything, biological absorption was a side issue to the main thrust of the conference's vision of the future of Native Americans.

Although the IRA often used the word *absorption* in its annual reports, it rarely did so when specifically referring to interracial relationships. Although it was dedicated to turning the Native American as "rapidly as possible into a civilized white man" and was "content to let the tribe go," it positioned itself as wanting "to do all that can be wisely done to save and guard the individual Indian."[14] So while the IRA's constantly stated aim was the "absorption into the common life of our people," it saw the process as one involving transformation rather than extinction. "The Indian as a savage member of a tribal organization cannot survive, ought not to survive the aggressions of civilization," opined the 1884 annual report, "but his individual redemption from heathenism and ignorance, his transformation from the condition of a savage nomad to that of an industrious American citizen, is abundantly possible."[15]

This did not mean that the IRA was hesitant to publish the biological absorptionist views of individual reformers in its many pamphlets. Charles C. Painter, one of the IRA's Washington lobbyists, wrote openly of the predominant view in the Indian Territory that "the Indian problem would be wiped out in blood within a few generations" in a report of a field trip published in 1886.[16] In the same year, Elaine Goodale, who had not yet met and married Charles Eastman, described Richard Pratt as not having "a particle of sentiment about 'a peculiar people,' 'preserving the identity of other races,' and so on. His healthy and inevitable and philosophical theory is the annihilation of the Indian and his salvation as an American citizen."[17] After his field trip to reservations in the Southwest, Samuel Chapman Armstrong described the so-called Five Civilized Tribes as "steadily improving, learning from the whites in their midst, becoming more and more Anglo-Saxon than Indian by admixture of blood," and then predicted that "we shall ultimately have in this Territory an Indian problem without Indians; Indian blood may be practically extinct, while Indian rights may exist in full force."[18]

In its annual reports, however, which might be read as expressing the organization's official line, the IRA's leadership preferred to resort to vague metaphors. A favorite was that of the "encroaching waves" of civilization, which were steadily eating away at reservations "like islands in a tempestuous sea."[19] "The sea of civilization is completely surrounding [the Indian]," said the 1910 annual report, "and the time is not far distant when he must 'sink or swim.'"[20] The IRA positioned itself as "true and wise friends [who] desire to watch every step" in the process by which "the Indian and his island reservation must be gradually absorbed in the sea of white civilization which surges about him" and "to defend the Indian, so far as possible, from every real wrong, to guard his individual rights and turn him as rapidly as possible into a civilized white man."[21] Whether this was to occur through interracial relationships was not specified.

Biological absorption similarly occupied a minor place in the reports made by the commissioners of Indian affairs to Congress. In these documents, the various commissioners attempted to demonstrate the successful application of uncontested and wide-ranging policies in all areas of the Indian office. They referred to their vision of the future for Native American people infrequently, reflecting the Bureau's concern with everyday administrative matters rather than with far-reaching policy. The short term of office enjoyed by most of these commissioners, and the inclusion of reports written by respected bodies such as the Board of Indian Commissioners as well as individual agents living in the West, meant that these reports also displayed a variety of opinions about interracial relationships and assimilation.

During the late 1880s and 1890s, official expressions of support for cultural assimilation were frequent, especially after the passing of the Dawes Act in 1887, and often drew on the same ideas and language that were applied to immigrants. In 1889, his first year as commissioner, Thomas J. Morgan wrote that he had held a strongly cherished conviction when he took on the responsibilities of the position that "logic of events demands the absorption of the Indians into our national life, not as Indians, but as American citizens."[22] A professional educator, Morgan embodied the latest views on the "Indian problem." He believed strongly in the ideals of patriotism and the powers of education and citizenship as tools of assimilation.[23] Morgan wrote of his plan for the "American Indian . . . to become the Indian American" and of the aim of the Bureau of Indian Affairs to "incorporate the Indians into the national life as independent citizens, so that they may take their places as integral elements in our society . . . as Americans, or rather as men, enjoying all the privileges and sharing the burdens of American citizenship."[24] Morgan's emphasis on the Americanization of Native Americans during his term of office (1889–93) influenced policies for decades to come. His successor, David M. Browning (1893–97) made few changes to the tenor of Morgan's policies.[25]

William A. Jones, who was commissioner from 1897 to 1904, was also a staunch cultural assimilationist, but with a slightly different emphasis: he was prepared to stop at making Native Americans financially self-supporting, rather than insisting on complete transformation. His administration marked a shift away from Morgan's emphasis on education toward encouraging able-bodied men to find employment. Jones wrote that under the current policy, the "Indian" would "pass out of our national life as a painted, feather-crowned hero of the novelist to add the current of his free, original American blood to the heart of this great nation. To educate the Indian in the ways of civilized life, therefore, is to preserve him from extinction, not as an Indian, but as a human being. As a separate entity he cannot exist encysted, as it were, in the body of this great nation."[26] Despite the mention of "blood," Jones made it clear in the following sentences that under his leadership the Bureau aimed to educate the Native American to "work, live, and act as a reputable, moral citizen, and thus become a self-supporting, useful member of society."

In 1905, the Board of Indian Commissioners included a long passage in its annual report that clearly argued against the necessity of completely removing Native American racial identity. Claiming that the many ethnic origins of the American people were among "the strength[s] of our American life," the Board urged that the "typical modern American is a fine 'composite,' with race elements drawn from many sources" and added: "We do not believe that the Government of the United States in dealing with its Indian wards would act righteously or wisely if it were to attempt to crush out from those who are of Indian descent all the racial traits which differentiate the American Indian from the other race stocks of the world."[27]

Jones's successor, Francis Leupp (1905-9), also did not believe it was necessary to transform Native Americans into white people, believing some of their culture to be worth preserving. Continually stressing the practical goal of self-support, Leupp argued in 1907:

> Everywhere I am striving to erase those lines which still rule off the Indian as a separate and distinct civic entity. Ethnically he will always remain an Indian. . . . But as a citizen of our Republic, and an equal sharer with his fellows of every

blood in the privileges and responsibilities of common citizenship, he is not an Indian but an American; and I should
be glad to see every mark expunged which tends to keep
alive in his mind any civil-distinctions to confuse his sense
of allegiance.[28]

Even more than the Lake Mohonk conference, therefore, the Bureau of
Indian Affairs was also concerned with forcing Native Americans to live
according to white standards. Both more practical and more money-con-
scious than the Mohonk reformers, the Bureau put in place policy after
policy to alter Native American ways of life, seemingly without finding
it necessary to speculate on the possibilities of biological absorption. The
continuing efforts to restrict rations, encourage labor, and impose white
moral systems upon Native Americans, not to mention the philosophy
of individual, family-based economic advancement that lay behind the
Dawes Act, all focused on cultural assimilation. Commissioner Robert
G. Valentine made this clear in his reports for 1909 and 1911. "The Indian Service," he said, "is a great outdoor-indoor school, with the emphasis on the outdoor. The students in this school are 300,000 individuals,
ranging in age from babes at the breast to the old men and women of the
tribes." The two main aims of the Bureau of Indian Affairs were "first, to
prepare the Indians for the lifting of the government's hand, and, second, to lift the hand."[29]

This is not to say there were no concerns about the growing number of
people of mixed descent or that incidences of interracial sexual relationships and marriages were missing from the annual reports. On the contrary, while often noting, as the Board of Indian Commissioners did in
1919, that "year by year the two races have been coming closer and closer together," white officials despaired on a moral level about the "practically open adultery within Indian reservations."[30] They attempted to
control immorality and sexually transmitted diseases by regulating reservation marriages and, when the increasing blurring of lines between
"white" and "Indian" became confusing, by discussing the legal definition of "Indian," the citizenship of white men who married Native American women, and the children of such marriages.[31] In 1918 the Board of
Indian Commissioners argued for legislation to "put an end to sexual

immoralities, such as illicit cohabitation, adultery, and other . . . offences of like character, and of the 'secret' and pseudo-religious dances and ceremonies which cloak bestial practices and gross immoralities and which would be particularly severe in its punishment of white men who prey on Indian women."[32] In the Christian, humanitarian context in which these reformers operated, the immorality of such relationships sometimes outweighed their interracial aspect.

The IRA also expressed concern about the "illicit intercourse between whites and Indian women" as early as 1883, its first year of operation.[33] In its early reports the IRA seemed concerned about the immorality and cruelty of the "brutal treatment" of Native American women by white men who "gave no sign of . . . devotion to any purpose in life beyond the gratification of their own undisciplined impulses."[34] It was not long, however, before the concerns about the financial considerations of these men and their children took precedent over anxieties about the suffering they may have inflicted on Native American women or the immorality of their actions.

Despite the IRA's endless rhetoric about assimilation and absorbing Native Americans into the economic mainstream, when white men married Native American women and created families of "half-breeds," these people were rarely seen as examples of assimilation despite their level of acculturation and financial success. Rather than seeing biological absorption as a solution, therefore, reformers and officials were often concerned about the "quality" of white people who entered into interracial relationships with Native Americans, and indeed their attitudes toward interracial sexual relationships varied according to the backgrounds of the white people involved. While there were certainly white women who married Native American men living on the reservations during this period, it was white men who married Native American women who came under constant attack, no doubt because of their far greater numbers. This was in part because they were seen as taking advantage of their wives in order to obtain their wives' rights to land, or perhaps government support, or to place themselves in a better position to exploit the local Native American community. White men who had long-term relationships with Native American women were scorned as "squaw men" and reviled as having forsaken the American work ethic in order to live as freeloaders on reservations. Soon after the Dawes Act was passed, certain white people expressed anxieties about such white men obtaining shares in the allotment of tribal lands. In 1888 a bill regulating marriages between "white men and Indian women" was introduced in the Senate. The act, which was approved in August 1888, prevented white men who married Native American women from becoming entitled to "any tribal property, privilege, or interest," and forced every Native American woman who married a white man to become an American citizen upon her marriage. The act excepted the "Five Civilized Tribes," a group which had a long history of intermarriage and powerful mixed-descent leaders.[35] In the same year agent Joseph W. Preston reported of the Mission Agency in California that "such men are rarely beneficial, and nearly always injurious to [their wives]. They, as a rule, marry the squaws for the advantages and the opportunities such a relation affords, and proceed to make the most of the situation. They manage to gobble up what the Indians make, and advise them to their hurt generally against the Government agencies, deal liquor [to] them and debauch their morals, and all this in such a manner as to evade the eye of the agent."[36]

The IRA's 1903 annual report all but mentioned by name a "certain intermarried citizen in Pickens county, Chickasaw nation" in a section that discussed the methods by which "Philistines, sharks, and robbers" deprived unwitting Native Americans of their most arable land.[37] Two years later the report outlined some "defects in the labor system" that included the case of a "well-to-do white man, married to a member of the Sioux tribe, [who] possesses a fine home and large stock interest worth many thousands of dollars" and who was receiving payment from the Indian labor fund. "Intermarried white persons who have certain influence with the agent in charge" were also seen to be exploiting the position of government farmer.[38]

At Lake Mohonk, Alice Robertson also voiced her concerns about the "quality" of white people engaging in interracial marriage in Indian Territory. "And what is this white blood?" she asked. "In some cases, it is the best blood of this country; but the majority of the intermarriages come from the class that is called "white renters." . . . The children of these renters, growing up among the Indians, will marry among them; and thus will necessarily be perpetuating the worse rather than the better traits of each."[39] Thus, in this racially charged period, concerns about class became racialized and imbued with ideas drawn from Darwinian philosophies and the eugenics movement.

Indeed, concerns about "squaw men" and their role in the process of assimilation prompted perhaps the clearest expression of absorptionist thinking by the leadership of the IRA. This occurred in 1897, when the Indian Appropriation Act reversed the central tenet of the 1888 act, placing all children of white and Native American parents "upon the same level as to the inheritance of tribal rights," removing, to the Indian Rights Association's disgust, the ability of interracial marriages to assimilate. "The law had worked well," the annual report recorded. "Its tendency was to prevent a self-seeking white man from marrying an Indian woman for the purpose merely of rearing a family of mixed-blood Indians, living on a reservation with their tribe, enjoying the product of their land, and drawing their annuities in their names." Now the IRA envisioned a "grand army of adventurers, who based their claims to tribal kindred on all kinds of absurd and round-about connections and who were ready to sweep down upon whatever was in sight and make off with it."[40] Philip C. Garrett and Herbert Welsh published an open letter to Congress in which they argued that the change was a "step backward," would encourage spurious claims for land from "adventurers claiming to have Indian blood," and would "overthrow well-established law, which, if left undisturbed, would in time bring about a social and political fusion of the Indian and White races."[41]

In a pamphlet addressing the same issue, Francis Leupp and Herbert Welsh more explicitly outlined how they saw the original act as being designed "to hasten the obliteration of all differences between the races and the absorption of the Indians into our body politic." "If the children of such a marriage remained Indians," they pointed out, there would be increase in the Native American population rather than a decrease, "their children and grandchildren would be Indians, and the anomalous status of these families under our laws would continue to vex us, and degrade them, through all time." Following lines of descent through Native American mothers was a backward step in civilization and in social purity: "The reason for the Indian practice is simple enough and entirely logical from an animal point of view[, but could] any idea do more to belittle the importance of social purity?" The authors were adamant that they did not wish to discourage interracial marriages, but wished only for those to take place which hastened absorption and assimilation—those which acted as a means by which to transform Native Americans into citizens, not the other way around. Not all marriages between white men and Native American women were to be condemned, but the "only marriages which will be encouraged by the legislation now proposed are the kind which both races would be better without—the kind that breed thriftlessness and swell the ranks of hereditary pauperism." Welsh joined Leupp in concluding, "The passage of the act of . . . 1888 was an important and long step toward the settlement of the mixed-blood question."[42]

Interracial marriages, however, which were at least recognized by church and state, were beginning to be seen as evidence of assimilation or as promoting its spread. Not all commentators thought ill of "squaw men"; such men could also be seen as agents of civilization. When he was still a U.S. civil service commissioner, Theodore Roosevelt told the Lake Mohonk conference in 1892 that he had become "rather a convert to that by no means always attractive specimen of the white race, the squaw-man." Roosevelt saw these men as providing opportunities for Native American women who had been partially assimilated at boarding schools to keep "up in the world, even if the man would not be, from our standpoint, a particularly attractive matrimonial venture. . . . He gives her a chance to use the gifts she has received at school. . . . You cannot form any idea of the terrible thing it is for a girl who has been eight or ten years at a non-reservation school to be thrown back into the life of the tepee."[43]

In 1911 the commissioners of the Bureau of Indian Affairs began including in their reports to the secretary of the interior a table giving the numbers of Native Americans who had married white people. Usually ranging between about 100 and 250 per year, these numbers were recorded alongside statistics of crimes and misdemeanors, arrests for drunkenness, and the number of missionaries working among the Native American communities. Also counted were the numbers of Native Americans who attended church (divided into Protestant and Catholic), could speak, read, and write English, wore European clothing, and were citizens who exercised their right to vote. The numbers of marriages were broken up into categories of "between Indians and whites" and "between Indians," and were further divided according to whether the marriage was by "tribal custom" or by "legal procedure."[44] The 1911 table was one of a series that attempted to record the numbers of Native Americans who were engaging in certain activities that ostensibly signaled their efforts to conform to white culture during the late nineteenth and early twentieth centuries. This project of the Bureau of Indian Affairs began in 1879, when it included a table that recorded the "number of Indians who wear citizen's dress," the "number of Indian families engaged in agriculture," the "number of mixed-blood families engaged in agriculture," and the "number of male Indians engaged in civilized pursuits." In addition it listed the numbers of Native Americans living in white-style houses, those who could read, and those attending school. These statistics were placed alongside basic information about births and deaths. They also recorded the level of white philanthropy in terms of "amount expended for education during the year by government" or "by religious societies," "number of missionaries," "number of church buildings," and "number of schools."[45] Other records in 1885 included the "number of Indian criminals punished during the year," "number of whisky sellers prosecuted," "number of whites killed by Indians during the year," and "freight transported by Indians with their own teams."[46] In 1892 these statistics included the number of marriages and divorces, along with the "number of men now living in polygamy."[47] The statistics of marriage recorded in 1911 and in subsequent years do not really indicate a deep concern about the numbers of interracial unions. They can be seen as demonstrating an ongoing concern with the extent to which the Native American population was becoming culturally assimilated into all aspects of white society, rather than as an attempt to record the extent to which biological absorption was taking place. As Nancy Cott has pointed out, simply encouraging or forcing Native Americans to practice monogamous marriage was an important aspect of cultural assimilation.[48]

This overall lack of emphasis on biological absorption and mixed feelings about interracial relationships make sense in the context of America's tri-racial population. Government officials and reformers' ideas about race were formed in a time in which issues of race dominated American ideas about their nation. When discussing Native American assimilation, both reformers and government officials often raised the example of the African American population, the majority of whom lived in the southern states, comparing the two groups in order to place them in a kind of racial hierarchy. There was already a long history of scientists measuring the physical and mental characteristics of African Americans and Native Americans in order to compare them with whites and find them inferior. In most cases, they gave Native Americans the second ranking after whites and placed African Americans at the bottom of the scale.[49] Nevertheless, for those interested in assimilation, African Americans occupied an ambiguous position in relation to Native Americans. They were a step "ahead" in their knowledge of white ways of living, but a long step "behind" in the hierarchy of races, and they were subject to a far harsher form of racism. After the Civil War and the failure of the Reconstruction period to convince white southerners they ought to treat African Americans as equals, numerous measures were implemented in the 1890s in the South to "replicate the slave period in everything but name."[50] While their legal domination had been undermined, southerners resorted to more intricate and insidious ways of emphasizing their superiority such as disenfranchisement, lynchings, and physical segregation in public places, the latter upheld in the Supreme Court's decision on *Plessy v. Ferguson* in 1896, which declared "separate but equal" facilities constitutional. Writing in 1903 as southern racism shifted and intensified, African American scholar W. E. B. Du Bois predicted correctly that the "problem of the twentieth century" would be the "color line."[51]

When addressing the "Indian problem," reformers were anxious to demonstrate the higher status of Native Americans when compared with African Americans. In 1905, for example, Commissioner Leupp stated: "The commonest mistake made by his white well[-]wishers in dealing with the Indian is the assumption that he is simply a white man with a red skin. The next commonest is the assumption that because he is a non-

Caucasian he is to be classed indiscriminately with other non-Caucasians, like the negro, for instance. The truth is that the Indian . . . will never be judged aright till we learn to measure him by his own standards."[52]

But reformers also used African Americans as an example of a group of nonwhite people who had successfully made the transition into American citizenship. Commissioner John D. C. Atkins hoped in 1885 that "we shall hear no more of the Indian as a separate and distinct race . . . but like the alien and the negro, who by our laws are admitted to the great family of American citizens, each individual must stand upon his own bottom, enjoying equal rights and bearing equal responsibilities."[53] At Hampton Institute, as David Wallace Adams has demonstrated, staff had a propensity to "search for lessons for the Indian question in the black experience," so much so that when Booker T. Washington, the famous African American leader, began his career as a teacher at Hampton, he was surprised when an Indian student he was escorting home was allowed to eat with whites in a steamboat dining room, while he was not.[54]

When the topics of interracial marriage and biological absorption were broached, however, the African American example was often raised as a kind of worst-case scenario that made the Native American option seem just that much better. A. J. Standing, who gave some "Thoughts and Suggestions on Indian Affairs" to the Lake Mohonk conference in 1904, argued, for example, that "I have long regarded amalgamation as the final destiny of the Indian race, as there is no such antipathy as exists between the white and Negro races, and I know of no more reasons why the half-blood should be classed as an Indian than a white."[55] In 1886, Philip C. Garrett gave perhaps the most unmistakable description of such a future, in which the white and Native American peoples would be integrated geographically and also share a mixed ancestry. The fusion of the Native American population into the white one would not be "to the detriment of the latter." Garrett supported this notion with some simple mathematics:

> Suppose there are 250,000 Indians of pure blood and 50,000,000 in our population, the infusion would amount to ½ per cent, of the whole. The negro infusion amounts to nearly 10 percent,

and the Indians are possessed of noble traits not shared by their African brethren. Are we not "straining at a gnat and swallowing a camel"?[56]

Henry Dawes also was not afraid to use the African American example to advocate the loss of Native American physical characteristics through interracial sexuality. At the Lake Mohonk conference in 1890 he argued that the "Indian people will not remain as a separate race among us, as the black race must. These figures show where he is going. He is to disappear in the midst of our population, be absorbed in it, and be one of us and fade out of sight as an Indian. . . . Their blood, their sinew, their strength are needed, and will help us."[57]

The growing numbers of European immigrants also raised the specters of assimilation and interracial sex in the minds of white Americans dedicated to the "Indian problem." More than 18.2 million immigrants left depressed and overcrowded Europe and entered the United States between 1890 and 1920 to escape religious and political persecution and to seek a better life.[58] The sheer size of their numbers, combined with their settlement in the slums of northeastern cities, attracted the attention of progressive reformers and the racism of the native-born American population, who quickly came to see the immigrants as an economic threat. In 1924 these feelings culminated in legislation that put in place quotas that dramatically reduced the numbers of immigrants allowed into the country and restricted entry of certain ethnic groups more than others. Scholars have recently explored the way in which this group became caught up in the racial ideologies that governed American society, being perceived in some cases as "nonwhite."[59] Unlike African Americans, however, immigrants were generally seen as able to integrate into the mainstream population within a generation; intermarriage, employment, and education were enough to assimilate them in the eyes of most Americans. Gary Gerstle has argued that an important proponent of these views was President Theodore Roosevelt, who celebrated the "melting pots" from which the world's "greatest peoples" had emerged. Roosevelt was keen to celebrate the contribution that European immigrants would make to the strength of the American character and what Gerstle has termed the "racialized nation."[60]

Richard Pratt reasoned in 1896 that Native Americans were actually better candidates for assimilation than many recently arrived immigrants: "When we consider that there are only about 250,000 Indians and that we can annually take in 500,000 Italians, Hungarians, and other immigrants and scatter them about in our great American community, and when within two and a half centuries we can bring from the tropical zone and the other side of the earth eight million of black savages and civilize and "citizenize" them as a useful part of our population, it does seem that in three or four centuries our Indians ought to be brought in to the same condition."[61] A lesser-known reformer, Oscar E. Boyd, even envisaged using such immigrants as partners for Native Americans, arguing in 1897 that "the problem might have solved itself by this time, largely, perhaps, by amalgamation with immigrants from foreign lands."[62]

In contrast to these groups, on a national level the idea of removing the physical attributes of the smaller population of Native Americans seemed far more feasible. As historian Brian Dippie has argued: "The native population was small—just an infinitesimal fraction of the whole American population—and while a massive infusion of Indian blood might pollute the national type, the limited amount available could do no harm and might even do some good."[63] This attitude was encouraged by the persistence of the "noble savage" stereotype, which in some cases even made the idea of a small amount of Native American ancestry desirable.[64] Many white Americans would rather admit to a distant Native American relative than to one of African or Asian background.

While reformers rarely openly, and never unanimously, advocated the biological absorption of Native Americans, positive views about it certainly existed. Indeed, in a study of the opinions of novelists, anthropologists, missionaries, and reformers, historian David D. Smits concluded that "the power elite could reach no consensus on the relative merits of Indian-white race mixing."[65] These ideas, however, cannot be seen as isolated from the wider context of race relations in the United States at the time. In the hierarchy of racial thought in late nineteenth- and early twentieth-century America, it seems that Native Americans were more acceptable sexual partners and spouses for white people than

African Americans. As Brian Dippie has argued, "Even [their] ambivalence set [their opinion on biological absorption] apart from the issue of black-white intermixing, since it meant that there were positives as well as negatives to be pondered." After all, Dippie points out, "Red-white amalgamation was being proposed in a context of racial segregation in the South, imperialism abroad, and nativism at home, all entailing deep distrust, fear, suspicion, and loathing of darker, 'inferior' peoples."[66] On the other hand, with the arrival of very considerable numbers of immigrants from Europe, Americans were becoming more and more used to the general idea that "difference" could be absorbed into the American nation without altering it.

Australian scholar Patrick Wolfe has pointed out that the various ways in which nonwhite groups were viewed as potential sexual partners for white people in settler societies were dictated by the size and characteristics of their population. In the United States, the relative smallness of the already partially "mixed" indigenous population meant that the category "red" was "highly vulnerable to dilution" in the larger white population.[67] By contrast, the "one-drop" rule was applied to the larger, more threatening African American population (where any African American ancestors meant that the person was defined as "black"). When all people who were of mixed white and black ancestry were classified as "black," the possibility of compromising the "purity" of the white population was removed. White people, on the other hand, saw Native American physical characteristics as more "absorbable." In Oklahoma, for example, recent research has discovered that in the first half of the twentieth century, Native Americans were classified as white in interracial marriage legislation, whether of mixed descent or not. This definition was not explicit, but was implicit in the law's distinction between those "of African descent" and those "not of African descent" rather than white people from nonwhite people.[68]

Population size was not the only factor, however. Wolfe has argued that a reason for these different racial codings can be found in the different roles that white people envisioned for these groups in their settler societies. While African Americans had been brought to the United States as a labor force, Native Americans' only commodity was land. This could be taken away all the more easily if indigenous identity was slowly disappearing through interracial sexual relationships. In this light, Wolfe argues, "the varying miscegenation policies make immediate sense, since assimilation reduces an Indigenous population with rival claims to the land whilst an exclusive strategy enlarges an enslaved labour force."[69] Native American leader Arthur C. Parker made exactly this point in 1916, when he compared the "unequal basis of assimilation" directed at immigrants, the Chinese, Native Americans, and African Americans:

> To the European Immigrant we say, "Come we want you in this free country . . . you are a commercial asset." To the Negro we say, " . . . we will tolerate you for after all you are a convenient laborer and may do even more for us, in time." To the Chinaman we say, "Stay away . . . We know your civilization is old and that you can teach us much—but your ideals—we are afraid." . . . To the Indians we say, " . . . learn to live and think like us, or—well, you'll become extinct."[70]

Issues of cultural assimilation and social class were not far away, however, and in the end they outweighed the diverse views about biological absorption. If an interracial couple were sufficiently assimilated and exhibited qualities associated with the middle classes, they were more likely to be viewed favorably. Sexual relationships between white people and Native Americans sat uncomfortably among a number of issues involving different groups of people. American reformers, therefore, concentrated on the more comfortable aim of culturally assimilating Native Americans. This was certainly not a gentle process. As Richard Pratt was famously quoted as saying, it still involved a drastic end to Native American identity. Agreeing to a certain extent with the attitude of those who had used guns to solve the "Indian problem" early in the century, Pratt repeated the old adage "There is no good Indian but a dead Indian." But, he added, the reformers were planning something a little milder: to "kill the Indian and save the Christian man."[71]

9. Absorbing the "Aboriginal Problem" in Australia

What did the word *assimilation* really mean to white Australians when they referred to Aboriginal people in the late nineteenth and early twentieth centuries? What future did they imagine for the original owners of the continent? In previous chapters, I have argued that cultural assimilation was in most instances nothing more than a broken promise made to the indigenous peoples of Australia. But if cultural assimilation was not the focus in Australia, then what was? To answer this question, in this chapter I undertake a state-by-state analysis of exactly how the incorporation of Aborigines into mainstream Australian society was imagined by those who created the many pieces of legislation aimed at indigenous people. Known as "protection" acts, the actual protection of indigenous rights, bodies, and land was far from the outcome of these laws. Australian historians have, for the most part, studied the separate sets of legislation passed by individual states and territories. A nationwide investigation of this legislation demonstrates that, although white Australians often spoke about their obligation to "civilize" the indigenous peoples they had displaced, they demonstrated little faith in the possibilities of cultural assimilation. Instead, Australian policies swiftly began to emphasize biological absorption of the mixed descent population and only rarely contained measures designed to encourage the three aspects of cultural assimilation: Christianization, education, and the ownership of private property. Indeed, the word *assimilation* was itself only very rarely used.

In the late nineteenth and early twentieth centuries, Australian policy makers planned the disappearance of the Aborigines, but not through their adoption of white ways of earning a living and their incorporation into the nation's economy. Rather, it was to be a two-stage process: first, the "doomed race" theory posited that people of full descent would soon "die out," and second, through biological absorption it was believed that Aboriginal physical characteristics and, it was hoped, Aboriginality itself would disappear altogether.[1] The latter theory relied on the dubious scientific idea that Aboriginal genes would not create any "throwbacks," or children who physically resembled stereotypes of "the Aboriginal," after a few generations of "interbreeding."[2] Ideas about who was or was not "fit" to "breed" were closely related to the rhetoric of eugenics, which had been filtering into Australia since the 1890s and gained in popularity during the interwar years.[3] Emphasis on biological absorption was more conspicuous in some states than in others, but in combination with the idea that Aborigines of full descent would "die out," it dominated the strategies that white Australians devised to rid themselves of their "Aboriginal problem."

In the Northern Territory and Western Australia, clauses in protection legislation that allowed one of the many forms of control over Aboriginal people's lives—control over whom they could marry—were the basis of the system of biological absorption in these places. Interracial relationships were both a source of anxiety about racial purity and a means through which the demise of the Aboriginal population could be imagined. In the southeastern states (South Australia, New South Wales, and Victoria—Tasmanian Aborigines were supposedly "extinct"), slightly different methods were adopted, but these were still on the whole driven by the underlying aim of biologically absorbing the indigenous population. Only the state of Queensland, discussed last, did not accede to this policy. These variations between the states cannot be explained by the varying times in which they put in place their policies, nor by the size of their white or indigenous populations. Instead, a crucial factor in each state or territory's particular solution to the "Aboriginal problem" was the size of its nonwhite, nonindigenous population, for the most part Pacific Islander and Asian men who had immigrated to Australia, particularly to the north and west, in search of work or had been brought there by force as slave labor. The presence of these populations was closely connected to the existence of legislation restricting whom Aboriginal people could marry. Thus this chapter is organized by region in order to demonstrate how the unique characteristics of local populations dictated how legislators envisioned the disappearance of Aboriginal identity.

As the twentieth century began in Western Australia, politicians' anxiety intensified about the prevalence of interracial sexual relationships between white men and Aboriginal women. In 1904 Walter Roth, the protector of the indigenous peoples of Northern Queensland since 1899, worked for a royal commission that inquired into the condition of Western Australian Aborigines.[4] Much to white settlers' discomfort the evidence taken by Roth included graphic stories of the sexual habits of Western Australian white men, not just itinerant workers and shepherds, but also station owners and police. "'Kombo'-ism [casual relationships between white men and Aboriginal women]," said Roth bluntly in his report, which was presented to Parliament in 1905, "is rife."[5]

Legislation focused on regulating Aboriginal employment was first passed in Western Australia in 1886, and the Western Australian Aborigines Act of 1905 was based partly on this earlier act, partly on an act passed by Queensland in 1897 and was partly a response to Roth's report. It attempted to regulate casual liaisons between white men and Aboriginal women by a variety of measures. These included the creation of reserves that anyone other than an Aborigine was forbidden to enter without good reason; provisions designed to force white fathers to support their children financially; and the transfer of guardianship of mixed-descent children to the protectors, who consequently acquired the power to remove them from their mothers and send them to live in government institutions. The act also made the chief protector's approval a requirement for all marriages of Aboriginal women to non-Aboriginal men. Like Anna Haebich, most historians have seen this last measure as one of a group of "sweeping powers allowing for the rigid control of Aborigines," and as yet another way of reducing the births of children fathered by white men with Aboriginal women.[6] However, while certainly related to the growing mixed-descent population, the section of the act that dealt with the institution of marriage was not specifically directed at the problem of casual liaisons between white men and Aboriginal women. Rather, its inclusion reveals much about the significant role that the presence of other ethnic groups played in the minds of legislators aiming to control the Aboriginal population.

As a result of its rich mineral resources and pearling industry, Western Australia had a small but significant Asian and Pacific Islander population, mostly men employed in these lucrative industries. The 1901 census recorded that out of a total population of 184,124 there were 3,615 people who were born in one of the "Asiatic" countries.[7] This group came to dominate the discourse about interracial relationships. No doubt the fact that this population was almost completely adult males contributed to legislators' anxieties. In evidence given before the Roth Royal Commission, both those answering questions and those posing them frequently mentioned this group of men when discussing problems of interracial sex and the production of mixed-descent children. Despite their comparatively small numbers, this group was singled out with extraordinary frequency in the minutes of evidence.[8]

Similarly, in parliamentary debates Asian and Pacific Islander men served as convenient scapegoats when sensitive topics were being discussed. In 1905 Frederick Piesse, the member of the Legislative Assembly for Katanning, blamed the "unfortunateness of natives" on their "connection with the darker races from the Islands of the East."[9] In 1929 when Edward Angelo quite rightly blamed the decimation of the Aboriginal population of Western Australia on diseases introduced by Europeans, a colleague interjected, "What about the diseases introduced by Asiatics?"[10] Surprisingly, given the very considerable number of children born of white and Aboriginal parents, it was the growing, but still small, population of children of Aboriginal and Asian or Pacific Islander parents which obsessed parliamentarians and motivated the legal controls on interracial marriage. For example, parliamentarian James Isdell concluded a diatribe against marriages between Aboriginal women and Asian men in 1905 with a simple warning: "We are talking about a White Australia, and we are cultivating a piebald one."[11] Isdell was not worried so much about the shades of "black" and "white"; it was the possibility of other hues introduced by Asian and Pacific Islander men that raised his ire.

In the Northern Territory (which was administered first by South Australia and, after 1911, by the Commonwealth government), white people had similar concerns about interracial sexual relationships. In the very first chief protector's report for 1910, William Stretton expressed his belief that the "aboriginal is, undoubtedly, capable of great improvement, but this can only be effected by separating them from their intercourse with Asiatic races. . . . Among these people a most undesirable race is rapidly increasing."[12] A clause controlling interracial marriage remained unchanged from its original appearance in the South Australian Northern Territory Aboriginals Act of 1910, the first and only piece of legislation South Australia passed concerning Northern Territory Aborigines.[13] The clause simply forbade the celebration of the marriage of a "female aboriginal with any person other than an aboriginal . . . without the permission, in writing, of a Protector."

In 1913, anthropologist and temporary chief protector Baldwin Spencer demonstrated clear bias against interracial sexual relationships between Aboriginal women and Asian men (as opposed to white men) in the Northern Territory, claiming that sexual contact with Chinese people caused "rapid degeneration of the native."[14] Spencer was specifically worried about mixed Aboriginal/Asian and Pacific Islander children. He recommended that the legislation "be amended to include a more clear definition of a half-caste than it now does. . . . It must be remembered that they are also a very mixed group. In practically all cases, the mother is a full-blooded aboriginal, the father may be a white man, a Chinese, a Japanese, a Malay, or a Filippino."[15]

While much of the legislation passed by Western Australia and the Northern Territory contained clauses that attempted to regulate nonmarital interracial sex between white men and Aboriginal women, the clauses specifically targeting marriage were aimed mostly at Asian and Pacific Islander men. It was not envisioned, in any case, that many white men would stoop to make their relationships with Aboriginal women public and long-term, but a vague feeling that these relationships and their offspring were integral to the demise of Aboriginal identity was also at work. Marriages between Aboriginal women and "alien" men could only complicate this process. This vague feeling, however, was soon given more explicit expression in the policies of two particular chief administrators.

In the late 1920s and 1930s, both the Northern Territory and Western Australia were under the direction of strong-willed chief protectors who attempted to use the anti-interracial marriage clauses in the legislation to promote biological absorption. Auber O. Neville in Western Australia and Cecil E. Cook in the Northern Territory endeavored to set up a process by which the mixed-descent population would gradually be "absorbed" into the white population through interracial sexuality. These men were perhaps the most influential advocates of the elimination of Aboriginal physical characteristics during this period.

In a book published in 1947, Neville outlined his views on the future of the Aboriginal population, policies which he had tried to implement during his administration:

> It would seem proper that like should mate with like—full-blood with full-blood, half-blood with half-blood or lighter—but because so many are near-white we must expect, and have experienced already, legal unions between us and them. It is to the benefit of our own race that the full-blood should not any longer be encouraged to mate with other than full-blood; on the contrary, he should be rigidly excluded from any association likely to lead to any other union.[16]

Neville was instrumental in the decision to include a clause in the Western Australian Aborigines Act Amendment Act of 1936 which dictated that no marriage of *any* Aboriginal person could be celebrated without the permission of the chief protector. Previously the restrictions had related only to Aboriginal women's marriages to non-Aboriginal men. Biological absorption depended on those of mixed Aboriginal and white descent having children with those who had fewer Aboriginal ancestors than themselves. Control of marriages was necessary to implement this theory, as was the separation of those of mixed descent from those of full descent. As J. Craig argued in 1936, "The colour must not be allowed to drift back to black. If we can only segregate the half-castes from the full-bloods we shall go a long way towards breeding the dark blood out of these people."[17] Far from an earlier moral concern to prevent "miscegenation" between white men and Aboriginal women, by 1936, according to the government, "the best thing that can happen to a half-caste [was] to marry a white."[18]

Dr. Cecil E. Cook, who held his dual posts of chief protector and chief medical officer of the Northern Territory from 1927 until 1939, was another outspoken advocate of biological absorption. Perhaps to a greater extent than any other high status official on record, Cook subscribed to the philosophy that the Aboriginal people could be absorbed into the white population through interracial marriage. Cook was open about his belief that people of mixed descent should marry each other or white partners, but not Aborigines of full descent, and used the powers granted to him by the Aboriginal Ordinance of 1911 to attempt to ensure that this would occur. Like his colleague in Western Australia, Cook was also adamant in his belief that this solution to the "Aboriginal problem" was being hampered by the births of children with Asian or Pacific Islander fathers. In 1930, immediately after he wrote of the permission he had given to the marriage of seven "female half-castes with persons other than aboriginals," he recorded that "action was taken to discourage any association which was calculated to result in or encourage marriage between coloured persons other than half-castes and female aboriginals."[19] Tony Austin argues that, especially in the early years of his office, Cook was careful not to make overly strong statements of his views in his official writing because of his many vociferous critics. In private correspondence, however, he was wont to argue openly, for example, that:

> In the Territory . . . the preponderance of coloured races, the prominence of coloured alien blood and the scarcity of white females to mate with the white male population, creates a position of incalculable future menace to the purity of race in tropical Australia. . . . If [women of mixed descent are] permitted to mate with alien blood, the future of this country may very well be doomed to disaster.[20]

It is hardly surprising that the Northern Territory, whose population included large proportions of Asian and Pacific Islander people, produced a chief protector with views as strong as Cecil Cook. In 1911, the census recorded that only 1,729 white Australians, most of whom were men, lived in the territory. A total of 1,633 Chinese people lived there, along with unrecorded numbers of Japanese, Pacific Islander, Maori, and various other peoples. The Aboriginal population was estimated at between 20,000 and 50,000.[21]

The extent to which the Western Australian and the Northern Territory legislation actually prevented people from marrying interracially is difficult to document. It seems clear that many couples wishing to marry were refused permission, but many couples surely lived together without marrying at all. Historian Christine Choo argues that the Western Australian application process "prohibited a great many from even attempting to formalize their marriage . . . [and] created a climate in which casual sexual relations were condoned while stable de facto marriages were destroyed."[22] There is considerable evidence that Neville did indeed use the legislation to encourage those of mixed descent to marry white or whiter. The chief secretary boasted to the Western Australian state parliament in 1936 that "the department now ha[s] a list of some 61 white men married to half-caste women, and the list is known to be incomplete."[23] Rare testimony from Aboriginal women living under the control of the legislation in Western Australia also exists, demonstrating that this legal prohibition did indeed make it difficult for Aboriginal women to marry non-Aborigines. In 1935 a group of young Aboriginal women told a Royal Commission: "Sometimes we have the chance to marry . . . a white man or an educated Asiatic, but we are again rejected, because that man does not wish to ask the chief protector's consent."[24] Still, Choo has argued, it was "virtually impossible" to prevent Aboriginal women and Asians from having relationships.[25] A recent study by Pamela Rajkowski examines in detail the impact of the Western Australian law on one particular couple, Jack and Lallie Akbar, who moved to South Australia so they could be married after Neville refused their application because of Jack's Afghan heritage.[26] In their autobiographies, which were recorded and edited by Gillian Cowlishaw, Tex and Nelly Camfoo described their difficulties in marrying in the Northern Territory.[27] There is some evidence that as early as 1912 Chief Protector Baldwin Spencer had been using his power to dictate whom Aboriginal women might marry.[28] Also in the Northern Territory, in 1932, Alfred Anderson of Borroboola applied to Cook for permission to marry an Aboriginal woman of full descent and received the reply: "All applications made by white men for permission to marry female Aboriginals are unequivocally refused. . . . You may regard this as definite and final." Anderson protested in writing against this decision, accusing Cook of "adopting a dictatory attitude."[29]

Legislation concerning Aborigines in the Northern Territory and Western Australia, with their considerable nonwhite populations, reflected a multiracial rather than a biracial society. While government rhetoric often indicated an implicit acceptance of interracial sexual relationships between white men and Aboriginal women, it remained adamant in its condemnation of relationships between men of other ethnic backgrounds and Aboriginal women. Legislators fought a losing battle to create a society that would eventually be "bred" white. When the 1937 Aboriginal Welfare Conference, at which all the state administrators had gathered, recommended that the destiny of Aborigines of mixed descent was their "ultimate absorption by the people of the Commonwealth," it was Neville who claimed that "Western Australia ha[d] gone further in the development of such a long-range policy" than any other state with its policy of controlling marriages, and emphasized the inevitability of the process. "How can we keep them apart from the community?" he asked. "Our own population is not increasing at such a rapid rate as to lead us to expect that there will be a great many more white people in the area fifteen years hence than there are at present."[30]

Cook also supported the idea of absorption as the only alternative to the horrifying possibility that "in fifty years, or a little later, the white population of the Northern Territory will be absorbed into the black."[31] To these men, responsible for the control of significant Aboriginal populations and familiar with the results of casual interracial sex on the frontier, biological absorption through the birth of more and more mixed-descent children seemed the obvious solution. It was an answer, however, which had some drawbacks. One of these was the "pollution" of indigenous blood with Pacific Islander and Asian blood. Hence the effort to prevent these unions through the restriction of whom Aboriginal people could marry.

In the southeastern states biological absorption was promoted using slightly different methods. Rather than controlling the parenting of mixed-descent children, politicians tried to engineer the "disappearance" of their indigenous populations by physically dividing Aborigines from one another, removing families and individuals from the reserves, and removing children from their families. These solutions to the "Aboriginal problem" were certainly a response to the characteristics of white settlement in these areas. Not only did white settlement happen earlier than in the northern and western states, but it grew faster. In Victoria, New South Wales, and South Australia, the period during which white settlers and Aboriginal groups physically and violently clashed was short and devastating for the Aboriginal populations. By the time Victoria, for example, began legislating to control its indigenous population in the 1860s, the Aboriginal population officially numbered only 1,869.[32] Furthermore, unlike those in the northern and western states, the southern and eastern states did not have significant nonwhite, non-Aboriginal populations.[33] Consequently these states displayed fewer anxieties about controlling or preventing interracial sexual relationships and, unlike the northern and western states, did not enact legislation that imposed official control on interracial marriages.

In New South Wales, Victoria, and South Australia, the humanitarian idea that white people owed Aborigines something for the theft of their land quickly dissipated and was replaced by resentment of Aborigines' supposed "cost" to the state. It was this problem which obsessed white administrators. Two solutions were found for the financial aspect of the "Aboriginal problem," both of which were applied in varying degrees in all the Australian states at different times. The first method attempted to divide indigenous populations along racial lines into "mixed-descent" and "full-descent" groups and to remove financial support from the former (the latter were expected to succumb to the "doomed race theory"). The second method divided the indigenous community in a different way, by singling out children, again mostly according to racial classification. The models for this policy were the acts passed by New South Wales in the early twentieth century. Although very different from the methods of biological absorption championed by Cook and Neville, these policies, too, with their emphasis on merging those of lighter skin with the white community, are clear applications of an absorptionist philosophy.

In Victoria in the 1870s and early 1880s, what historian Michael Christie has called "a fully-fledged absorptionist policy" was developed and dually enshrined in law by the Aborigines Protection Act of 1886. This act, Christie has argued, "virtually ensured that 'Aborigines' . . . would eventually die out."[34] In various debates in the Victorian parliament and in evidence taken by an 1877 royal commission on the Aborigines, white people repeatedly expressed their opinion that Aborigines of full descent were destined to succumb to the "inevitable fate of an inferior race to disappear before a superior," as C. M. Officer, the member for Toorak, put it.[35] By contrast, those of mixed descent were increasing in numbers, and the solution proposed for these people was to deprive them of the government support to which they had previously been entitled by removing them from the reserves and stopping their rations. In other words, as one of the authors of the policy explained, these people should be "treated as Europeans" and separated from the "pure blacks."[36] On the surface this form of "absorption" appeared to imply little more than assimilation into the white economies. Mixed-descent people were denied their Aboriginal identity, and the government support that went with it, and were sent out into mainstream society to sink or swim. However, the racial categorization on which the policy was based (those of mixed descent, who already had some white ancestry, were targeted) indicates its similarity to the methods of biological absorption attempted in Western Australia and the Northern Territory. Not only would these people live and work alongside white people, but their partially white ancestry rendered them possible contributors to a process of absorption, should they marry each other or white people. To encourage this process, the Board for the Protection of Aborigines prevented them from marrying those of "full-descent."

Although the Victorian 1886 act failed, for a variety of reasons, to force Aborigines of mixed descent to support themselves financially, the cruel and pragmatic nature of Victorian policy became, as has been recognized by John Chesterman and Brian Galligan, an important "precursor" to practices in the other states.[37] Thus it was clear that the New South Wales

Board for the Protection of Aborigines was from its inception aware of and in complete agreement with the ideas circulating in Victoria. From 1898 the New South Wales Board had sent out circulars to missionaries and station managers asking them to ensure that no able-bodied Aboriginal people were receiving government assistance.[38] Removing people from the stations, however, could not be achieved with encouraging circulars, and the board's report for 1908 lobbied for the introduction of legislation giving the board power "more especially with respect to the children, who, under existing conditions, must sooner or later become a burden on the State."[39] The New South Wales government's legislative attempts to control the lives of Aboriginal people in the early part of the twentieth century, while similar to those made in Victoria, are also unique in their blatant and single-minded focus on absorbing the Aboriginal population by means of removing children from their parents. Although all Australian states participated in the removal of children from their parents, the New South Wales government placed the earliest and greatest emphasis on this method of destroying Aboriginal identity. Pale-skinned children were targeted for removal in the hope that they would "pass" for white, and boys and girls were sent to different regions of the state to keep them apart.[40] Bain Attwood has shown that this time was one in which the lives of New South Wales Aborigines steadily worsened. "Hundreds, even thousands, of Aboriginal men and women were prohibited from remaining on or entering into reserves," while the amount of land reserved for Aborigines was halved between 1910 and 1928. Approximately 2,000 Aboriginal children were separated from their families by the board between 1909 and 1938.[41] By 1937 New South Wales felt that it came second only to Victoria in having found a solution to the "Aboriginal problem." Board member B. S. Harkness told the 1937 Aboriginal welfare conference, "Our problem is not so difficult as that of other States, excepting Victoria," and he added his support to the prevailing view that people of mixed descent should be "merged" with the white population.[42]

South Australia put in place policies of dispersal and removal similar to those applied in New South Wales and Victoria. South Australia originally considered restricting the marriages of Aboriginal women when it was still in control of the area that became the Northern Territory. Indeed, South Australia's period of governing this area (1863–1911) provides a revealing case study of the differences in policy between the southeastern and northwestern regions of Australia. Perhaps calmed by the same forces that delayed the development of Aboriginal policy in New South Wales and Victoria, it was not until 1911, just after the legislation for the transfer of control of the Northern Territory to the Commonwealth had been passed, that the South Australian government enacted legislation for the "Aboriginal and Half-Caste Inhabitants of the State of South Australia."[43] The clauses omitted from this legislation, compared with those included in the Northern Territory legislation, are revealing. South Australian parliamentarians obviously believed their constituents to be better employers than those in the Northern Territory, and the possibility of violence by Aborigines in possession of firearms was seen as less substantial. More significantly, and no doubt due to the smaller populations of Asians and Pacific Islanders in the southern state, there was seen to be no need to monitor the marriages of Aborigines with other persons.[44]

A royal commission to investigate the Aboriginal population of South Australia was appointed just after the 1911 act was passed. In 1913 it produced a progress report that suggested policies similar to those operating in Victoria and New South Wales in the previous decades: people of mixed descent were not to be supported by the government, and the merging of the populations was to be accomplished by removing children from their parents. As in Victoria and New South Wales, it was thought that there should not "be an obligation on the general taxpayer to support the people of [another] race as loafers."[45] By 1923 the South Australian government felt it necessary to enact legislation that concentrated on the removal and institutionalization of Aboriginal children, its main provision allowing the chief protector to place any Aboriginal children in an institution until they turned eighteen.[46] South Australia's firm commitment to biological absorption was reaffirmed at the 1937 conference, at which a federal Aboriginal policy was discussed for the first time. The South Australian representative, Professor J. B. Cleland, expressed concerns about a growing mixed-descent population in his state that was not the result of an "additional influx of white blood, but following on inter-marriage with themselves." He asked for Commonwealth funding for a study about the "best method for the gradual absorption of the half-caste" and suggested that a scheme be implemented "by which the two sexes can have opportunities of meeting and so marrying."[47]

The removal of children became common practice in all Australian states as the century progressed. Historian Peter Read has described the impact of the policies in this way:

> It used to be said that by the end of the First World War, there wasn't a single British family that had not been touched, by injury or death, by the fighting in Europe. It is probably fair to say that except for the remotest regions of the nation, there was not a single Aboriginal family which had not been touched by the policy of removal. Everybody had lost someone.[48]

White Australians are only just beginning to learn of the extent of Aboriginal peoples' suffering as a result of these policies. In 1997, the Human Rights and Equal Opportunity Commission released a report which investigated the removal of Aboriginal and Torres Strait Islander children from their parents. One of its many conclusions was that the removal of children was an act of genocide according to the Convention on Genocide ratified by Australia in 1949. "The essence of genocide is acting with the intention to destroy the group," the report argued. "The Inquiry's process of consultation and research has revealed that the predominant aim of indigenous child removals was the absorption or assimilation of the children into the wider, non-indigenous community so that their unique cultural values and ethnic identity would disappear."[49]

That racial policies, particularly those which restrict interracial marriage, cannot be explained without examining the entire racial landscape in which they were adopted (in other words, all the racial groups that lived in that particular area) is borne out by the huge body of anti-interracial marriage legislation passed in the United States, from 1661, when the Maryland General Assembly passed the first colonial antimiscegenation statute, and were operational until 1967, when the U.S. Supreme Court declared such laws unconstitutional. Created to keep the white race "pure," these laws varied greatly in terms of the restrictions and punishments put in place and the groups targeted (although the majority of these laws focused on African Americans). They make the Australian legislation, which restricted but did not forbid interracial marriages in three of the seven colonies/states, look mild by comparison. They also served a very different purpose: to prevent interracial marriages rather than to encourage certain types of them, as occurred in Western Australia and the Northern Territory. In Queensland, however, although a clause restricting interracial marriage almost identical to that enacted in Western Australia and the Northern Territory was included in its protection legislation, initial anxieties about racial mixing resembled those in the United States more than those in neighboring Australian states. As in many American states, the object of the law was to prevent interracial marriages altogether, rather than to encourage certain types that would lead to biological absorption.

Queensland was the first state to pass a law that enabled the chief protector to control the marriages of Aboriginal people. The 1901 act, which amended the Queensland government's first attempt at protection legislation (the 1897 Aboriginals Protection and Restriction of the Sale of Opium Act), contained a clause that made the marriage of female Aborigines to any person other than an Aborigine conditional on written permission from a protector.[50] In debating the clause, however, legislators displayed subtly different anxieties about interracial relationships between Aboriginal women and Asian and Pacific Islander men than those prevalent in Western Australia and the Northern Territory.[51] Although men of nonwhite ethnicities (mostly Pacific Islander and Asian) who lived in Queensland in significant numbers were still regarded in some quarters as undesirable sexual partners for Aboriginal and mixed-descent women, the good qualities of Pacific Islander husbands were a familiar refrain in the protector's reports over the next few years. Between 1899 and 1913, the reports of the chief protectors displayed an implicit acceptance of marriages between Aboriginal or mixed-descent women and Pacific Islanders, Asians, or Europeans. The concern of Walter Roth and Richard B. Howard, the chief protectors for this period, was the prevention of immorality and cruelty, not the long-term consequences of the sexual mixing of the different groups. In his report for 1899, which attempted to estimate the number of mixed-descent children in the North, Roth's preoccupation was not with their growing numbers but with alleged infanticide and the "future welfare, care, and happiness of the children themselves."[52] In the next year's report he called interracial marriages "a great moral wrong" not because of anxieties about "miscegenation" but because they might take place "without previous careful inquiry being made as to whether [Aboriginal women] are not already married in the tribal sense of the term."[53] He complained that "the general morality of some of the settlers etc., in these same districts is at so low an ebb that the presence of such (especially half-caste) [female] children acts as a sort of premium on 'kombo'-ism. For as long as the Asiatic or low-class European realises that no Governmental action is taken with regard to his half-caste children, he will continue cohabiting with his aboriginal paramour."[54]

So while anxieties certainly existed about a growing "hybrid popu-lation," Roth did not use the law restricting marriages to try to prevent Aboriginal–Pacific Islander marriages altogether.[55] After describing nine such "marriages, etc." between Aboriginal women and Chinese or Pacific Islander men in which the women worked as prostitutes, Roth revealed that his personal agenda was always to "exert my influence in the direc-tion of trying to put a stop to these mixed marriages, but cases repeated-ly occur where they may be considered both expedient and justifiable." When deciding whether to allow a marriage Roth gave great weight to the "general character and repute of both individuals, the number of years during which there has been cohabitation, and, where children have been born, the manner in which they have been reared, cared for, and schooled."[56] He had given permission for forty such marriages that year. In each case he listed the district, ancestry of both husband and wife, and occupation of the husband. In some cases Roth even saw marriage as the least of a number of evils. "It is a practical impossibility to prosecute all the men—Europeans, Asiatics, and Islanders—living with aboriginal females, under the harbouring clauses of the Act," he wrote in his report for 1905, "and hence my action has been to encourage marriage where the parties persist in cohabiting, rather than lay my department open to the reproach of sanctioning concubinage and prostitution."[57]

The appointment of John W. Bleakley to the office of chief protector in 1913-14 heralded a new era that put Queensland even further out of line with the rest of Australia. In his first report for the year 1913, Bleakley wrote of his belief that mixed-descent women should marry only Aboriginal or mixed-descent men.[58] It appears that Bleakley did his best to discourage interracial relationships. In 1916, he mentioned that a "policy of encouraging legal marriage to [Aboriginal women's] own country men is proving successful, as in twenty-eight cases the husbands chosen were aboriginal or half-castes."[59] By 1928 his policy had become "to check as far as possible the breeding of half-castes, by firmly discouraging miscegenation, and, in conformity with this, every effort is made to encourage marriage of those now with us to people of their own race."[60] By 1931 Bleakley was even attributing the success of this policy to the desires of the Aboriginal women themselves. "It is noteworthy," he wrote in his report for 1931, "that in very few instances any desire has been shown to marry outside of their own race; in fact, in the institutions, they seem to show a preference for the full-blood."[61] Finally in 1932 he noted the change in departmental policy toward marriages with white men:

> The efforts of this Department in the past have been directed to the checking of this evil, by sternly preventing miscegenation, as far as the limited machinery made possible. The marriage of whites and aboriginals, unfortunately not discouraged in the earlier years, has been absolutely prohibited, and every encouragement given to these women to marry amongst their own race.[62]

Far from encouraging the idea of absorbing Aboriginal identity altogether, Bleakley went out of his way to rid Queensland of its mixed-descent population by absorbing it into the indigenous population rather than the white.[63] In this, he made Queensland the exception to every other Australian state and territory.

Although Bleakley's policies certainly showed the same anxieties about the problem of a growing mixed-descent population, he was not in agreement with the chief protectors of Western Australia and the Northern Territory, Neville and Cook, who by this time were advocating the absorption of Aboriginal physical characteristics into those of the white population. The reasons for Bleakley's unconformity can perhaps be found in his 1936 and 1937 reports, as he grappled with his unpopular ideas about the future of Australia's multiracial society. "Considerable interest in the case of the half-caste has been awakened by suggestions from different quarters," he wrote in 1936, "resulting in a side controversy, that the solution of the problem of their future lay in their absorption into the white race by marriage of young women to white men." His reason for objecting to this idea was also regarded as one of the biggest "problems" faced by supporters of the absorption policy—the "impurity" of mixed-descent "blood":

> Unfortunately, such a proposal, although suitable in some special cases of quadroon and lighter types with definite European characteristics, overlooks the many complexities of this difficult problem. Not every half-caste is the product of European breeding—quite a large proportion are of alien blood more akin to the aboriginal race itself, such as Pacific Island, African, Malay, and others of Asiatic origin.[64]

The following year Bleakley reiterated this objection when commenting on the 1937 Aboriginal Welfare Conference's support of the policy of "absorption." According to Bleakley, "Queensland's cross-breed problem was probably more complex than that of any other State, owing to the greater percentage of Pacific Island and Asiatic crosses, and the views of most of the authorities on the subject in this state disputed the wisdom of measures to encourage the absorption of these breeds."[65] Despite, or perhaps because of, the lack of unease about Aboriginal and Asiatic relationships voiced in Queensland, it appears that the phenomenon had reached greater prominence in that state. At the conference itself, Bleakley recommended that people of mixed descent should be absorbed not by the white population but by the "native community."[66]

There does not appear to be one simple explanation for Queensland's aberrant use of its ability to control indigenous marriages. Although it is arguable that the difference in Queensland's policy can be attributed to the opinions of Bleakley personally, his belief that Queensland's 'crossbreed problem' was more 'complex' than any other state suggests that the white population of Queensland was also perhaps not so confident of being able to absorb such a large indigenous community. It has been estimated that the area that later became the state of Queensland was home to 100,000 Aborigines at the time of initial white settlement. Although by 1901 that figure had fallen to 26,670, it was still the largest recorded Aboriginal population of any state in Australia.[67] Queensland also had a significant Chinese population and a sizeable Pacific Islander minority population created by the sugar industry.[68] Just as in the United States, nonwhite populations of significant size caused the idea of biological absorption to be vetoed by Queensland administrators.

According to the discussions surrounding the legislation, Queensland adopted the 1901 interracial marriage clause to prevent Aboriginal women who were already married according to their own traditions from marrying a different man under the laws of the state and to prevent men from using marriage to escape prosecution for "harbouring" Aboriginal women. Bleakley then used it to prevent interracial marriages between Aboriginal and mixed-descent women and non-Aboriginal men, thus impeding rather than encouraging biological absorption. This model was then taken over by other states and manipulated to fit their own anxieties about interracial "miscegenation," anxieties that only appeared in Queensland much later. So the laws prohibiting marriage of Aboriginal women to non-Aborigines actually grew from quite different concerns in the various states. Although, as many historians have noted, the Queensland legislation was the basis of that of Western Australia, South Australia, and the Northern Territory, in practice legislators and administrators interpreted clauses with similar wording to suit their own ends.

Perhaps another explanation can be found in the argument of several Australian historians, most recently Nikki Henningham, that relationships between white settlers and Aboriginal people in Queensland, particularly in the north, were in many ways unlike that in other regions in Australia. Henningham argues that, as well as the anxieties created by the isolation and small size of the white population, labor shortages in the early years of settlement had produced a unique situation in which Aboriginal people were indispensable, unpaid "family members" on many outback Queensland stations.[69] Although, as Henningham points out, this situation was one of the reasons why many Queensland white men resented the 1897 act for interfering in what they saw as their personal lives, its blurred racial boundaries might also have been behind the reluctance of Queensland administrators and politicians to consider biological absorption as a solution to their "Aboriginal problem." As late as the 1960s—in the United States a period of increasing racial tolerance—Bleakley was still arguing that because of the inferior natures of white people willing to engage in interracial sexual relationships and "the present half-civilized state of the aborigines, the process of absorption would be through the least desirable channels on both sides. There is much to be eliminated from, or changed in, the aboriginal ideology before the race can mate on a level with that of a higher culture without incurring grave social dangers."[70] Despite the genocidal implications of biological absorption, as these comments imply, it can also be seen to entail a kind of equality: the equality of two groups of people who felt compatible enough to allow for intimate acquaintances to be formed. Such issues demonstrate the complexities of comparative history. This kind of equality was a rare occurrence in the United States' "Jim Crow" South, infamous for its intolerance of interracial marriages. In Queensland, too, it was unthinkable.

Leaving aside Queensland, therefore, a broad comparison of Australian state policies reveals some subtle national differences. White Australians relied on interracial sexual relationships to bring about assimilation through a generation-by-generation loss of Aboriginal physical identity. In Western Australia and the Northern Territory, where large nonwhite, nonindigenous populations existed (such as Pacific Islander or Asian peoples), controls were put in place to prevent the production of children with mixed Asian or Pacific Islander descent, who did not fit into the absorption project. In the southeastern states of Victoria, New South Wales, and South Australia, smaller populations of Aboriginal people allowed white people to be quite content to let biological absorption occur "naturally," helping it along with methods such as dispersal and the removal from Aboriginal homes of children of mixed descent, but not feeling the need to control marriage through legislation. Only policy makers in Queensland were squeamish about the absorptionist project and tried to prevent racial mixing and to ensure the "purity" of the white race.

It is not surprising, then, that in the 1930s, when arguments about the biological absorption of mixed-descent Aborigines were at a peak, Aboriginal activists organized themselves to begin commenting public-ly on the issue, offering yet another perspective as to what assimilation meant in the Australian context. Although on the other side of the world and in a different decade, the Aborigines' Progressive Association (APA) had a similar agenda to the Society of American Indians (SAI), discussed in chapter 3. The APA was established in Dubbo, New South Wales, in 1937. It had several branches on different reserves and held five annual conferences in various country towns. President John Patten's friendship with the editor of a radical nationalist monthly, the *Publicist*, helped the APA gain publicity and influence, and William Ferguson assisted him in leading the organization. Its manifesto "Citizen Rights for Aborigi-nes!" pointed out that for the indigenous people of Australia, January 26, 1938, the 150th anniversary of the landing of Captain Cook, was not a cause for celebration and demanded "equal education, equal oppor-tunity, equal wages, equal rights to possess property, or to be our own masters—in two words: *equal citizenship!*"[71] The APA was also concerned with stressing the abilities of its members to fit into white society. "The overwhelming majority of us" they argued "are able and willing to earn our living by honest toil, and to take our place in the community, side by side with yourselves."[72]

The members of the APA were less visible than members of the SAI—not through lack of effort but as a result of the much smaller white humanitar-ian reform movement that existed in this country to take up the cause of Aboriginal rights. In comparison with the several large organizations and the powerful and educated reformers who ran them in the United States, white Australia had only a few lone voices raised in support of Aborigi-nal people. Far from being seized on as shining examples of assimilation, the APA had to constantly demand the opportunity to prove that they could be assimilated, stressing their willingness to join "Modern Austra-lia." Patten's efforts to collect evidence for his and Ferguson's testimony before the Legislative Assembly select committee on the administration of the Aborigines Protection Board in 1938 were to no avail, and deputations to the premier of New South Sales, to two prime ministers, and the "Day of Mourning" protest on Australia Day did little to relieve the conditions suffered by the Aboriginal people of New South Wales. Tragically, their protests fell, for the most part, on deaf ears.[73]

The APA had a unique perspective on the issue of biological absorption. In 1938 Patten and Ferguson argued: "The existence of 20,000 and more half-castes in Australia is a proof that the mixture of Aboriginal and white races is practicable . . . the Australian Aboriginal is somewhat similar in blood to you yourselves, as regards inter-marriage and inter-breeding. We ask you to study this question, and to change your whole attitude towards us, to a more enlightened one."[74] Also in 1938 an anonymous author argued in the *Australian Abo Call* for the suitability of both full and mixed-descent Aboriginal people as partners for whites: "The halfcastes are 'half' white, that is, *they have the virtues of both races.* A Half-caste has the inherited intellect of the white man as well as the noble ancestry of the Aboriginal."[75] While some scholars have seen these discussions as claims that "Aborigines easily bred white, an argument that no self-respecting Aborigine would countenance," they can be read at least as an effort to claim racial equality.[76] Like the SAI, the APA spoke about the qualities of Aboriginal people—albeit with less confidence than the Native Americans, who had a much stronger version of the "noble savage" to draw upon. "Do you really believe that . . . half-castes are 'naturally backward' and lacking in natural intelligence?" Patten and Ferguson asked. "If so, you are completely mistaken. When our people are backward, it is because your treatment has made them so. Give us the same chances as yourselves, and we will prove ourselves to be just as good, if not better, Australians than you!"[77] Ferguson was even more blunt in an article published in the *Daily Telegraph* in 1937, in which he argued that the "end of the race problem must be absorption of the black people. Let them intermarry and intermarry. We are not animals, not vile creatures. . . . We want you to realise that we are your brothers."[78]

Part of the APA's concern was simply to make White Australia acknowledge that miscegenation existed. The *Abo Call* published numerous extracts from Xavier Herbert's novel *Capricornia*, which described in (for the time) shocking detail the world of the "combo" in a fictitious Northern Territory and, as the editors put it, the "callousness of whitemen in regard to their [own] children."[79] As well as recognition of the cruelties inflicted, however, miscegenation was presented as a positive. "The whiteman is proud of his Harbour Bridge," ran one memorable passage, "but he is not proud of his greatest product—20,000 Halfcastes."[80] In the late 1930s, caught between racist opinions about their lack of desirability as marriage partners (despite generations of sexual exploitation) and government policies which had absorptionist ideals at their heart, the APA opted to use biological absorption as a basis for emphasizing racial equality.[81]

In Australia, therefore, as Patrick Wolfe has argued, a small indigenous population in conjunction with various scientific works proposing the suitability of Aboriginal "blood" for absorption led to the same belief as in the United States, that "the category 'White' [could] stand admixture" of indigenous identity without its purity being compromised. On the other hand, "Aboriginality," like "Indianness," could not; it immediately became "half-caste," "quadroon," or "octoroon" by the addition of white "blood."[82] The intensity of the effort to absorb Aborigines biologically is thrown into relief when the inadequate efforts to culturally assimilate them are compared with the more concerted efforts in the United States. In addition, the Australian emphasis on absorption can be partially explained by comparing Australian racial landscape with that of the United States. Wolfe proposes that the absence of an Australian equivalent of the African American population meant that white American anxieties were diffused over a number of groups. In Australia, Wolfe has argued, the lack of a significant "third race" meant that "miscegenation discourse focused from the outset on Indigenous people" and emphasized their segregation from the smaller numbers of Asian and Pacific Islander people who might "pollute" the process of their absorption.[83]

While on the surface similar strategies were put in place to control and assimilate Aborigines and Native Americans—such as reserves, agents/protectors, and educational institutions where children lived separately from their parents—white Australians established far fewer avenues for assimilation than white Americans. The Dawes Act at least offered land and citizenship for those who were willing and able to comply with the demands of the assimilationists; American educational institutions could act as a stepping-stone for a select few into mainstream institutions of higher learning. Instead, protection legislation concentrated on controlling the lives of Aboriginal people—where they lived, the conditions under which they were employed, whether they could buy alcohol, and even whether or not they were defined by the state as "Aboriginal" at all. In practice, the legislation hindered Aborigines' efforts and reduced their opportunities to participate in the white economic system in many ways. Stringent employment regulations discouraged white people from employing Aboriginal workers. Aboriginal women (and often girls) sent to be servants often returned to the reserves pregnant.[84] Efforts to educate Aboriginal people were severely limited. It is little wonder, then, that I found no Australian couples equivalent to the educated Native American men married to white women in the archives.

Conclusion

It was no less a man than Theodore Roosevelt who said to me once in the White House that he would give anything to have a drop of Sioux or Cheyenne blood in his veins. It is a fact that the intelligent and educated Indian has no social prejudice to contend with.

Charles Eastman, The Indian To-day

Even in twenty-first-century Australia it is difficult to imagine an Australian prime minister telling an Aboriginal leader that he wished he had indigenous ancestry, as Charles Eastman claimed President Roosevelt once did. White Europeans settled in North America and Australia with the same disdain for the rights of the indigenous owners of the lands, and similar ideas about their "savage" and "uncivilized" nature, despite significant differences in the social and intellectual context of the periods in which they began their colonial projects. For the most part they attempted to remove these obstacles to their expansion with acts of violence and brutality, but an ideology of assisting un-Christian peoples to "find" God also existed and gave some colonial projects a humanitarian aspect. Eventually some white people became publicly dedicated to the idea of teaching Native Americans and Aborigines to live as white people and assimilating them into what had become the dominant mainstream society. Many acts of cruelty were committed in the name of these ideas. But despite these basic similarities in the treatment of the indigenous peoples of the North American and Australian continents there are telling differences in the status accorded to Native Americans and Australian

Aborigines by white people, even in the present day. One particular difference has shaped this study.

While both white Australians and white Americans realized the importance of education to the success of assimilation, they saw indigenous people as intellectually inferior, and they mostly constructed curricula that privileged manual training. In the United States, however, for a brief period at the end of the nineteenth century, attitudes among humanitarian reformers were slightly more egalitarian. Reformers and government officials encouraged and assisted a select few (though the majority were, it must be remembered, not so lucky) to be "leaders" of their people, attend institutes of higher learning, and perhaps even gain a profession. In Australia, where the first Aborigines graduated from universities in the 1960s, these "elites" had no equivalent in this period. White people envisioned Aboriginal people joining the laboring classes at best, and even this was problematic as the Australian working class began to make their opposition to this plan known. These particularities impacted on the social status of participants in marriages between white women and indigenous men. In America, despite the strong taboos against interracial relationships involving white women, some high-profile, middle-class unions of educated Native American men and white women occurred. This was not so in Australia. This comparison of the assimilation policies of both nations has suggested some reasons for this disparity, one of the main ones being the significant numbers, amounting to a critical mass, of Christian, humanitarian reformers that existed in the United States and their rarity in Australia. Another explanation is the differing emphasis on the two types of assimilation: cultural assimilation, which found its strongest expression in the United States, and biological absorption, which underlay many of the policy "solutions" proposed in Australia.

The presence of other nonwhite populations was important in shaping white attitudes toward sexual relationships with indigenous peoples. The hierarchy of different ethnic groups, which obsessed scientists in the late nineteenth and early twentieth centuries, shaped the ideologies of assimilation in each country. Where two nonwhite peoples existed simultaneously, white government officials and reformers, it seems, could not help but compare them. This was especially true in the United States, with its large black and immigrant populations. In 1904 Commissioner of Indian Affairs William A. Jones noted the reasons why the Native American "race is worthy of all the time, money, and labor expended on it by a generous Congress and people." Unlike African Americans, he argued:

> The Indian has always been a free man. He was never a slave to master or potentate. He chose his rulers, who ruled because of their ability. You might degrade, but not enslave him. The American Indian retains his pride of ancestry and glories in the fact that he is an Indian. No blush of shame mangles his face when he is designated by his racial name.[1]

Native Americans, in general, occupied a higher status than African Americans in the racial hierarchies that dominated white American thinking of the time. I have argued that this partially explains why marriages could take place between white women and Native American men, even in the strictly segregated state of Virginia where Hampton Institute was located.

That these marriages took place highlights the difference made by the presence of a larger nonwhite, nonindigenous population in America to the way in which interracial relationships between white people and indigenous people were perceived. Marriages and sexual relationships between white people and indigenous people were among the most acceptable of interracial unions. As scholars such as Ward Churchill have noted, white Americans often hinted that the absorption of the small amount of Native American "blood" into the large white population would not only make little difference to the "whiteness" of Americans but might also be a solution to the "Indian problem."[2] It was harder to imagine such a solution in relation to the much larger black population, and this was reflected in white attitudes toward interracial sexual relationships with that group. In addition, according to Winthrop Jordan, as early as the beginning of the eighteenth century, white Americans had found themselves in a dilemma regarding the slave population. If African Americans were freed, it was believed that racial intermixture and the "pollution" of white America would result. If they were not, then the white American could not remain, as Jordan put it, "faithful to his own image as the world's exemplar of liberty and equalitarianism." "Whatever path he took," Jordan says, "he seemed to abandon part of himself, so that neither could be taken with assurance."[3] Interracial mixing with African Americans had a long, sensitive, and resonant history.

A similar phenomenon existed in the Australian states of Western Australia, Queensland, and the Northern Territory, which also had significant nonwhite populations (mostly Asian and Pacific Islander). The presence of these people also affected the way in which interracial relationships were viewed by white authorities. In Western Australia and the Northern Territory, this presence prompted white officials to place stringent controls on the men Aboriginal women could marry in the hope that the process by which Aboriginal identity would be "absorbed" into the white population would be simplified. Different attitudes to interracial sexuality existed in different areas in Australia. Particularly unusual forms existed in Queensland, where, as in the United States, proportionately larger nonwhite populations made white people more afraid of interracial sexual relationships, and in Victoria, where the 1886 Aborigines Protection Act made marriages between white women and men of mixed descent less anxiety-producing than other forms of interracial marriage. Both in America and Australia the emphasis on "absorbing" indigenous identity often made concerns about relationships between members of nonwhite groups—for example, African and Native American students at Hampton or Aboriginal and Pacific Islander people in Queensland—far more intense than in connection to relationships between indigenous and white people. The former kind of union would produce, it was thought, "unabsorbable" physical types who would be more difficult, if not impossible, to assimilate.

Overall, white Australians were more enthusiastic than white Americans about the prospect of interracial sexual relationships leading to a loss of distinctive Aboriginal physical characteristics. The lack of a large nonindigenous, nonwhite population in Australia was a significant reason for this difference. American reformers were more dedicated to the idea of cultural assimilation, partly, it seems, because they knew that they would never be able to achieve a "white America," thanks to the presence of the black population, which was simply too large to be "absorbed." On the other hand, a "white Australia" was a real possibility, as reflected by the passing of legislation commonly known by that very name in 1901. From a comparative perspective, it appears that the black presence made a significant difference to the way that the white–Native American relationships were perceived. This difference is the subtext to an exchange between Charles Eastman and Booker T. Washington:

> Dr. Booker Washington is in the habit of saying jocosely that the negro blood is the strongest in the world, for one drop of it makes a "nigger" of a white man. I would argue that the Indian blood is even stronger, for a half-blood Negro and Indian may pass for an Indian, and so be admitted to first-class hotels and even to high society.[4]

The less menacing, more manageable size of the Native American population, compared with the African American, is one explanation for these varying levels of racism. As Patrick Wolfe has argued, however, it was not simply population size that dictated these attitudes; it was also the relationship these nonwhite groups had to the dominant white majority. African Americans were not simply more threatening because of their larger numbers. Their position as providers of cheap labor required their continuing existence as well as their social relegation. The absorption of indigenous people into white society, on the other hand, would hasten the ultimate, uncontested possession of their land.[5]

This book has described many processes, policies, and beliefs that could be associated with the ideology of assimilation. At its essence, though, assimilation was a means to an end, and in that sense, no discussion of it would be complete without some acknowledgment of its genocidal implications. This book was researched and written against a background of debates in Australia about the "stolen generations." In 1997 the Human Rights and Equal Opportunity Commission released its report on the government's practice of removing Aboriginal children of mixed descent from their parents, and argued that the practice was genocidal and calling for reparations and apologies, neither of which have been fully given.[6]

As I wrote, many Australians questioned the commission's argument about whether the policies of the Australian government can be labeled "genocide," and many others sought ways to make the reparations called for by the commission. Part of my motivation for this study, therefore, was to explore the underlying premise of the commission's report: that assimilation, which can be seen as a benign ideology compared with some of the more violent aspects of colonization, could also lead to unbelievably cruel and inhumane practices. Assimilation policies in the United States and Australia were often justified on Christian and humanitarian grounds. A small number of white Americans, and even fewer white Australians, cared about the future position of colonized indigenous peoples in what so quickly became the dominant white society, and believed that Aboriginal and Native American people were capable of learning the white way. Assimilationist methods were not always imposed on indigenous peoples against their will. Yet the assimilationists' assumption that to claim their full humanity, Native American and Aboriginal people had to embrace the ways of white society, often led them to treat indigenous people with breathtaking injustice, to show little understanding or respect for indigenous culture, and to have no qualms about advocating its complete destruction. The endpoint of an assimilationist policy, after all, is the disappearance of a distinct people, not, as Robert Niezen puts it, "through massacre but a bloodless process of education and 'development.'"[7] In Australia, however, the process was not quite as "bloodless" as Niezen describes. Quite apart from the terrible massacres (which were common to both countries), Australian absorptionists relied very much on mixing Aboriginal with white "blood" to accomplish their objectives.

For this reason, I and other scholars have explored the ideology of assimilation beginning with the premise that the laws and policies described here were attempts at genocide, as defined by Raphaël Lemkin in his 1944 book, *Axis Rule in Occupied Europe.* Lemkin's definition includes "cultural genocide."

> Generally speaking, genocide does not necessarily mean the immediate destruction of a nation except when accomplished by mass killings of all members of a nation. It is intended rather

to signify a coordinated plan of different actions aimed at
the destruction of essential foundations of the life of national group, with the aim of annihilating the groups themselves
(even if all individuals within the dissolved group physically survive). The objectives of such a plan would be a disintegration of political and social institutions, of culture, language, national feelings, religion, and the economic existence
of national groups, and the destruction of personal security,
liberty, health, dignity, and even the lives of the individuals
belonging to such groups.[8]

Nevertheless, the degree to which genocide is seen as taking place in
each country is still a matter for scholarly debate. Policies of cultural genocide certainly existed in the United States and Australia, and scholars
such as Ward Churchill and Henry Reynolds have convincingly labeled
the excessive violence perpetuated on Native American and Aboriginal people genocidal.[9] Moreover, white Australians have their system-
atic attempts at biological absorption to add to their already tarnished
record. Nevertheless, it is my understanding that not many Americans or
Australians, then or now, would concur in the unconditional application
of the label "genocide."[10] The legal, cultural, and historical intricacies of
the crime of genocide are beyond the scope of this study.[11] But it cannot
be denied that for white people in both countries assimilation policies
were part of a solution that included actual killing as an answer to the
problem posed by the presence of groups of people with prior claims to
land and puzzlingly different ways of living.

It is just as important to note, however, that the history of interracial
relationships reveals that indigenous people and white people were not
always on different sides of the fence and the important insights this
gives us into the gendered nature of colonialism. The colonizer/colonized
dichotomy obscures the complexity of settler societies, in which more
often than not more than two ethnic groups interacted with each other
as well as with white people on the same soil. Settler society was a web
of interactions in which issues of race, gender, and class all impacted on
people's lives; a phenomenon illustrated by the high level of racial mixing took place. Barriers of race could be overcome by people's feelings

for each other. This truth undermines the notion that relationships between white women and indigenous men "never happened"—that the special place white women had in the colonizing imagination as symbols of the purity and power of the white race implied a taboo too strong to allow such relationships to occur. Thus the history of white women who married indigenous men is an important addition to our understanding of the active role white women played in the imperial project, the documenting of which has been an important feminist project over the last few decades. Like white men, white women had a variety of relationships with indigenous peoples. As I have shown, they could be employers, neighbors, teachers, philanthropists, public servants, social workers, wives, and lovers. In all these roles, their whiteness dictated both their actions and the reaction of the world to them. But in some instances, human feeling could cross seemingly unsurpassable barriers of racial difference. So many of the histories of assimilation in the United States and Australia have dealt mainly with government legislation and social policy. The human story of how people negotiated their lives within that framework is often neglected. I hope I have provided a small part of that other story by charting the lives of people who made an unusual, sometimes subversive, choice of spouse.

Comparing the two nations at this microcosmic level leads to a closer understanding of the similarities and differences in their treatment of indigenous populations. Analysis that crosses national boundaries also has implications for the way in which Australians and Americans view their own histories. As citizens of a larger and more economically powerful nation whose history is often portrayed as exceptional, Americans may profit from the realization that their origins lie in a global process of colonization by Europeans. In Australia, where the cruel treatment of indigenous people has frequently been rationalized as the product of "good intentions at the time," white Australians would do well to realize that dealings with the original owners of the land might have been different—that other possibilities were explored elsewhere, and that the situation in which we found ourselves in the year 2006 was not always the inevitable outcome of the past.

Source Acknowledgments

Chapter 1, "Native American Education and Marriages at Hampton Institute," previously appeared as "Interracial Marriage and the Ideology of Assimilation: Hampton Institute, 1878–1923," in *Virginia Magazine of History and Biography* 108, no. 3 (Autumn 2000): 279–303.

Parts of chapters 3, "Educated Native American Men and Interracial Marriage," and 7, "White Women Married to Aboriginal Men," previously appeared as "Margins of Acceptability: Class, Education, and Interracial Marriage in Australia and America," in *Frontiers* 23, no. 3 (2002): 55–75.

Chapter 4, "A Middle-Class White Woman Philanthropist and Interracial Marriage," previously appeared as "Reading the Personal as Political: The Assimilationist Views of a White Woman Married to a Native American Man, 1880s–1940s," in *Australasian Journal of American Studies* 18, no. 2 (1999): 23–41.

Chapter 6, "Regulating Aboriginal Marriages in Victoria," previously appeared as "Regulating Koori Marriages: The 1886 Victorian 'Aborigines Protection Act,'" in *Journal of Australian Studies* 67 (2001): 22–29.

Chapter 9, "Absorbing the 'Aboriginal Problem' in Australia," previously appeared as "Absorbing the Aboriginal Problem: Controlling Marriage in Australia in the Late Nineteenth and Early Twentieth Century," in *Aboriginal History* 27 (2003): 185–209.

Notes

Introduction

1. Mumford, *Interzones*, xi.

2. Ideas about race have changed since the marriages described in this book took place. Race is no longer seen as a biological truism but as a set of social constructs grounded in time and place. These shifts have complicated the language used to talk about the phenomenon of interracial marriage. The word *race* has been in English usage since the sixteenth century, and although its meaning has continued to fluctuate, it has generally referred to groups of people who were believed to differ culturally, physically, and even intellectually. This idea is behind the cruel and unequal treatment that some groups of people have

received from others, most notably in the last three centuries in which complex belief systems based on these assumptions justified colonialism, systems of slavery in the United States and the Caribbean, apartheid in South Africa, and the Nazi attempt at genocide of the Jews in 1940s Germany. For this reason many scholars now believe that history written using the concept of race can only be backward-looking in terms of the human rights and social equality of all people. But without race, the topic of interracial marriage is meaningless and could not be written. However amorphous ideas of race were, for those who lived in Australia and the United States in the late nineteenth and early twentieth centuries, they were a reality. Legislation governing interracial marriage was couched in racialized terms. Racial ideology, therefore, impinged on the lives of the people who are at the core of this book, and it was also an integral part of their view of the world and the social mores that constrained their lives. There is inherent worth in exploring and interrogating the ways in which the constantly reinvented category of race was defined by Australians and Americans. Therefore, I have used both the word *race* and the word *interracial* to refer to the relationships discussed in this book. See Martha Hodes's study of illicit sex between black men and white women in the nineteenth-century American South for a different approach to this problem with language. Hodes, *White Women, Black Men*, 9. See Banton, *Racial Theories*, for a detailed study of the varying philosophies of race held in the western world over the last few centuries, and Matthew Frye Jacobson's introduction to *Whiteness of a Different Color*, 1–12, for more discussion of the issue of using the concept of race in historical scholarship.

3. There have been some smaller studies of white women's relationships with Native American men. See Alexander, "Elaine Goodale Eastman" and "Finding Oneself through a Cause"; Dobrow, "White Sister of the Sioux"; Jacobs, "The Eastmans and the Luhans"; and McGrath, "White Brides." Glenda Riley briefly addressed the topic of white women who married Native Americans in *Women and Indians on the Frontier*, 181–83, and Ruth Frankenberg devoted a chapter of *White Women, Race Matters: The Social Construction of Whiteness* to white women who married interracially or adopted nonwhite children. Some case studies of white women who had relationships with black men have been explored. See Diedrich, *Love across Color Lines: Ottilie Assing and Frederick Douglass*, and Horowitz and Peiss, *Love across the Color Line*. There has, of course, been important work on interracial relationships in United States in general. All historians of interracial relationships between settlers and indigenous people are indebted to Sylvia Van Kirk's groundbreaking study *Many Tender Ties: Women in Fur-Trade Society, 1670–1870*. Other works include Forbes, *Africans and Native Americans*; Hurtado, *Intimate Frontiers*; Mumford, *Interzones*; Nash, *Red, White, and Black*; Romano, *Race Mixing*; and Spickard, *Mixed Blood*. Nancy Cott has woven interracial marriage into *Public Vows*, her history of marriage and the American nation.

4. Two exceptions are Haskins and Maynard, "Sex, Race, and Power," and Spencer, "The Lives of Jim Page and Rebecca Forbes in the Adnyamathanha Community." Jan Ryan has done important work on marriages of white women and Chinese men in "'She Lives with a Chinaman': Orient-ing 'White' Women in the Courts of Law."

5. Reynolds, *With the White People*, 111, 114.

6. See, e.g., Grimshaw, "Interracial Marriages and Colonial Regimes in Victoria and Aotearoa/New Zealand"; Hurtado, *Intimate Frontiers*; Stoler, "Sexual Affronts and Racial

Frontiers"; Williamson, *New People*; Wolfe, "Nation and MiscegeNation"; and Young, *Colonial Desire*.

7. Stoler, "Tense and Tender Ties," 829. See also the roundtable on "Empires and Intimacies: Lessons from (Post)Colonial Studies," based on Stoler's article.

8. Kerber, "The Meanings of Citizenship," 839.

9. In 1855, Congress created a statute declaring that any woman "who might lawfully be naturalized under existing laws who had married or would marry an American man gained American citizenship in doing so." As Nancy Cott has argued, this "act was remarkable in its gender specificity" and understood "male headship of the marital couple as a *civic* and *political* norm." Cott, "Marriage and Women's Citizenship in the United States, 1830–1934," 1456.

10. Baldwin, "Subject to Empire," 555.

11. Ryan, *Womanhood in America*, 139.

12. See esp. Chaudhuri and Strobel, *Western Women and Imperialism*; Midgley, *Gender and Imperialism*; Strobel, *European Women and the Second British Empire*; Ware, *Beyond the Pale: White Women, Racism, and History*; and Stoler, "Carnal Knowledge and Imperial Power."

13. Loomba, *Colonialism/Postcolonialism*, 159.

14. Dyer, *White*, 29.

15. Cott, *Public Vows*, 1.

16. I follow Martha Hodes's reasoning regarding the use of the term *toleration* to refer to relationships of white women and nonwhite men. Toleration, she says, "suggests a measure of forbearance for that which is not approved. . . . [T]he phenomenon of toleration, no matter how carefully defined, cannot convey the complexity of responses: white neighbors judged harshly, gossiped viciously, and could completely ostracize the transgressing white woman." Hodes, *White Women, Black Men*, 3.

17. Hodes, *White Women, Black Men*, 211.

18. See, e.g., the special issue of the *Journal of American History* 86, no. 3 (December 1999) on "The Nation and Beyond," which included reflections on transnational history by David Thelan, Robin Kelly, and Ian Tyrrell; Adas, "From Settler Colony to Global Hegemony"; Bender, *Rethinking American History in a Global Age*; and Russo, *American History from a Global Perspective*.

19. Australian scholar Ian Tyrrell is perhaps the best example, both in exploring methodologically how this kind of history might be written and then putting it into practice. See Tyrrell, "Comparing Comparative Histories: Australian and American Modes of Comparative Analysis," "American Exceptionalism in an Age of International History," "Making Nations/Making States," and "Peripheral Visions."

20. David Goodman has explored the similarities and differences between the responses to the gold rushes in mid-nineteenth-century Victoria and California. Goodman, *Gold Seeking*. Tyrrell has compared the environmental movements in California and Australia in the late nineteenth century in *True Gardens of the Gods*. Women's organizations and the struggle for suffrage are topics with analogous features in America and Australia. Grimshaw, "Writing about White Women in New Societies" and "Reading the Silences"; Tyrrell, *Woman's World/Woman's Empire*; and Deacon, "Politicizing Gender." See also Campbell, "Irish Nationalism and Immigrant Assimilation: Comparing the United States and Australia." In addition, *Australasian Journal of American Studies* 9, no. 2 (December 1990)

explored "Comparative U.S.–Australia Themes."

21. Turner, *The Significance of Sections in American History* (1932) as quoted in W. Turrentine Jackson, "A Brief Message for the Young and/or Ambitious," 5. Some early comparative historians concluded that the frontiers of America and Australia were not sufficiently similar to apply Turner's limited definition of the frontier based on census statistics. More recent definitions of the frontier, however, are applicable to many geographical areas. Annette Kolodny has defined a frontier as either "a zone of successive interpenetrations" or as a "locus of first cultural contact." Kolodny, "Letting Go Our Grand Obsessions," 2–3. For a discussion of new meanings of *frontier*, see Limerick, *The Legacy of Conquest* and "Turnerians All: The Dream of a Helpful History in an Intelligible World."

22. See Alexander, *Moving Frontiers*; Allen, *Bush and Backwoods*; Burt, "If Turner Had Looked at Canada, Australia, and New Zealand When He Wrote about the West"; Ward, *The Australian Legend*; and Winks, *The Myth of the American Frontier*.

23. Jackson, "A Brief Message for the Young and/or Ambitious," 13, and Fredrickson, "Comparative History," 464.

24. Wolfe, "Land, Labor, and Difference."

25. Stanley, *The Bible and the Flag*, chap. 3. For an examination of the way in which evangelical religion transformed British society in the early nineteenth century, see Bradley, *The Call to Seriousness*. See also Porter, "Trusteeship, Anti-Slavery, and Humanitarianism" and "Religion, Missionary Enthusiasm, and Empire." For an exploration of Enlightenment ideas in a context of colonialism, see Hulme and Jordanova, *The Enlightenment and Its Shadows*, esp. 1–46.

26. Senate, *Annual Report of the Commissioner of Indian Affairs*, 35th Cong., 1st sess., 1857, 292.

27. In Australia, the most emphatic purveyor of these ideas has been the Human Rights and Equal Opportunity Commission in its 1997 report, *Bringing Them Home: Report of the National Inquiry into the Separation of Aboriginal and Torres Strait Islander Children from Their Families*. In the United States, there has been no similar nationwide, government-funded study. Instead, the accusation of ethnocide is made by scholars such as José Barreiro, the editor-in-chief of *Native Americas*. See José Barreiro, "First Words: When Education Became Ethnocide." Scholars in Australia and the United States have also argued that outright genocide was a part of the colonial project in both nations. See esp. Reynolds, *An Indelible Stain?* and Churchill, *A Little Matter of Genocide*.

28. Grew, "The Comparative Weakness of American History," 98.

29. Most Australian Aboriginal people find reference to "degrees" of Aboriginality offensive because, historically, notions of "blood" were used to divide them. Native Americans have also suffered through white definitions of "degrees" of indigeneity, although in recent decades they have adopted notions of "blood" to simplify the processes of tribal enrollment. Unfortunately I cannot discuss assimilation or interracial marriage without reference to the phenomenon of "mixed ancestry." As I have argued, ideas of the dilution of indigenous blood were inherent to assimilation ideology. I have tried to keep the use of the many offensive terms related to this subject to a minimum. See Pettman, "Race, Ethnicity, and Gender in Australia," 75. For a discussion of the historical background to tribal use of blood quantum requirements, see Meyer, "American Indian Blood Quantum Requirements."

30. Reynolds, *An Indelible Stain?* 177.

31. Haebich, "Imagining Assimilation."

32. Anderson, *The Cultivation of Whiteness*, 216–43; Beresford and Omaji, *Our State of Mind*; McGregor, *Imagined Destinies*, chap. 4; McGregor, "'Breed Out the Colour'"; Wolfe, *Settler Colonialism*, 175–76; Manne, "The Stolen Generations."

33. Human Rights and Equal Opportunity Commission, *Bringing Them Home*. For a description of the public debate about the report, see Bradfield, "From Empires to Genocide Chic."

34. See Ahern, "Assimilationist Racism: The Case of the 'Friends of the Indian,'"; Dippie, *Vanishing American*; Harmon, "When Is an Indian Not an Indian?"; Kazal, "Revisiting Assimilation"; and Smits, "'Squaw Men,' 'Half-Breeds,' and Amalgamators."

35. Limerick, *Legacy of Conquest*, 338.

36. Mihesuah, "American Indian Identities," 13.

37. Sturm, *Blood Politics*, 2.

38. Jaimes, "Federal Indian Identification Policy."

39. Churchill, "Nobody's Pet Poodle: Jimmie Durham," 485.

40. Adams, *Education for Extinction*, 8.

41. See Davenport, *State Laws Limiting Marriage Selection: Examined in the Light of Eugenics.*

42. Only two scholars have attempted a state-by-state description of these laws. Franklin Johnson included them in his *Development of State Legislation Concerning the Free Negro*, and in 1989 David H. Fowler explored the laws in detail in his *Northern Attitudes towards Interracial Marriage*. There is also a significant body of scholarship dedicated to implications of the existence of miscegenation laws. See Moran, *Interracial Intimacy*; Kennedy, *Interracial Intimacies*; Pascoe, "Race, Gender, and Intercultural Relations"; Pascoe, "Miscegenation Law"; Pascoe, "Race, Gender, and the Privileges of Property"; and Wallenstein, *Tell the Court I Love My Wife.*

43. Cott, *Public Vows*, 41.

44. Hispanics were also rarely included. Pascoe, "Race, Gender, and Intercultural Relations," 7.

45. Pascoe, "Miscegenation Law," 49.

46. Prucha, *Great Father*, 2:765–67.

47. House, *Annual Report of the Commissioner of Indian Affairs*, 60th Cong., 1st sess., 1907, 21.

48. *Proceedings of the Second Annual Lake Mohonk Conference, 1884*, 14, 21, and *Proceedings of the Tenth Lake Mohonk Conference, 1892*, 13.

49. *First Annual Report of the Indian Rights Association, 1883*, 6, IRAP.

50. *Eleventh Annual Report of the Indian Rights Association, 1893*, 20, IRAP.

51. Dippie, *Vanishing American*; Smits, "'Squaw Men,' 'Half-Breeds,' and Amalgamators."

52. Morris, *Domesticating Resistance*, 93–97.

53. When the first federal government introduced an act in 1902 to establish a common federal franchise, white women received the vote and Aborigines of Queensland and Western Australia were explicitly excluded. As a flow-on effect, Aborigines were excluded elsewhere not only as federal voters but also in state legislatures where they had not previously been debarred. For further discussion of the legal implications of the Australian

constitution for Aboriginal people, see Chesterman and Galligan, *Citizens without Rights*, chap. 3.

54. Henry Reynolds, *This Whispering in Our Hearts*. It is significant that Reynolds's book, the only general history of humanitarianism in Australia, is really a series of biographies of individuals rather than a discussion of large organizations. A similar approach is taken by John Harris in *One Blood*, his history of Australian missionaries.

55. For information about the Aborigines' Protection Society and the historical context in which it was formed, in particular the House of Commons committee appointed in 1836–37 to examine imperial relations in several British settlements, see Laidlaw, "Integrating Metropolitan, Colonial, and Imperial Histories."

56. Reynolds, *This Whispering in Our Hearts*, 1–21.

57. Commonwealth of Australia, *Aboriginal Welfare*.

58. Markus, *Australian Race Relations, 1788–1993*, 154.

59. Commonwealth of Australia, *Aboriginal Welfare*, 29.

60. Chesterman and Galligan, *Citizens without Rights*, chap. 6.

61. *Commonwealth Parliamentary Debates*, 1951, 875, quoted in Ramson, *The Australian National Dictionary: A Dictionary of Australianisms on Historical Principles*, 16–17.

62. "Protection of the Aborigines (Annual Report of the Board for the Year Ended 30th June 1939)," and "Protection of Aborigines (Annual Report of the Board for the Year Ended 30th June 1941)," *Joint Volumes of Papers Presented to the Legislative Council and Legislative Assembly of New South Wales* 1, pt. 2 (1941–42): 1.

63. Clark, *A History of Australia*, 5:200.

64. Markus, *Australian Race Relations*, 110–54.

1. Education and Marriages at Hampton Institute

1. Peabody, *Founder's Day at Hampton*, 13–26.

2. See Brown, *Good Wives, Nasty Wenches, and Anxious Patriarchs*; Higginbotham and Kopytoff, "Racial Purity and Interracial Sex in the Law of Colonial and Antebellum Virginia"; Johnston, *Race Relations in Virginia and Miscegenation in the South, 1776–1860*; Smits, "'Abominable Mixture,'"; Walter Wadlington, "The Loving Case"; and Wallenstein, "Race, Marriage, and the Law of Freedom."

3. Hultgren and Molin, *To Lead and to Serve*, 33, and *Twenty-two Years' Work*, 451–52.

4. *Twenty-two Years' Work*, 340–41; Hultgren and Molin, *To Lead and to Serve*, 22, 33; student file of George Bushotter, HUA, *Twenty-two Years' Work*, 349, 387–88; student file of Thomas C. Miles, HUA; *Twenty-two Years' Work*, 435; student file of Wesley Huntsman, HUA; and *Twenty-two Years' Work*, 456. In her introduction, Folsom wrote, "When I speak in my records of a 'good home,' I refer more to the home life than to the building that shelters it." *Twenty-two Years' Work*, 320.

5. See Mathes, "Nineteenth-Century Women and Reform," 2, 12–13.

6. See Alexander, "Elaine Goodale Eastman" and "Finding Oneself through a Cause"; Dobrow, "White Sister of the Sioux"; and Eastman, *Sister to the Sioux*.

7. Lindsey, *Indians at Hampton Institute*, 165; Tingey, "Indians and Blacks Together," 222–48; and *Southern Workman* 46 (December 1917); 47 (January 1918): 47; 48 (May 1919): 255; 48 (November 1919): 623; and 49 (September 1920): 431, HUA.

8. Rideout, *William Jones*, 7–8, 27.

9. *Nineteenth Annual Report of the Indian Rights Association, 1901*, 34–35, IRAP. The IRA was also involved in raising money to help Jones with his academic career. See *Twenty-first Report of the Indian Rights Association, 1903*, 34–35, IRAP.

10. Henry Owl, "Some Successful Indians," *Southern Workman* 47 (1918): 537–38.

11. *Southern Workman* 51 (November 1922): 532.

12. Samuel Chapman Armstrong to Richard Henry Pratt, August 18, 1878, folder 11, box 1, RHPP.

13. "Report of E. Whittlesey and Albert K. Smiley," *Annual Report of the Commissioner of Indian Affairs, 1888*, 50th Cong., 2d sess., appendix C, 741.

14. "Proceedings of the Board of Indian Commissioners at the Seventeenth Lake Mohonk Indian Conference," *Annual Report of the Commissioner of Indian Affairs, 1899*, 56th Cong., 1st sess., appendix D, 31.

15. ARHI, 1912, 11, HUA.

16. *Southern Workman* 41 (1912): 546.

17. ARHI, 1912, 11–12, HUA.

18. Hultgren and Molin, *To Lead and to Serve*, 18.

19. *Southern Workman* 8 (1879): 77

20. *Ten Years' Work for Indians at Hampton Institute, Virginia, 1878–1888*, 3.

21. Faculty Records, 13, 15, August 16, 1888; Discipline Books 1887–88, 214, 310, HUA. See also Lindsey, *Indians at Hampton Institute*, 156, 168, and Tingey, "Indians and Blacks Together," 181–83.

22. Tingey, "Indians and Blacks Together," 181–82.

23. "Report of Indian Records 1919," Caroline Andrus Collection, HUA.

24. Lindsey, *Indians at Hampton Institute*, 261.

25. Student files of Maude Abbie Goodwin and Elsie Greene Doxtater, HUA. The marriages were *reported* in January 1914 and December 1917 respectively. It is not known whether they took place before Hampton's denials of instances of interracial marriages were made in 1912.

26. Richard Pratt to Arthur C. Parker, December 11, 1912, *PCM*.

27. ARHI, 1878, 11.

28. *Twenty-two Years' Work*, 318.

29. ARHI, 1879, 16.

30. ARHI, 1884, 71.

31. *Southern Workman* 9 (1880): 63.

32. *Proceedings of the Second Annual Meeting of the Lake Mohonk Conference, 1884*, 27.

33. Hultgren and Molin, *To Lead and to Serve*, 37–39.

34. *Annual Report of Commission of Indian Affairs, 1886*, 49th Cong., 2d sess., 101.

35. Byron M. Cutcheon to Richard Henry Pratt, April 1, 1886, folder 64, box 3, RHPP.

36. *Proceedings of the Third Annual Meeting of the Lake Mohonk Conference, 1885*, 52.

37. *Sixth Annual Report of the Executive Committee of the Indian Rights Association, 1888*, 49, IRAP.

38. ARHI, 1886–87, 49.

39. Faculty records, August 15, 1888, HUA.

40. Armstrong quoted in Lindsey, *Indians at Hampton Institute*, 196–98.

41. ARHI, 1888, 42.

42. *Talks and Thoughts of the Hampton Indian Students* (March 1887): 4 and (July 1887): 2.

43. *Talks and Thoughts of the Hampton Indian Students* (August 1888): 3.

44. ARHI, 1881, 13.

45. ARHI, 1892, 86.

46. See Adams, *Education for Extinction*, 173–81.

47. *Ten Years' Work*, 42–43.

48. *Twenty-two Years' Work*, 393.

49. Hoxie, *A Final Promise*, 4–9.

50. *Southern Workman* 10 (December 1881): 120.

51. Adams, "Fundamental Considerations," 3.

52. Adams, *Education for Extinction*, 58.

53. Katznelson and Weir, *Schooling for All*, 24–25, 45; Katz, *Reconstructing American Education*, 15–16.

54. *Proceedings of the Seventh Annual Meeting of the Lake Mohonk Conference of the Friends of the Indian, 1889*, 17–21.

55. *Proceedings of the Second Annual Meeting of the Lake Mohonk Conference, 1884*, 14.

56. *Second Annual Report of the Indian Rights Association, 1884*, 5, IRAP.

57. *Sixtieth Annual Report of the Board of Indian Commissioners to the Secretary of the Interior, 1929*, 10.

58. *Proceedings of the Seventh Annual Meeting of the Lake Mohonk Conference, 1889*, 17–21.

59. *Report of the Thirty-first Annual Lake Mohonk Conference of Friends of the Indian and Other Dependent Peoples, 1913*, 7.

60. Adams, *Education for Extinction*, 57.

61. Adams, *Education for Extinction*, 63.

62. Churchill, "The Crucible of American Indian Identity," 52. In an earlier text, Churchill gave a slightly different figure, arguing that "from roughly 1890 to 1970, an average of more than 70 percent of each succeeding generation of native youngsters was subjected to the boarding school experience." Churchill, *A Little Matter of Genocide*, 285n.

63. Genevieve Bell estimates that 10,000 students spent time at Carlisle. Bell, "Telling Stories," 331.

64. House, *Annual Report of the Commissioner of Indian Affairs*, 47th Cong., 1st sess., 1881, 338–39.

65. Littlefield, "Learning to Labor."

66. Churchill, "The Crucible of American Indian Identity," 51.

67. See, e.g., Benson, *Children of the Dragonfly*.

68. Barreiro, "First Words," 2. See also Churchill, *A Little Matter of Genocide*, 83–84, 366n, 414, and Noriega, "American Indian Education in the United States: Indoctrination for Subordination to Colonialism."

69. Hoxie, *A Final Promise*, 191–92.

2. Interracial Marriages of Carlisle Alumni

1. File of John Walker, Mani, Labatte, Sioux, CSR, 1879–1918, RG 75, National Archives and Records Administration, Washington DC.

2. Adams, *Education for Extinction*, 299. For a discussion of the controversies over returned students, see Adams, 283–92.

3. Dyer, *White*, 29.

4. File of John Walker, Mani, Labatte, csr.

5. Files of John Bongo, Chippewa, Raleigh Jackson, Seneca, and John. W. Parker and Simon Blackstar, Caddo, csr. Admittedly, not all read the question in this way—"Yes I am married. She is nice woman," "Have not went courting yet," and "Not on your life" were all memorable answers. Files of Samuel Cook, Nez Perce, John F. Suseip, Penobscot, and Robert McLean, Sioux, csr.

6. Files of Millard Hendrick, Ella Stander, Arapahoe, Harry Shawbush, Lucius Aitsan, Kiowa, Ned Brace, Kiowa, and John Schenandore, Oneida, csr.

7. File of Jacob White Cow Killer, Sioux, csr.

8. Bell, "Telling Stories," 354.

9. Mihesuah, *Cultivating the Rosebuds*, 105–6.

10. File of John Big Fire, Winnebago, csr.

11. Newspaper clipping from *Harrisburg (pa) Telegraph*, April 19, 1912, in file of Rosetta Pierce, Seneca, csr.

12. File of Henry E. Roberts, Pawnee, csr.

13. File of Daphne Waggoner, Sioux, csr.

14. File of Jefferson Miquel, Yuma, csr.

15. File of Helen J. Kimmel, Sioux, csr.

16. File of Emil Hauser, Cheyenne, csr.

17. File of Lewis Thompson, Navajo, csr.

18. File of Minnie Onhand, Osage, csr.

19. File of Nellie White Clay, Crow, csr.

20. Child, *Boarding School Seasons*, 77–79. See also Carol Devens, "'If We Get the Girls, We Get the Race.'"

21. Bell, "Telling Stories," 351.

22. See, e.g., the files of Lucinda Reed, Cherokee, and Amelia Hewitt, Tuscarora, csr.

23. Files of Grace Warren, Colville, Sophia Wilkins, Klamath, Zenobia Barcia, Mission, Ellen Martin, Osage, Minnie Paul, Seneca, and Emma Millie Marrel, Spokane, csr.

24. File of Etta Crow Batson, Cherokee, csr.

25. Krupat, *Red Matters*, 91n30.

26. Adams, *Education for Extinction*, 282–83.

27. Files of George Marks, Ottawa, and Eben Beads, Apache, csr.

28. Scholars differ in their estimates of how many students attended Carlisle. Bell claims that 10,000 Native American children spent time at Carlisle, while Brian Dippie counted 4,903. David Wallace Adams counted 3,800 up until 1899. There are thousands of Carlisle student files held in the National Archives in Washington dc. Many contain very little information at all, and there were no doubt many more interracial marriages of Carlisle students than those recorded there. Bell, "Telling Stories," 333; Dippie, *Vanishing American*, 119; Adams, *Education for Extinction*, 63.

29. File of Joseph Sheehan, Alaskan, csr.

30. File of William Moses Patterson, Tuscarora, csr.

31. File of Harry West, Washie, csr.

32. File of Russel White Bear, Crow, csr.

33. File of Edward Fox, Shawnee, csr.

34. File of Henry K. Fox, Skokomish, CSR.

35. Files of Walter Paul, Seneca, John Suseip, Penobscot, Maud Allen, Seneca, and Wilson Silas, Oneida, CSR.

36. Files of Clarke Asbury, Pueblo, Isiah Wasaquam, Ottawa, Bruce Fisher, Pueblo, John Thompson, Mohawk, and Betsy Collins, Chippewa, CSR.

37. Files of Cordelia Hicks, Wyandotte, and Peter J. Powlas, Oneida.

38. Vasha Nakootkin, Alaskan, CSR.

39. Some examples are Allen, *Blood Narrative*, Krupat, *Red Matters*, and Hilden, *When Nickels Were Indians*.

3. Educated Native Men and Interracial Marriage

1. *Proceedings of the Seventh Annual Meeting of the Lake Mohonk Conference*, 1889, 18–22.

2. Fletcher, "The Preparation of the Indian for Citizenship," 65.

3. *Annual Report of the Commissioner of Indian Affairs*, 1892, 52nd Cong., 2d sess., 1271.

4. Women's National Indian Association, *Our Work—What? How? Why?* 23–24.

5. Hertzberg, *Search for an American Indian Identity*, 36.

6. *QJSAI* 1, no. 1 (January–April 1913): 69.

7. "Constitution," 1911–16, folder 1, box 10, SAIR.

8. Chauncey Yellow Robe to Carlos Montezuma, August 6, 1911, PCM.

9. Pratt to Fayette A. McKenzie, November 2, 1912, folder 356, box 10, RHPP.

10. *QJSAI*, 1, no. 3 (July–September 1913): 282.

11. Arthur C. Parker to Elias M. Ammons, March 28, 1913, box 1, folder 1, SAIR.

12. Parker to Gertrude Bonnin, August 23, 1915, box 1, folder 8, SAIR.

13. Carlos Montezuma and Charles Eastman were founding members of the Society of American Indians, and Thomas Sloan and Sherman Coolidge, a lawyer and a preacher, who both also married white women, were part of the leadership of the organization. Montezuma corresponded with Eastman, Sloan, and Coolidge, and Sloan and Eastman often visited the Montezumas in Chicago. Thomas Sloan and Elaine Goodale Eastman both lived at Hampton before their marriages. Elaine Goodale Eastman wrote a biography of Richard Pratt, Montezuma's mentor. The Eastmans, Carlos Montezuma, Thomas Sloan, and Sherman Coolidge all corresponded with Richard Pratt. For further exploration of the links between educated Native Americans in the early twentieth century, see Hoxie, "Exploring a Cultural Borderland," and Hertzberg, *Search for an American Indian Identity*.

14. Hertzberg, *Search for an American Indian Identity*, 58.

15. *QJSAI* 1, no. 4 (October–December 1913): 371.

16. J. E. Armstrong to Carlos Montezuma, May 4, 1917, enclosing George W. Ingalls to J. E. Armstrong, October 16, 1878, PCM.

17. Speech made before Protestant ministers, 1891, folder 649, box 19, RHPP.

18. *QJSAI* 1, no. 1 (January–April 1913): 52.

19. Pratt to Montezuma, September 14, 1891, PCM.

20. Pratt to Henry Dawes, March 24, 1892, enclosing Montezuma to Pratt, March 15, 1892, PCM.

21. Speech made before Protestant ministers, 1891, folder 649, box 19, RHPP.

22. Pratt to Montezuma, November 17, 1890, PCM.

23. Montezuma to Hal J. Cole, June 15, 1893, PCM.

24. Montezuma to Pratt, June 21, 1892, folder 213, box 6, RHPP.

25. Montezuma to Thomas J. Morgan, May 14, 1890, emphasis in original, and Montezuma to Morgan, June 27, 1890, PCM.

26. Olive Harrison to Montezuma, December 2, 1899, PCM, emphasis in original.

27. Jesse M. Schultheis to Montezuma, January 8, 1900, PCM.

28. Fred Merrifield to Montezuma, November 22, 1899, PCM.

29. Montezuma to Pratt, November 30, 1921, PCM.

30. See, e.g., the *Grand Rapids Herald*, July 14, 1912, 4, PCM.

31. Maria Ruiz to Montezuma, October 19, 1898, PCM.

32. Montezuma to Pratt, March 20, 1916, PCM.

33. Montezuma, *Wassaja* 1, no. 1 (April 1916): 1, PCM.

34. *Wassaja* 1, no. 8 (November 1916): 3, PCM.

35. Montezuma, *The Indian Problem from an Indian's Standpoint*, speech given on February 10, 1898, PCM.

36. Richard Pratt, "The Dependent Races in our Midst," speech given in Philadelphia, January 13, 1913, PCM.

37. Pratt to O. H. Lipps, December 14, 1915, PCM.

38. Pratt, "Address of Brigadier General Richard H. Pratt, U.S.A. Retired, Made before the Pennsylvania Commandery, Military Order of Region Wars of the United States at the Belvue Straftford [Bellevue-Stratford] Hotel, Philadelphia, 14 January 1913," PCM.

39. Pratt to Montezuma, January 11, 1912, PCM.

40. Montezuma to Marie Montezuma, September 22, 1913, PCM.

41. Pratt to Montezuma, October 31, 1913, PCM.

42. Pratt to Montezuma, November 7, 1913, PCM.

43. Eastman, *From the Deep Woods to Civilization*, 31–32.

44. Eastman, *From the Deep Woods*, 46–47.

45. Wilson, *Ohiyesa*, 25–26.

46. Eastman, *From the Deep Woods*, 59–60.

47. Wilson, *Ohiyesa*, 41.

48. Eastman, *From the Deep Woods*, 114.

49. Wilson, *Ohiyesa*, 67. The dispute was over money allocated to "nonhostile" Sioux to compensate for their property losses during the troubles surrounding the Wounded Knee massacre.

50. "Announcement for the Season of 1904–5, Dr. Charles A. Eastman (Ohiyesa)," pamphlet held in the Eastman Collection, Jones Library, Amherst MA.

51. F. A. McKenzie to A. C. Parker, October 31, 1911, folder 1, box 6, SAIR.

52. Wilson, "Dr. Charles A. Eastman," 11. For discussions of Eastman's writings, see Copeland, *Charles Alexander Eastman (Ohiyesa)*, vol. 33; Krupat, *Native American Autobiography*; Peterson, "'An Indian . . . an American'"; and Stensland, "Charles Alexander Eastman: Sioux Storyteller and Historian."

53. Eastman, *From the Deep Woods*, 195.

54. Quoted in Hertzberg, *Search for American Indian Identity*, 69.

55. Quoted in Hertzberg, *Search for American Indian Identity*, 186.

56. Deloria, *Playing Indian*, 123.

57. *The Indian's Friend* 26, no. 6 (March 1914): 7–8.

58. Eastman, *Indian To-day*, 3-4.

59. Hertzberg, *Search for American Indian Identity*, 41-42.

60. Eastman, *From the Deep Woods*, 138.

61. Eastman, *Soul of the Indian*, 24.

62. Eastman, *Indian To-day*, 120.

63. Eastman, *Indian To-day*, 147.

64. Hertzberg, *Search for an American Indian Identity*. See also Deloria, *Playing Indian*.

65. *QJSAI* 7, no. 3 (Fall 1919): 159. For insight into Grace Coolidge's views on the "Indian problem" and her experiences at the Wind River reservation in Wyoming (although not on her marriage), see Coolidge, *Teepee Neighbors*.

66. One of the earliest issues of the *QJSAI* proclaimed, *"There Must Be a Uniform Civilization,"* adding that the basis of "that civilization, better termed *ethnic culture*, was and is English." *QJSAI* 1, no. 2 (April–June 1913): 104, emphasis in original. Arthur Parker later argued that the "future of the Indians is with the white race and in a civilization derived from the old world." *QJSAI* 4, no. 1 (January–March 1916): 8.

67. *QJSAI* 1, no. 1 (January–April 1913): 2.

68. *QJSAI* 1, no. 4 (October–December 1913): 362-63.

69. M. B. Hannah, "Absorbing the Indian," *QJSAI* 5, no. 2 (April–June 1917): 118.

70. *QJSAI* 2, no. 1 (January–March 1914): 3.

71. *QJSAI* 2, no. 1 (January–March 1914): 67.

72. *QJSAI* 4, no. 4 (October–December 1916): 299, 303-4, emphasis in original.

73. See Smits, "'Squaw Men,' 'Half-Breeds,' and Amalgamators."

74. Kimmel, *Manhood in America*, 81-102.

75. Bederman, *Manliness and Civilization*, 170-216.

76. Montezuma to Pratt, March 15, 1892, *PCM*.

77. *Boston Sunday Post*, June 20, 1915, folder 34, box 3, EGEC. See also pamphlet *Oáhe: A Camp for Girls*, Eastman Collection, Jones Library.

78. *Boston Sunday Post*, June 20, 1915.

79. See Deloria, *Playing Indian*.

80. Hertzberg, *Search for an American Indian Identity*, 213-36.

81. Deloria, *Playing Indian*, 188.

82. See Devens, "'If We Get the Girls, We Get the Race.'" For information about Susette La Flesche Picotte, the first Native American woman to graduate from medical school, see Pascoe, *Relations of Rescue*, 112-45.

83. Eastman, *From the Deep Woods*, 105-6.

84. Walter R. Johnson and D. Michael Warren, eds., *Inside the Mixed Marriage*, 7.

85. Iverson, *Carlos Montezuma*, 33. For further autobiographical information about Zitkala-Ša, see her collection of *American Indian Stories*. See also Zitkala-Ša, *Old Indian Legends*.

86. Zitkala-Ša to Montezuma, June 1901, *PCM*.

87. Zitkala-Ša to Montezuma, March 5, 1901, *PCM*.

88. Zitkala-Ša to Montezuma, April 12, 1901, *PCM*.

89. Zitkala-Ša to Montezuma, February 20, 1901, *PCM*.

90. Zitkala-Ša to Montezuma, April 19, 1901, *PCM*, emphasis in original.

91. Zitkala-Ša to Montezuma, ca. April 1901, *PCM*.

92. Zitkala-Ša to Montezuma, ca. April 1901, *PCM*.

93. Zitkala-Ša to Montezuma, May 20, 1901, *PCM*.

94. Zitkala-Ša to Montezuma, May 2, 1901, *PCM*.

95. Zitkala-Ša to Montezuma, May 1, 1902, *PCM*.

96. Zitkala-Ša to Montezuma, June 1901, *PCM*.

97. For further discussion of Zitkala-Ša's philosophies as revealed by her correspondence with Montezuma, see Spack, "Dis/engagement."

98. Montezuma to William H. Underwood, before May 4, 1904, *PCM*.

99. Montezuma to Underwood, before May 4, 1904, *PCM*.

100. Hertzberg, *Search for an American Indian Identity*, 10.

101. See Foreman, "Reminiscences of Mr. R. P. Vann," 842, and Shirley, *Belle Starr and Her Times*.

102. For information about the Luhan marriage, see Jacobs, "The Eastmans and the Luhans." For Carobeth Laird, see her books *Encounter with an Angry God: Recollections of My Life with John Peabody Harrington, Limbo*, and *Mirror and Pattern: George Laird's World of Chemehuevi Mythology*.

103. Iverson, *Carlos Montezuma*, 99.

104. Carlos Montezuma to Marie Montezuma, August 22, 1921, *PCM*

105. Marie Montezuma to Carlos Montezuma, c. September 1921, *PCM*.

106. Carlos Montezuma to Marie Montezuma, September 3, 1921, *PCM*.

107. Marie Montezuma to Carlos Montezuma, September 19, 1921, *PCM*.

108. Carlos Montezuma to Marie Montezuma, September 5, 1921, *PCM*.

109. Carlos Montezuma to Marie Montezuma, September 28, 1921, *PCM*.

110. Carlos Montezuma to Marie Montezuma, September 3, 1921, *PCM*.

111. Carlos Montezuma to Marie Montezuma, October 3, 1921, *PCM*.

112. Marie Montezuma to L. V. McWhorter, c. February 4–14, 1923, *PCM*.

113. Richard Pratt to Marie Montezuma, February 9, 1923, folder 425, box 12, RHPP.

114. Marie Montezuma to Will C. Barnes, October 24, 1934; Gladys Brown to Marie Montezuma, July 29, 1924, *PCM*.

115. See Carlos Montezuma to Richard Pratt, October 1 and 10, 1901, folder 214, box 6, RHPP.

116. Commissioner Chas. H. Burke to the Secretary of the Interior, June 12, 1922, *PCM*.

117. Carlos Montezuma to Joseph W. Latimer, June 24, 1922, *PCM*. In contemporary Australia, members of the stolen generation are experiencing similar problems with identity and claims to land rights.

118. Carlos Montezuma to Marie Montezuma, January 1923, *PCM*.

119. Iverson, *Carlos Montezuma*, 173.

120. Hertzberg, *Search for an American Indian Identity*, 44–45.

121. Wilson, *Ohiyesa*, 191–92.

122. Fanon, *Black Skin, White Masks*, 46.

123. Mihesuah, "American Indian Identities," 23.

4. Woman Philanthropist and Interracial Marriage

1. For a discussion of the origins of these terms and their treatment by historians, see Cott, *The Bonds of Womanhood*, esp. 1–18, 197–206. For explorations of the ideology itself, see Kraditor, *Up from the Pedestal*, and Welter, *Dimity Convictions*.

2. Mathes, "Nineteenth-Century Women and Reform," 2.

3. Pascoe, *Relations of Rescue*, 112–45.

4. *Fourth Annual Report of the Women's National Indian Association, 1884*, 49.

5. Jacobs, "The Eastmans and the Luhans," 34–35.

6. *Proceedings of the Ninth Annual Meeting of the Lake Mohonk Conference, 1891*, 88. Elaine Goodale Eastman believed strongly in the "cult of true womanhood" and its usefulness in "Indian reform." When writing of her experiences in the West she argued that "the influence of a pure woman . . . (h)er superior knowledge, her fearlessness, and her goodness seem to fill [Native Americans] with admiration and almost awe, and she can persuade them to study and to think and to give up some of their old bad habits when an equally good *man* would not influence them at all." Eastman concluded this piece with a call for the government to send as many female Indian agents, inspectors, school superintendents and supervisors, teachers, and field matrons to the West as possible. If this was done, she argued, then there was no doubt "that the day of salvation for the red man would be brought much nearer." Eastman, "The Indian—A Woman among the Indians," 136, 140.

7. "Solution of the Indian Problem," *Red Man* 10, no. 9 (December 1890–January 1891): 4.

8. Carter, "Completely Discouraged."

9. Betzinez and Nye, *I Fought with Geronimo*, foreword, 174, 203–5; Jason N. Betzinez to Richard Pratt, December 1901, folder 12, box 1, RHPP.

10. Welsh, *Four Weeks among Some of the Sioux Tribes of Dakota and Nebraska*, 3, and Harrison, *Latest Studies on Indian Reservations*, 42–43.

11. Coolidge, *Teepee Neighbors*, 59.

12. Theodore Roosevelt, *Report of Hon. Theodore Roosevelt Made to the United States Civil Service Commission, upon a Visit to Certain Indian Reservations and Indian Schools in South Dakota, Nebraska, and Kansas*, 10, IRAP.

13. *Proceedings of the Fourth Annual Lake Mohonk Conference, 1886*, 43–44.

14. Unreferenced and undated newspaper clipping, Newspaper Clippings, HUA, and *Southern Workman* 20 (July 1891): 212; *Indian's Friend* (journal of the Women's National Indian Association) 8, no. 7 (March 1896): 9; Eastman, *Sister to the Sioux*, 169–72. It is worth noting that Eastman chose not to call her memoirs by the more accurate title of "Wife to a Sioux." This was perhaps to highlight her political alliance with all Native Americans rather than her more personal connections to individuals.

15. *Indian Helper* 6, no. 19 (January 16, 1891): 3.

16. Eastman, "Sioux Indian Women," *Woman's Signal* 4, no. 94 (October 17, 1895): 247.

17. Eastman, "The Indian—A Woman among the Indians," 129. See Dobrow, "White Sister of the Sioux"; Alexander, "Elaine Goodale Eastman"; Alexander, "Finding Oneself through a Cause"; and Georgi-Findlay, *Frontiers of Women's Writing*.

18. Eastman, *Sister to the Sioux*; Elaine Goodale Eastman to her sister Rose, April 23 c. 1945 from a private collection of Eastman's letters held by Theodore D. Sargent. My sincere thanks to him for allowing me access to this material.

19. Eastman, *Sister to the Sioux*, 21. See, e.g., Elaine Goodale, "How to Americanize the Indian."

20. Eastman, *Sister to the Sioux*, 65.

21. Alexander, "Elaine Goodale Eastman," 92. Elaine later wrote about her experiences at Pine Ridge: Eastman, "The Ghost Dance War and Wounded Knee Massacre of 1890–91."

22. *New York Times,* June 7, 19, 1891

23. Eastman to her sister Rose, 1936, Sargent Collection. See Wilson, *Ohiyesa,* 163–65, 191. Eastman published several novels: *Journal of a Farmer's Daughter, Little Brother o' Dreams, Yellow Star, Indian Legends Retold, The Luck of Oldacres,* and *The Voice at Eve.*

24. Eastman to her sister Rose, June 24 c. 1928 and c. 1930; Eastman to her sister Dora, December 26, 1930, Sargent Collection.

25. Eastman, "Our New-Old Indian Policy," *Christian Century,* November 27, 1929, scrapbook 3, box 5b, EGEC.

26. Eastman to John Collier, July 8, 1933, and Paul Hutchinson to Harold L. Ickes, May 31, 1934, *Native Americans and the New Deal: The Office Files of John Collier, 1933–1945.*

27. Eastman, "Does Uncle Sam Foster Paganism?" 1016; Collier, "A Reply to Mrs. Eastman," 1018–19; Eastman to Collier, August 15, 1934, *Native Americans and the New Deal.*

28. Collier to Eastman, August 17, 1934, *Native Americans and the New Deal.* For examples of Elaine's continuing critique of Collier's work, see Eastman, "Indians Are People," *Advance,* October 4, 1934; "Indian 'New Deal': How It Works with the Navahoes Reported by Former Correspondent," *Springfield Daily Republican,* May 24, 1935; "A Dissenting View," *Zion's Herald,* June 5, 1935; "The Status of the Indian," *New Republic,* January 1, 1936; "The American Indian and His Religion," *Missionary View of the World,* March 1937, all in scrapbook 3, box 5b, EGEC. For the exchange in the *Atlantic,* see Collier to Eastman, February 27, 1941, folder 33, box 3, EGEC, and Eastman, "Indians Come Alive," *Atlantic,* November 1942, scrapbook 3, box 5b, EGEC.

29. Prucha, *Great Father,* 2:952.

30. Newman, *White Women's Rights,* esp. chaps. 2 and 5.

31. Eastman, *Sister to the Sioux,* xi, 43.

32. *Proceedings of the Fourth Annual Lake Mohonk Conference, 1886,* 4–5; Elaine Goodale to Richard Pratt, July 14, 1890, folder 85, box 3, RHPP; Eastman, *Pratt: The Red Man's Moses,* 10. This tension is also evident in Eastman's correspondence with Pratt's family, to whom she sent the final drafts of her book for approval. In reply to Nana Pratt Hawkins's criticism that "when speaking of [Pratt] you so often use adjectives before his name such as 'bellicose,' 'combative,' etc., which does not bring the reader in sympathy with him," Eastman argued that "it would be a serious mistake to omit, as you suggest, every word or line implying anything but unqualified admiration and praise. The public nowadays doesn't want to read about 'noble, self-sacrificing,' or practically perfect characters." Hawkins to Eastman, April 16, 1934, and Eastman to Hawkins, April 21, 1934, RHPP; Elaine Goodale, "The Documents in the Case," *Christian Union,* n.d., scrapbook 1, folder 4, EGEC.

33. Georgi-Findlay, *Frontiers of Women's Writing,* 263; Eastman, *Sister to the Sioux,* 33, 169.

34. *Independent,* February 7, 1889, scrapbook 1, folder 2, EGEC.

35. Alexander, "Finding Oneself through a Cause," 36.

36. Eastman, "The American Indian and His Religion."

37. Wilson, *Ohiyesa,* 81n; Dippie, *Vanishing American,* 262; Eastman, *Pratt,* 197; Eastman, "Our Forward-Looking Indians," *Unity,* September 1942, scrapbook 3, box 5b, EGEC.

38. Eastman, "To the Editor," *Word Carrier,* April 2, 1936; Eastman, "Not So Many Indians," *New York Herald Tribune,* September 12, 1943. See also "Exploiting Indian Blood," *Springfield Republican,* July 11, 1933; "Future of the Indian, *Springfield Republican,* May 31,

1941; and "Is the American Indian a Citizen?" *New York Call*, November 20, 1942, all in scrapbook 3, box 5b, EGEC.

39. Eastman, *Pratt*, 204, 191; "Alturian Club Hears Mrs. Elaine G. Eastman," scrapbook 3, box 5b, EGEC.

40. Eastman, "Future of the Indian," *Springfield Republican*, May 31, 1941, scrapbook 3, box 5b, EGEC; Eastman, "American Indian Soldiers," *Springfield Republican*, September 22, 1943, scrapbook 3, box 5b, EGEC; Eastman, "Indians Come Alive." Elaine's daughter Irene later utilized her Native American background to promote her singing career, using the stage name "Taluta" and singing Native American ballads in traditional dress. An advertising pamphlet claiming that "through songs and legends we may look into the minds of a race utterly unlike that of any other in the world" is held in the Eastman Collection, Jones Library.

41. Eastman, "Indians Are People," *Advance*, October 4, 1934, scrapbook 3, box 5b, EGEC.

42. Smith, *The View from Officer's Row*, 45–46; Summerhayes, *Vanished Arizona*, 156, 158–59.

43. Gladys H. Brown to Maria Montezuma, July 29, 1924, PCM.

5. Broken Promise of Aboriginal Education

1. Senier, *Voices of American Indian Assimilation and Resistance*, 4

2. "Royal Commission on the Aborigines," VPP 3 (1877–78): 82.

3. Reynolds, *Black Pioneers*, 284.

4. Reynolds, *Black Pioneers*, 7–12.

5. Reynolds, *With the White People*, 99–109.

6. Morris, *Domesticating Resistance*, 124.

7. Barcan, *A History of Australian Education*, 7–8.

8. Trudinger, "Education of Aborigines," 45.

9. *Report of the Parliamentary Select Committee on Aboriginal Tribes (British Settlements)*, 119.

10. Lord John Russell to Sir George Gipps, August 25, 1840, Commonwealth of Australia, *Historical Records of Australia* 20, ser. 1, 775–76.

11. "Report of the Select Committee on Aborigines," *Votes and Proceedings (Victoria)*, 1858–59, 46–47 as quoted in Fletcher, *Documents in the History of Aboriginal Education in New South Wales*, 50.

12. Elkin, "Native Education, with Special Reference to the Australian Aborigines," *Oceania* 7, no. 4 (June 1937): 489.

13. Barcan, *A History of Australian Education*, 130–54. Even so, state-funded secondary schools would not become numerous until after the Second World War.

14. See Peter Biskup, *Not Slaves, Not Citizens*, 148–49.

15. Secretary of the Board for the Protection of Aborigines to the Secretary of the Education Department, March 29, 1934, item 67, box 4, B313/1, NAAV.

16. Trudinger, "Education of Aborigines," iv; and Milnes, "A History of Aboriginal Education in the Goldfields District of Western Australia since 1927," 90–91, 145–46. See also Partington, *Perspectives of Aboriginal and Torres Strait Islander Education*, 42.

17. Ryan, *Aboriginal Tasmanians*, 230–31.

18. "Aborigines Protection Board (Report for the Year Ended 1938)," *NSWPP* 1, pt. 2 (1941–42): 1.

19. Secretary of the Department of Public Instruction to Miss A. N. Brown, Hon. Secretary of the Victorian Aboriginal Group, August 8, 1933, Unit 225, VPRS 796, Board of Education, Outward Correspondence—Primary Schools 1868–1938, PROV, 96.

20. Secretary of the Department of Public Instruction to Mr. J. D. Haddow, October 20, 1936. The request was refused on the grounds that the assistant "is not required to perform any duties other than those laid down in the School curriculum." Secretary of the Department of Public Instruction to Secretary of the Victorian Teacher's Union, December 31, 1936, Unit 225, VPRS 796, PROV, 119, 123.

21. R. Stewart, A. Combs, and P. Cameron to the Victorian Board for the Protection of Aborigines, September 22, 1879, item 95, box 4, B313/1, NAAV.

22. "Protection of the Aborigines (Report of the Board for 1885)," *JLCNSW* 39, pt. 2 (1885): 2.

23. Fletcher, *Clean, Clad, and Courteous* and *Documents in the History of Aboriginal Education*, esp. 73–105.

24. "Protection of Aborigines (Report of Board for 1892)," *JLCNSW* 50, pt. 2 (1892–93): 3.

25. "Aborigines Protection Board (Report for the Year 1901)," and "Aborigines Protection Board (Report for the Year 1902)," *New South Wales Votes and Proceedings* 2 (1903): 2.

26. "Aborigines (Report of Board for the Protection of, for year 1910)," *NSWPP* 2 (1911–12): 3. For more information about expulsions, see Fletcher, *Clean, Clad, and Courteous*, 171–205; Goodall, *Invasion to Embassy*, 109–11; and Cowlishaw, *Black, White, or Brindle: Race in Rural Australia*, 86.

27. Milnes, "A History of Aboriginal Education," 124–25, 154–56.

28. See Broome, *Aboriginal Australians*, 166; Milnes, "A History of Aboriginal Education," 61–62, 272; and Howard, *Aboriginal Politics in Southwestern Australia*, 15. For information about the incident at Wagin, see *Argus*, August 3, 1933, 6, and Milnes, "A History of Aboriginal Education," 280–83.

29. Milnes, "A History of Aboriginal Education," 201.

30. Bennett, *Teaching the Aborigines*, 64–67.

31. John Glasgow of the Education Department to the Board for the Protection of Aborigines, November 17, 1890, Unit 1, Central Board for the Protection of Aborigines, Correspondence Files, VPRS 1694, PROV.

32. McGregor, *Imagined Destinies*, 96.

33. Broome, *Aboriginal Australians*, 106, 123, 132.

34. Bleakley, "The Aboriginals and Half-Castes of Central Australia and North Australia," 8.

35. Giese, "A Brief Study of Aboriginal Education in the Northern Territory," 81.

36. Bleakley, "The Aboriginals and Half-Castes," 31.

37. Ryan, *Aboriginal Tasmanians*, 225.

38. Gale, *A Study of Assimilation: Part-Aborigines in South Australia*, 239.

39. *South Australian Parliamentary Debates*, 1923, 711.

40. Huggins and Blake, "Protection or Persecution?" 50–51.

41. Broome, *Aboriginal Australians*, 149.

42. "Aboriginal Department—Report for the Year Ended 31 December, 1936," *QPP* 2 (1937): 10.

43. "Furneaux Islands Half-Castes: Report of Select Committee," *Tasmanian Parliamentary Papers* 91, no. 48 (1924–25): 4.

44. "First Report of the Central Board Appointed to Watch over the Interests of the Aborigines in the Colony of Victoria," *VPP* 3 (1861–62): 11.

45. Report of the Board for the Protection of Aborigines, 1884, *New South Wales Votes and Proceedings* 2 (1885): 606, as quoted in Fletcher, *Documents in the History of Aboriginal Education*, 77.

46. Human Rights and Equal Opportunity Commission, *Bringing Them Home*, 170–71.

47. William Ferguson, "Give Us Justice!" *Daily Telegraph* (Sydney), October 15, 1937, as quoted in Attwood and Markus, *The Struggle for Aboriginal Rights*, 79.

48. There are also some examples of Aboriginal women being singled out for special attention. See, e.g., Attwood, "Biography of Bessy Cameron."

49. Meeting minutes of BPA, July 30, 1860, August 20, 1860, September 3, 1860, September 17, 1860, May 27, 1861, June 17, 1861, and July 29, 1861, item 1, B314, NAAV. See also Christie, *Aborigines in Colonial Victoria*, 173. In 1821 two Tasmanian Aboriginal boys were sent to England for further education by Robert Knopwood, who ran the Orphan School in Hobart. One died in England, and the other died soon after his return to Hobart six years later. Ryan, *Aboriginal Tasmanians*, 79.

50. Secretary of the Department of Education to Mr. W. Dunstan, Head Teacher, Lake Condah Primary School, January 10, 1887, item 585, VPRS 796, PROV, 19.

51. Walter M. Gamble, Inspector of Schools to F. A. Hagenauer, March 21, 1899, Unit 1, VPRS 1694, PROV.

52. "Thirty-fifth Report of the BPA," *VPP* 4 (1899–1900): 5; "Thirty-seventh Report of the BPA," *VPP* 3 (1900–1901): 5; and "Forty-fourth Report of the BPA," *Victorian Votes and Proceedings* 1 (1909): 6.

53. Fletcher, *Documents in the History of Aboriginal Education*, 112–14.

54. *Australian Dictionary of Biography*, 12:303–5.

55. "Aboriginal Department—Information Contained in Report for the Year Ended 31st December, 1924," *QPP* 1 (1925): 6.

56. Paddy Cahill to Baldwin Spencer, November 18, 1916, item 4, box 1, Spencer Papers, Australian Institute of Aboriginal and Torres Strait Islander Studies, as quoted in McGregor, *Imagined Destinies*, 96.

57. "Annual Report of the Chief Protector of Aboriginals for 1904," *QPP* 1 (1905): 17.

58. "Report on the Administration of the Northern Territory for the Year Ended 30th June, 1932," *CPP* 3 (1932–33): 8.

59. M. Moorhouse, protector of Aborigines to chief protector of Aborigines, Port Phillip, April 10, 1849, colonial secretary's in-letters, 4/1141.2, New South Wales State Archives as quoted in Fletcher, *Documents in the History of Aboriginal Education*, 38.

60. William Shelley to Governor Macquarie, April 8, 1814, Commonwealth of Australia, *Historical Records of Australia* 7, ser. 1, 370–71.

61. Petition of white residents of Gulargambone to Minister of Education, September 10, 1919, Gulargambone School Files, box 5, New South Wales State Archives, as quoted in Fletcher, *Documents in the History of Aboriginal Education*, 123. See this volume and Fletcher, *Clean, Clad, and Courteous* for many more examples.

6. Regulating Aboriginal Marriages in Victoria

1. Statement of the BPA, May 7, 1884, Unit 266, VPRS 10265, PROV, emphasis in original, quoted in Chesterman and Galligan, *Citizens without Rights*, 19.

2. Aborigines Act, 1869, section 8.

3. "Twenty-third Report of the Board for the Protection of Aborigines," *Victorian Parliamentary Papers* 2 (1887): 3.

4. Often these so-called orphans were merely children the BPA felt were more likely to be assimilated away from their parents.

5. "Thirty-fourth Report of the Board for the Protection of Aborigines," *VPP* 3 (1898): 4.

6. Memo to H. P. Keogh, March 14, 1910, item 8, BPA Letterbooks, B329, Central Board for the Board for the Protection of Aborigines, Correspondence Files, NAAV.

7. See, e.g., Minutes of the meetings of the BPA, February 3, 1876, May 11, 1881, November 1, 1882, December 6, 1882, and June 8, 1905, items 3 and 5, B314, NAAV.

8. "Coranderrk Aboriginal Station: Report of the Board," *VPP* 2, no. 5 (1882–83): 91.

9. A. M. A. Page to John Heinrich Stähle, August 28, 1888, item 4, B329, NAAV.

10. Friedrich A. Hagenauer to Tocas Johnson, May 28, 1897, item 7, B329, NAAV.

11. Hagenauer to Constable J. Akeroyd, June 1, 1897, item 60, box 4, B313/1, NAAV, emphasis in original.

12. Hagenauer to Miss Agnes Hamilton, March 24, 1893, item 180, B329, NAAV.

13. Memo to H. P. Keogh, March 14, 1910, item 8, B329, NAAV.

14. Hagenauer to Page, June 9, 1886, item 180, box 11, B313/1, NAAV.

15. "Twenty-fourth Report of the BPA," *VPP* 2 (1888): 3.

16. Minutes of meeting of the BPA, June 6, 1888, item 4, B314, NAAV.

17. "Twenty-fourth Report of the BPA," *VPP* 2 (1888): 8.

18. Minutes of meeting of the BPA, October 15, 1869, item 2, B314; Thomas Harris to BPA, February 26, 1882; and Strickland to A. M. Page, March 13, 1882, items 192 and 193, box 11, B313/1, NAAV.

19. Apart from the four men described in this chapter, there is mention of "Young Robertson," son of a "half caste man and a white mother" who lived on a farm near Ballarat. Hagenauer to BPA, May 31, 1892, Unit 1, VPRS 1694, PROV. A "George Youle" is listed as married to a white woman in the census table published in the BPA's annual report for 1877. "Thirteenth Report of the BPA," *VPP* 3 (1877–78): 12. In 1861 it was reported that a young white girl had left her home near the Goulburn River and "fled to the Bush" with a Aboriginal man. Minutes of meetings of BPA, September 16, 1861 and November 4, 1861, item 2, B314, NAAV.

20. "Royal Commission on the Aborigines," *VPP* 3 (1877–78): 3.

21. "Thirteenth Report of the BPA," *VPP* 3 (1877–78): 12, and "Fourteenth Report of the BPA," *VPP* 3 (1878): 12.

22. T. Braham to J. Dwyer, April 15, 1877, item 50, box 3, B313/1, NAAV.

23. Form from the Office of Lands and Survey, Melbourne, reg. no. 3576, item 50, box 3, B313/1, NAAV.

24. W. Goodall to A. M. A. Page, July 4, 1877, item 50, box 3, B313/1, NAAV.

25. James Acussin[?], William Good, Frank Blair, John Ross, and Harry Sanders to Page, July 4, 1877, item 50, box 3, B313/1, NAAV.

26. J. E. Goodall to Page, July 9, 1877, item 50, box 3, B313/1, NAAV.

27. Minutes of meeting of the BPA, July 20, 1877, item 3, B314, NAAV.

28. John Dawson, William Manfold, Jonny Castello, Pompy Austin, Jonny Stuart, Thomas Kid, Sam Robinson, John Brawn, Ricke Manfold, Colin Hood, John Ross, William Good, Henry Dawson, James Dawson, James Lancaster, Baxter Gouner, Jack Gibe, Tommy Willow, King Dave, Walter Johnson to Page, July 27, 1877, item 50, box 3, B313/1, NAAV.

29. Alex Dennis to Page, June 29 and July 10, 1879, item 39, B313/1, NAAV.

30. "(Eliminyt) Colac Inspection, 1922," item 227A, B313/1, NAAV.

31. The Victorian Birth, Death, and Marriage Records have registrations of George, born 1874, Louisa Catherine, born 1877, Richard, born 1878, Henry, born 1882, and Ellen, born 1884. All were registered in Colac. The BPA's minutes mention that the Sharps had eight children in September 1892. Minutes of meeting of BPA, September 7, 1892, item 4, B314, NAAV.

32. See minutes of meeting of BPA, October 1, 1879, item 3; February 14, 1890, item 4, B314; and "(Eliminyt) Colac Inspection, 1922," item 227A, box 14, B313/1, NAAV. The surname of this family was spelled in various ways in the records of the BPA. I have adopted the spelling used by Joseph Crough in the most recent correspondence I could find in 1919. The name was also spelled Crow and Crowe.

33. Minutes of meeting of BPA, November 5, 1890, item 4, B314, NAAV.

34. F. A. Hagenauer to the Chief Secretary, July 29, 1902, item 227A, box 14, B313/1, NAAV.

35. Hagenauer to J. Crow, August 12, 1892, item 5, B329, NAAV. The Croughs were again threatened with the loss of their land to "another . . . family who will be glad to receive it" if they did not stop "continually absenting" themselves from the reserve in April 1894. W. J. Dickenwood to Mrs. J. Crowe, April 6, 1894, item 6, B329, NAAV.

36. Wm. J. Dickenwood to J. Crowe, March 8, 1893, item 6, B329, NAAV.

37. Hagenauer to Mrs. J. Crowe, June 16, 1893, item 6, B329, NAAV.

38. For example, in 1910 J. Ditchburn of the BPA wrote to Joseph Crough to inform him that as Mrs. Crough was in Colac Hospital suffering from some kind of fever, it had been decided that four of his children should be sent to Coranderrk. J. Ditchburn to J. Crowe, March 9, 1910, item 8, B329, NAAV.

39. In 1892 Hagenauer paid for the construction of an additional room in the Sharps' house for Richard's brother Jack to live in. This generosity was no doubt prompted by the fact that Jack was classified as full descent and was therefore entitled to support by the BPA under law. See F. A. Hagenauer to R. Sharp, August 17, 1892, item 5, B329 and minutes of meeting of the BPA, September 7, 1892, item 4, B314, item 4, NAAV.

40. Hagenauer to Sharp, July 4, 1893, item 6, B329, NAAV.

41. Minutes of meeting of the BPA, June 4, 1890, item 4, B314, NAAV.

42. Minutes of meeting of the BPA, March 6, 1895, item 4, B314, NAAV.

43. Hagenauer to Sharp, January 18, 1896, item 7, B329, NAAV.

44. Hagenauer to Mrs. C. Sharp, March 19, 1896, item 7, B329, NAAV.

45. Hagenauer to J. Crough, May 7, 1897, item 7, B329, NAAV.

46. Joseph Crough to E. H. Parker, August 12, 1919, item 227A, box 14, B313/1, NAAV.

47. Undated note, item 227A, box 14, B313/1, NAAV.

48. According to the records, the Robinsons' first two children, Emily and William, had been born in 1870 and 1871, respectively, and so were adults at this time. It is not clear

whether they were still living with their parents, and a gap of twenty or so years between children seems improbable. The possibility exists that William was the "Young Robertson" mentioned in Hagenauer to BPA, May 31, 1892, Unit 1, VPRS 1694, PROV. Their third child, Mary Edith, was born on the first day of 1893.

49. Hagenauer to Mr. J. Robinson, January 22, 1892, item 5, B329, NAAV.

50. Minutes of meeting of the BPA, August 1, 1894, item 4, B314, NAAV.

51. Minutes of meeting of the BPA, March 6, 1895, item 4, B314, NAAV.

52. Hagenauer to Mrs. Saunders, August 2, 1894, item 6, B329, NAAV.

53. D. J. Slattery, J. Akeroyd and I. Helpman to the BPA, October 1, 1898, item 60, box 4, B313/1, NAAV.

54. Hagenauer to D. J. Slattery, July 13, 1897, item 7, B329, NAAV.

55. Hagenauer to Slattery, September 23, 1897, item 7, B329, NAAV.

56. Minutes of meeting of BPA, October 13, 1897, item 5, B314, NAAV.

57. Akeroyd and Slattery to Hagenauer, January 10, 1898, item 60, box 4, B313/1, NAAV.

58. Minutes of meeting of BPA, February 9, 1898, item 5, B314, NAAV.

59. "Robinson Family," October 1, 1898, item 638, Aboriginal Case Files, B337/0, NAAV.

60. J. Ditchburn, acting secretary, to Mrs. J. Crowe, August 10, 1909, item 8, B329, NAAV.

61. "Coranderrk Aboriginal Station. Report of the Board," VPP 2, no. 5 (1882–83): 193. George Briggs told the committee that his family was originally from Tasmania, most probably the same Briggs family that Norman B. Tindale identified in his exhaustive study of the genealogical history of the small community of people living on the Bass Strait Islands in the 1930s. Tindale recorded that the Briggs family went to Victoria before 1865 and their descendants had mostly congregated at Cumeragunja in New South Wales. See Tindale, "Growth of a People: Formation and Development of a Hybrid Aboriginal and White Stock on the Islands of Bass Strait, Tasmania, 1815–1949: Results of the Harvard–Adelaide Universities Anthropological Expedition, 1938–1939," 21. Diane Barwick mentioned that Briggs was of Woiworung descent in her *Rebellion at Coranderrk*, 186.

62. Blake, *Place Names of Victoria*, 160, 235.

63. Female Patient Case Books, Kew Asylum, vol. 6, VPRS 7397/P1, PROV.

64. Police Report of Lunatic Prisoner, June 21, 1881, Admittance Warrants, Kew Asylum, box 18, VPRS 7456/P1, PROV.

65. Female Patient Case Books, Kew Asylum, vol. 6, VPRS 7397/P1, PROV.

66. Leave of Absence Register, Kew Asylum, vol. 1, VPRS 7451/P1, PROV.

67. Strickland to Page, July 27, 1881, item 191, box 11, B313/1, NAAV.

68. Strickland to Page, February 6, 1882, item 191, box 11, B313/1, NAAV.

69. Maria L. Beggs to Mrs. Briggs, September 1882, item 199, box 12, B313/1, NAAV.

70. Page to Mrs. Maria L. Beggs, September 9, 1882, item 3, B329, NAAV.

71. M. Woods to A. M. A. Page, September 25, 1882, item 199, box 12, B313/1, NAAV.

72. M. L. Beggs to BPA, September 14, 1882; A. M. A. Page to Sgt. M. Woods, September 27, 1882; M. Woods to A. M. A. Page, September 30, 1882, item 199, box 12, B313/1, NAAV.

73. William Goodall to A. M. A. Page, September 29, 1882, item 199, and Mrs. D. Brand to A. M. A. Page, October 18, 1882, item 200, box 12, B313/1, NAAV.

74. Coranderrk Dormitory Reports, 1884, item 218, box 13, B313/1, NAAV.

75. A. M. A. Page to Mrs. Maria Beggs, n.d., item 4, B329, NAAV.

76. Crawford Paseo, Industrial and Reformatory Schools Department to the BPA, December 10, 1885, item 219, box 13, B313/1, NAAV.

77. William Moss, Hon. Sec of Victorian Deaf and Dumb Institution to A. M. Page, January 19, 1882, item 192, box 11, B313/1, NAAV.

78. Minutes of meeting of BPA, February 11, 1908, item 6, B314.

79. *Victorian Parliamentary Debates*, 1910, 1386

80. *Victorian Parliamentary Debates*, 1910, 1599.

7. White Women Married to Aboriginal Men

1. Fraser, *Husbands*, 32.

2. Hill, *Great Australian Loneliness*, 244–46. Hill did, however, publish a photograph of the couple in the book.

3. Kate Darian-Smith, "'Rescuing' Barbara Thompson and Other White Women: Captivity Narratives on Australian Frontiers," 110.

4. Hill, *Great Australian Loneliness*, 247.

5. His father was a Queensland-born Aboriginal man whose occupation as an itinerant rural worker had caused Jimmy's frequent changes of school. His mother's father was an Irishman named Jack Fitzgerald, from whom Jimmy is supposed to have inherited his red hair. Cameron Roy and Kathielyn Job, *Around the Black Stump*, 97.

6. "Aborigines (Report of Board for Protection of, for 1883–84)," *JLCNSW* 26, pt. 3 (1883–84): 1649.

7. "Aborigines (Report of Board for Protection of, for 1898)," *JLCNSW* 61, pt. 1 (1899): 3.

8. See Read, *A Hundred Years' War: The Wiradjuri People and the State.*

9. *Sydney Morning Herald*, November 23, 1900, 7–8.

10. *Sydney Morning Herald*, November 24, 1900, 5–6.

11. *Sydney Morning Herald*, November 23, 1900, 7–8.

12. *Sydney Morning Herald*, November 24, 1900, 5–6.

13. Keneally, "Doing Research for Historical Novels." See Keneally, *The Chant of Jimmy Blacksmith* and the full-length feature film based on the book, produced and directed by Fred Schepisi, Arthouse Productions, 1978.

14. Keneally, *The Chant of Jimmie Blacksmith*, 59.

15. See Reynolds, "Jimmy Governor and Jimmy Blacksmith"; Tiffin, "Victims Black and White: Thomas Keneally's *The Chant of Jimmy Blacksmith.*"

16. See, e.g., Clune, *Jimmy Governor*, 13.

17. Rolls, *A Million Wild Acres*, 222; Reynolds, "Jimmy Governor and Jimmie Blacksmith," 20; and Wood, "The 'Breelong Blacks,'" 99–100.

18. *Sydney Morning Herald*, July 25, 1900, 8. Ethel also testified that "Mrs. Mawbey and Miss Kerz never said anything to me about Jimmy. They said it was a wonder a nice looking girl like me would throw myself away on a blackfellow. They only said that once to me. That did not make me unhappy, nor did I grow unhappy at Breelong because of the taunts. It made no difference between me and my husband." *Sydney Morning Herald*, November 23, 1900, 7.

19. *Sydney Morning Herald*, November 24, 1900, 11.

20. Morris, *Domesticating Resistance*, 44–48.

21. "I was two years at Cassilis police station, employed as a tracker and then went back to Wollar. After a time I went to Gulgong wood-cutting for a man named Starr; then I went wool-rolling at Digilibar, then back to Gulgong. I got married and followed various occupations up to the time I went to work for Mr. Mawbey." *Sydney Morning Herald,* October 29, 1900, 7–8.

22. *Mudgee Guardian,* August 16, 1900, 3, 21; September 3, 1900, 2; September 24, 1900, 2; October 1, 1900, 2.

23. Fletcher, *Documents in the History of Aboriginal Education,* 86–87, 107–9.

24. *Dubbo Liberal,* July 25, 1900, 2.

25. Morris, *Domesticating Resistance,* 110–15.

26. *Mudgee Guardian,* August 9, 1900, 3.

27. *Mudgee Guardian,* August 16, 1900. 21.

28. *Mudgee Guardian,* September 3, 1900, 3.

29. Corrective Services, Darlinghurst Goal, *Condemned Prisoners' Daily Record, 1892–1903,* 5/1739, and *Diary Kept by Officer Doing Duty over Jimmy Governor, 6 December 1900–12 January 1901,* 6/1029, Archives Office of New South Wales, Sydney.

30. Personal communication with Cathy Dunn, May 10, 1997 and *Australian Dictionary of Biography,* 9:62.

31. Halse, "The Reverend Ernest Gribble and Race Relations in Northern Australia," 55.

32. Halse, "The Reverend Ernest Gribble," 188–92, and Registration of Marriage Certificate, no. 150, 1907, New South Wales Registry Office.

33. E. R. Gribble, Journal 1902, ABMP, box 35(69), item 10/7, Mitchell Library, Sydney.

34. Thomson, *Reaching Back,* 37.

35. The minutes of a meeting of the Executive Council of the Australian Board of Missions held on November 8, 1907, records an application by Ernest for a leave of absence for his sister. It was granted for a period of three months. ABMP, box 35 (69).

36. ABMP, box 35 (69), and Halse, "The Reverend Ernest Gribble," 191.

37. Halse, "The Reverend Ernest Gribble," 190.

38. Halse, "The Reverend Ernest Gribble," 190–91. This is hardly surprising when the extensive rules and regulations for mission workers at Yarrabah included admonitions to "Remember that 'Example' is better than Precept," "Be careful in manner, work, habits, and conversation," and "Be patient, watchful, prayerful, and zealous." *Yarrabah, Church of England Aboriginal Mission: Rules and Regulations.*

39. "Aborigines (Report of Board for the Protection of, for year 1910)," NSWPP 2 (1912): 3.

40. "Aborigines (Report of Board for the Protection of, for year 1911)," NSWPP 1 (1912): 3.

41. *Sydney Morning Herald,* November 13, 1928, January 12 and 31, 1929.

42. Julie Marcus, "The Beauty, Simplicity, and Honour of Truth," 117–18.

8. Solving the "Indian Problem"

1. Prucha, *Great Father,* 2:618.

2. Adams, *Education for Extinction,* 9–10.

3. *Twenty-first Annual Report of the Indian Rights Association, 1903,* 3, IRAP.

4. *Proceedings of the Ninth Annual Meeting of the Lake Mohonk Conference, 1891,* 113.

5. *Proceedings of the Eleventh Annual Meeting of the Lake Mohonk Conference, 1893,* 143.

6. *Proceedings of the Third Annual Meeting of the Lake Mohonk Conference, 1885*, 27–28.

7. Garrett, "The Indian Policy in Its Relations to Crime and Pauperism," 25, 29.

8. *Proceedings of the Fourth Annual Lake Mohonk Conference, 1886*, 9, 43–44; *Proceedings of the Seventh Annual Meeting of the Lake Mohonk Conference, 1889*, 117–18.

9. Lyman Abbott to Richard Henry Pratt, June 30, 1904, box 1, folder 4, RHPP.

10. Leupp, *The Indian and His Problem*, 343.

11. *Proceedings of the Thirteenth Annual Meeting of the Lake Mohonk Conference, 1895*, 25.

12. *Proceedings of the Third Annual Lake Mohonk Conference, 1885*, 44.

13. *Address to the Public of the Lake Mohonk Conference, 1883*, 9–10.

14. *Fourteenth Annual Report of the Indian Rights Association, 1896*, 10, 12, IRAP.

15. *Second Annual Report of the Indian Rights Association, 1884*, 5, IRAP.

16. Painter, *A Visit to the Mission Indians of Southern California, and Other Western Tribes*, 5, IRAP.

17. Various authors, *Captain Pratt and His Work for Indian Education*, pt. 2, 7, IRAP.

18. S. C. Armstrong, *Report of a Trip Made in Behalf of the Indian Rights Association to Some Indian Reservations of the Southwest by S. C. Armstrong, Principal of Hampton School, Va.*, 26, IRAP.

19. *Twenty-ninth Annual Report of the Indian Rights Association, 1911*, 5, IRAP.

20. *Twenty-eighth Annual Report of the Indian Rights Association, 1910*, 3, IRAP.

21. *Fourteenth Annual Report of the Indian Rights Association, 1896*, 10, IRAP.

22. House, *Annual Report of the Commissioner of Indian Affairs*, 51st Cong., 1st sess., 1889, 3.

23. Prucha, *Great Father*, 2:701.

24. House, *Annual Report of the Commissioner of Indian Affairs*, 51st Cong., 2d sess., 1890, vi, and House, *Annual Report of the Commissioner of Indian Affairs*, 52nd Cong., 1st sess., 1891, 4.

25. Prucha, *Great Father*, 2:723.

26. House, *Annual Report of the Commissioner of Indian Affairs*, 58th Cong., 2d sess., 1903, 2–3.

27. House, *Annual Report of the Commissioner of Indian Affairs*, 59th Cong., 1st sess., 1905, 17

28. House, *Annual Report of the Commissioner of Indian Affairs*, 60th Cong., 1st sess., 1907, 21.

29. House, *Annual Report of the Commissioner of Indian Affairs*, 62d Cong., 2d sess., 1911, 3.

30. House, "Fiftieth Annual Report of the Board of Indian Commissioners," in *Annual Report of the Commissioner of Indian Affairs*, 66th Cong., 2d sess., 1919, 218.

31. See, e.g., House, *Annual Report of the Commissioner of Indian Affairs*, 46th Cong, 2d sess., 1879, 77; House, "Rights of Children of Indian Women and U.S. Citizens Married since August 9, 1888," in *Annual Report of the Commissioner of Indian Affairs*, 53rd Cong., 3d sess., 1894, 65–66; Senate, *Memorial of Wilbur F. Bryant, in Case of Louis Riel, on Naturalization of Persons of Mixed Indian and White Blood*, 50th Cong., 2d sess., 1888; Senate, *Correspondence on Sioux Mixed Bloods*, 53d Cong., 2d sess., 1894; and Senate, *Report by Mr. Allen from the Committee on Indian Affairs*, 52d Cong., 1st sess., 1896, which noted that the term *Indian* "does not seem at all times to have been accurately defined in our legislative history" and attempted to use legal decisions concerning African American identity as precedents.

32. House, *Annual Report of the Commissioner of Indian Affairs*, 65th Cong., 3d sess., 1918, 336.

33. *First Annual Report of the Indian Rights Association, 1883*, 25, IRAP.

34. *Second Annual Report of the Indian Rights Association, 1884*, 19; *Fifth Annual Report of the Indian Rights Association, 1887*, 21, IRAP.

35. House, *Annual Report of the Commissioner of Indian Affairs*, 50th Cong., 2d sess., 1888, 940.

36. *Annual Report of the Commissioner of Indian Affairs*, 1888, 13.

37. *Twenty-first Annual Report of the Indian Rights Association, 1903*, 18, IRAP.

38. *Twenty-third Annual Report of the Indian Rights Association, 1905*, 46, 67, IRAP.

39. *Proceedings of the Seventh Annual Lake Mohonk Conference, 1889*, 117–8.

40. *Fifteenth Annual Report of the Indian Rights Association, 1897*, 28, IRAP.

41. *Letter of Philip C. Garrett and Herbert Welsh to the Members of the Fifty-fourth Congress, Feb. 13, 1897*, 1–2.

42. Leupp and Welsh, *Let There Be No Backward Step*, 2–5, IRAP.

43. *Proceedings of the Tenth Annual Meeting of the Lake Mohonk Conference, 1892*, 87.

44. *Annual Report of the Commissioner of Indian Affairs*, 1911, 71.

45. House, *Annual Report of the Commissioner of Indian Affairs*, 47th Cong., 2d sess., 1882, 334–35.

46. House, *Annual Report of the Commissioner of Indian Affairs*, 49th Cong., 1st sess., 1885, 582–83.

47. House, *Annual Report of the Commissioner of Indian Affairs*, 52d Cong., 2d sess., 1892, 760–61.

48. Cott, *Public Vows*, 26, 120–23.

49. Gould, *The Mismeasure of Man*.

50. Cecelski and Tyson, *Democracy Betrayed*, x.

51. W. E. B. Du Bois, *The Souls of Black Folk*, 9.

52. *Annual Report of the Commissioner of Indian Affairs*, 1905, 1.

53. *Annual Report of the Commissioner of Indian Affairs*, 1885, 6–7.

54. Adams, "Education in Hues," 165, 175–76.

55. *Proceedings of the Twenty-second Annual Meeting of the Lake Mohonk Conference, 1904*, 35.

56. *Proceedings of the Fourth Annual Meeting of the Lake Mohonk Conference, 1886*, 9.

57. *Proceedings of the Eighth Annual Meeting of the Lake Mohonk Conference, 1890*, 84–85.

58. Archdeacon, *Becoming American*, 113.

59. The "nonwhite" status of immigrants during this period has been explored by a number of scholars including Karen Brodkin, *How the Jews Became White Folks and What That Says about Race in America*; Ignatiev, *How the Irish Became White*; Jacobson, *Whiteness of a Different Color*; and Roediger, *The Wages of Whiteness*.

60. Gerstle, *American Crucible*, 45.

61. *Proceedings of the Fourteenth Annual Meeting of the Lake Mohonk Conference, 1896*, 37.

62. *Proceedings of the Fifteenth Annual Meeting of the Lake Mohonk Conference, 1897*, 73–74.

63. Dippie, *Vanishing American*, 248.

64. The most blatant example of this kind of thinking is the 1924 Virginian antimiscegenation statute that excepted white people with 1/16th Native American blood—a category that included many of the states' white elite who claimed descent from John Rolfe

and Pocahontas. See Wadlington, "The Loving Case"; Wallenstein, "Race, Marriage, and the Law of Freedom"; and Tilton, *Pocahontas*.

65. Smits, "'Squaw Men,' 'Half-Breeds,' and Amalgamators," 57.

66. Dippie, *Vanishing American*, 250, 257.

67. Wolfe, *Settler Colonialism*, 2.

68. Wallenstein, "Native Americans Are White, African Americans Are Not," 56.

69. Wolfe, "Land, Labor, and Difference," 867.

70. *QJSAI* 4, no. 4 (October–December 1916): 303–4.

71. *Annual Report of Board of Indian Commissioners*, 1885, 132.

9. Absorbing the "Aboriginal Problem"

1. Tasmania, the smallest state, had an important role to play in keeping what Russell McGregor has labeled the "doomed race theory" alive, having in a sense "proved" it by allowing the rest of the world to believe that the Tasmanian Aborigines had become "extinct" with the death on May 8, 1876, of the "last" full-descent person (a woman called Truganini). McGregor, *Imagined Destinies*, 50–51.

2. For example, it was argued in the South Australian state parliament: "Many well known ethnologists have advocated the assimilation of our Australian natives into the white race. Some people hold up their hands in horror at the thought of the black race mingling with the white, but ethnologists and archaeologists have agreed that it is a logical solution of this vexed problem. The Australian aboriginal is different from the negroid races of other countries, as he does not throw back." *South Australian Parliamentary Debates*, 1938, 845.

3. Tony Austin has analyzed the Northern Territory's policies under chief protector Cecil Cook as an "eugenicist solution." Austin, "Cecil Cook, Scientific Thought, and 'Half-Castes' in the Northern Territory, 1927–1939," and "Genocide and Schooling in Capricornia: Educating the Stolen Generation." Stephen Garton and Russell McGregor, however, have pointed out several reasons why absorption was not strictly eugenic thinking and stress the importance of not labeling it as such. Garton, "Writing Eugenics: A History of Classifying Practices," 9–18, and McGregor, "'Breed Out the Colour.'"

4. Aborigines Protection Act, 1886 (Western Australia). Accurate measurements of the size of the Aboriginal population living in Western Australia during this period do not exist. In 1891 and 1901, the state government counted only those "full-bloods" living in settled areas and included "half-castes" as part of the white population. They counted 6,245 and 6,212, respectively, while the white population hovered around 200,000. Fraser, *Western Australian Year-Book for 1902–04*, 110, and *Statistical Register of Western Australia for 1901 and Previous Years*, 5.

5. Roth, "Royal Commission on the Condition of the Natives," 25.

6. Haebich, *For Their Own Good*, 85.

7. Vanden Driesen, *Essays on Immigration Policy and Population in Western Australia, 1850–1901*, 158; Fraser, *Western Australian Year-Book for 1902–04*, 297.

8. See the evidence of Thomas Houlahan, John Byrne, Robert Anderson, and Henry Charles Prinsep, "Western Australian Royal Commission on the Condition of the Natives," *Report of the Royal Commission on the Condition of the Natives* (Perth: Government Printer, 1905), n.p.

9. *WAPD* 28 (1905): 324.

10. *WAPD* 83 (1929): 2105.

11. *WAPD* 28 (1905): 427.

12. "Report of the Government Resident for the Year 1910," *CPP* 3, no. 66 (1911): 42.

13. The Northern Territory Aboriginals Act of 1910 (South Australia) defined who was to be classed as Aboriginal, set up a department to control and "promote the welfare" of Northern Territory Aborigines, prevented white people from moving Aboriginal people around the country and from entering reserves, gave the chief protector the power to say where Aboriginal people could live and for whom they could work, made it an offense to sell a gun to an Aboriginal person, restricted Aboriginal women from marrying non-Aborigines, and set up a system to make the white fathers of mixed-descent children contribute to their maintenance. A 1911 ordinance, passed by the Commonwealth government, added to rather than replaced the 1910 act. It gave the chief protector greater powers over Aboriginal people's lives and changed the system of licensing white employers to use Aboriginal labor.

14. Spencer, "Preliminary Report on the Aboriginals of the Northern Territory," 43.

15. Spencer, "Preliminary Report," 46.

16. Neville, *Australia's Coloured Minority*, 56.

17. *WAPD* 98 (1936): 823.

18. *WAPD* 98 (1936): 987.

19. "Report on the Administration of North Australia for the Year Ended the 30th June, 1930," *CPP* 4, no. 216 (1929–31): 6.

20. Cook to Morley, April 28, 1931, as quoted in Austin, *I Can Picture the Old Home So Clearly*, 133–34.

21. Powell, *Far Country*, 126.

22. Choo, *Mission Girls*, 113–14.

23. *WAPD* 98 (1936): 987.

24. Petition presented to the Royal Commission into the Treatment of Aborigines at Broome by Aboriginal Women of the Town, 1935, held in the Betty Rischbieth Papers, National Library of Australia, quoted in Catriona Elder, "'It Was Hard for Us to Marry Aboriginal': Some Meaning of Singleness for Aboriginal Women in Australia in the 1930s," *Lilith* 8 (1993): 121. See also Choo, *Mission Girls*, 118–20, and "Report of the Royal Commissioner Appointed to Investigate, Report, and Advise upon Matters in Relation to the Condition and Treatment of Aborigines," *Western Australian Votes and Proceedings*, printed paper no. 2, 1936.

25. Choo, *Mission Girls*, 117.

26. See Rajkowski, *Linden Girl*.

27. Cowlishaw, *Love against the Law*, esp. 58–60, 72–75.

28. Home Affairs Department Files, Northern Territory, "Marriages with Aboriginals," A1 1912/3519, NAAC.

29. Cecil Cook to Alfred Anderson, May 31, 1932, and Anderson to the Minister of Internal Affairs, August 27, 1932, Home Affairs Department Files, Northern Territory, "A. Anderson Appln. Permission to Marry Female Aborigine (Alice)," A1 1932/3578, NAAC.

30. Commonwealth of Australia, *Aboriginal Welfare*, 10–11.

31. Commonwealth of Australia, *Aboriginal Welfare*, 14.

32. Christie, *Aborigines in Colonial Victoria*, 175.

33. There had been a large influx of non-European, predominantly Chinese, immigrants to Victoria during the gold rush decades (1850s–1880s), but by 1891 the Chinese population had fallen from 25,424 in 1857 to 7,349 in 1901, making up less than 0.8 percent of the total population. Cronin, *Colonial Casualties*, 136, 140. New South Wales did have a significant Chinese population during the mid-nineteenth century due to the gold rushes, when there were around 17,000 Chinese in the state. In 1881 white anxieties about this group resulted in the Chinese Influx Act, which restricted their immigration, all but solving the "problem" by the time the colony began to concentrate on assimilating its indigenous population.

34. Christie, *Aborigines in Colonial Victoria*, 201.

35. "Royal Commission on the Aborigines," *VPP* 3 (1877–78): 111.

36. "Royal Commission on the Aborigines," 52.

37. Chesterman and Galligan, *Citizens without Rights*, 20.

38. "Aborigines (Report of Board for 1898)," *JLCNSW* 61, pt. 1 (1899): 3.

39. "Aborigines (Report of the Board for the Protection of, for Year 1908)," *NSWPP* 2 (1909): 4.

40. Morris, *Domesticating Resistance*, 110. The 1909 act defined an "Aborigine" as any "full-blooded aboriginal native of Australia, and any person apparently having an admixture of aboriginal blood who applies for or is in receipt of rations or aid from the board or is residing on a reserve." The measures it put in place to remove "able-bodied" Aboriginal people from the reserves were even more drastic than Victoria's policies, which at least gave some years of warning before people of mixed descent had to vacate the reserves. The act also gave the board the power to dictate where Aborigines could camp, and made it illegal, as in the other states, to supply Aborigines with alcohol.

41. Attwood, Burrage, Burrage, and Stokie, *A Life Together, a Life Apart*, 8.

42. Commonwealth of Australia, *Aboriginal Welfare*, 14.

43. Like its rejected predecessor, the Aborigines Act, 1911 (South Australia) was very similar to the 1897 Queensland legislation. It created the Aborigines Department and a chief protector, who became the legal guardian of all children under twenty-one years. It made it an offense to remove any Aboriginal, female "half-caste," or child from a district; attempted to keep non-Aboriginals out of reserves, made provisions for treating contagious diseases, and attempted to regulate employment through inspections rather than a permit system. It gave the department the power to remove any Aboriginal person from a reserve or force them to stay on one, to move Aboriginal camps away from towns, and to allot blocks not exceeding 160 acres to Aboriginals. Provisions were also included which forced fathers of mixed-descent children to contribute to their maintenance.

44. See "Report of the Select Committee of the Legislative Council on the Aborigines Bill," *South Australian Parliamentary Papers* 2, no. 77a (1899); Austin, *Simply the Survival of the Fittest*, 168–69; *South Australian Parliamentary Debates*, 1899, 38, and 1911–12, 231.

45. "Progress Report of the Royal Commission on the Aborigines," *South Australian Parliamentary Papers* 2, no. 26 (1913): 12.

46. *Aborigines (Training of Children) Act, 1923* (SA).

47. Commonwealth of Australia, *Aboriginal Welfare*, 10.

48. Read, "The Return of the Stolen Generation," 9.

49. Human Rights and Equal Opportunity Commission, *Bringing Them Home*, 272–73.

50. The 1897 act was used as the model for legislation passed in Western Australia (1905), South Australia (1910), and the Northern Territory (1911). It defined "Aborigines" and "half-castes" (placing many of the second category into the first, and therefore subjecting them to the act), attempted to segregate the races by creating reserves, appointed protectors, and made the employment of Aborigines dependent on a permit issued by a protector. It also made it an offense to "harbor" Aborigines or female "half-castes" (a hint here of anxieties about sexual relationships between white men and Aboriginal women), or to remove Aborigines from one district to another or out of the state, or to supply Aborigines with alcohol or opium. It also tightened controls of the employment of Aborigines on pearling and béche de mer vessels, forbade female Aborigines or half-castes or children from being employed on ships, made it an offense for anyone (except a superintendent or protector) to frequent a place where Aborigines or female "half-castes" were camped, made fathers of mixed-descent children liable for their support, and placed the burden of proof of age onto men accused of having carnal knowledge of underage Aboriginal girls.

51. For a discussion of anxieties surrounding relationships of Aboriginal women and Asian men in the far North, see Ganter, "Living an Immoral Life."

52. "Report of the Northern Protector of Aboriginals for 1899," *QVP* 5 (1900): 10.

53. "Report of the Northern Protector of Aboriginals for 1900," *QVP* 4, pt. 2 (1901), 9.

54. "Annual Report of the Northern Protector of Aboriginals for 1901," *QPP* 1 (1902): 7.

55. "Annual Report of the Northern Protector of Aboriginals for 1901," 8.

56. "Annual Report of the Northern Protector of Aboriginals for 1901," 9.

57. "Annual Report of the Chief Protector of Aboriginals for 1905," *QPP* (1906): 15.

58. "I lean strongly to the view that it is less cruel to these unfortunates to keep them among the race to which they belong, half by blood and almost wholly by nature, than to expect them to take a place with their white sisters, where uncongenial conditions and company condemn them very often to what can only be an unhappy lonely existence." "Annual Report of the Chief Protector of Aboriginals for the Year 1913," *QPP* 3 (1914): 11.

59. "Annual Report of the Chief Protector of Aboriginals for the Year 1916," *QPP* 3 (1917): 8.

60. "Aboriginal Department—Information Contained in the Report for the Year Ended 31st December, 1928," *QPP* 1 (1929): 5.

61. "Aboriginal Department—Information Contained in the Report for the Year Ended 31st December, 1931," *QPP* 1 (1932): 8.

62. "Aboriginal Department—Information Contained in the Report for the Year Ended 31st December, 1932," *QPP* 1 (1933): 9.

63. Although the only official criteria for accepting or rejecting applications for interracial marriages expressed in the protector's reports remained those given by Roth in 1901 (character, length of cohabitation, children, etc.), the differing policies of the three protectors between 1884 and 1939 are reflected in numbers and kinds of marriages approved by them. Until 1916, under the protectorships of Roth and Howard, in the first few years of Bleakley's office, the majority of marriages approved were to Pacific Islanders. From 1917, the majority of approved marriages were between Aboriginal women and Aborigines, or "half-castes" (presumably descended from European and Aboriginal parentage). By

1928, only marriages between Aboriginal women and Aboriginal men or men of mixed descent were approved. In the following decade growing numbers of such marriages took place (reaching a peak of 113 in 1936), while there were at most one or two cases of interracial marriage between Aboriginal women and other ethnic groups.

64. "Aboriginal Department—Information Contained in the Report for the Year Ended 31st December, 1936," QPP 2 (1937): 10.

65. "Aboriginal Department—Information Contained in the Report for the Year Ended 31st December, 1937," QPP 2 (1938): 11–12.

66. Commonwealth of Australia, *Aboriginal Welfare*, 8.

67. Chesterman and Galligan, *Citizens without Rights*, 31. The Northern Territory's Aboriginal population was merely *estimated* to be between 20,000 and 50,000. Queensland's figure was based on more reliable statistics.

68. In 1906 a government report estimated that over 5,000 Melanesian men were resident in Queensland. Approximately 20,000 Chinese people arrived in Queensland in the last decades of the nineteenth century, many attracted by the gold rushes of the period, although many returned home again after a short stay. Evans, Saunders, and Cronin, *Race Relations in Colonial Queensland*, 218, 332.

69. Henningham, "Perhaps If There Had Been More Women in the North, the Story Would Have Been Different," 257–58.

70. Bleakley, *The Aborigines of Australia*, 314.

71. J. T. Patten and W. Ferguson, "Citizen Rights for Aborigines!" The APA was not the only Aboriginal-run organization who lobbied for indigenous rights in this period. The Victorian-based Australian Aborigines League was an earlier and better-known advocate of Aboriginal rights in the 1930s. See *Sydney Morning Herald*, January 27, 1938, 6; McGregor, *Imagined Destinies*, 249–52; Markus, *Blood from a Stone*.

72. Patten and Ferguson, "Citizen Rights for Aborigines!"

73. See the *Sydney Morning Herald*, December 1, 1937, 16; June 27, 1938, 6; February 27, 1938, 17; January 3, 1940, 10; and "Notes of Deputation from Aborigines Progressive Association, 1st February 1938," Premier's Letters Received, file no. A27/915, Premier's Special Bundles: Treatment of Aborigines in NSW 1936–63, reel 1862, New South Wales State Archives, Sydney. The Aborigines' Welfare Board recorded William Ferguson and the APA's actions in their minutes but did not appear to see the need to do anything to prevent the organization's efforts. See Aborigines' Welfare Board Minute Books, April 13, 1934, March 13, 1935, November 3, 1937, January 5, 1938, May 4, 1938, and July 6, 1938, 4/7126–7, 4/8544, 4/8553, reels 2792 and 2793, New South Wales State Archives, Sydney. For more information about the activities of the APA, see *Australian Dictionary of Biography*, 8:487–88, 11:162–63, and Horner, *Vote Ferguson for Aboriginal Freedom*.

74. Patten and Ferguson, "Citizen Rights for Aborigines!"

75. "Halfcastes. By One of Them," *Australian Abo Call* 2 (May 1938): 4, original emphasis.

76. Horner and Langton, "The Day of Mourning."

77. Patten and Ferguson, "Citizen Rights for Aborigines!"

78. Bill Ferguson, "Give Us Justice! An Aborigine Appeals for His People," *Daily Telegraph*, October 15, 1937, clipping in Premier's Letters Received, file no. A27/915, Premier's

Special Bundles: Treatment of Aborigines in NSW 1936–63, reel 1862, New South Wales State Archives, Sydney.

79. *Australian Abo Call* 4 (July 1938): 3.

80. "Halfcastes," 4.

81. Other Aboriginal activists saw it differently. William Cooper, who campaigned from Melbourne in the 1930s, opposed ideas of biological absorption. Coming from a very different perspective than that of Patten and Ferguson, Cooper read the argument for biological absorption as one which assumed that people of mixed descent were somehow "inferior" to those of full Aboriginal descent, a view which he strenuously denied. Markus, *Blood from a Stone*, 185.

82. Wolfe, "Nation and MiscegeNation," 116.

83. Wolfe, "Land, Labor, and Difference," 866–905.

84. Chesterman and Galligan, *Citizens without Rights*, 124. See the comments of Bailey and Neville at the 1937 conference. Commonwealth of Australia, *Aboriginal Welfare*, 12.

Conclusion

1. House, *Annual Report of Commissioner of Indian Affairs*, 58th Cong., 3d sess., 1904, 30.

2. Churchill, "The Crucible of American Indian Identity," 46.

3. Jordan, *White over Black*, 581

4. Eastman, *Indian To-day*, 119–20. Another version of this anecdote survives: "Washington: Negro blood is the strongest blood in the world because it only takes a drop of it to turn a white man into a Negro. Eastman: Indian blood is stronger than Negro blood because it only takes fifty per cent Indian blood to get a Negro into the best society." Ralph Henry Gabriel to Eastman, May 16, 1941, folder 22, box 2, EGEC.

5. Wolfe, "Land, Labor, and Difference."

6. Human Rights and Equal Opportunity Commission, *Bringing Them Home*.

7. Niezen, *Spirit Wars*, 8.

8. Quoted in Churchill, *A Little Matter of Genocide*, 70. In his final chapter Churchill discusses at length the way in which this, the original definition of the word *genocide*, was redefined by the United Nations and academics over the last five decades.

9. Churchill, *A Little Matter of Genocide*, Moses, *Genocide and Settler Society*; and Reynolds, *An Indelible Stain?*

10. One significant American exception is Keetoowah Cherokee scholar Ward Churchill, who points out that the United States is the only global "superpower" not to have ratified the Convention on Prevention and Punishment of the Crime of Genocide, adopted by the United Nations in 1948, and ratified by over one hundred UN member states, including Australia, by 1990. As David Stannard points out in the preface to this work, Churchill is "a man looking for trouble." Churchill, *A Little Matter of Genocide*, xiii, 363–98.

11. For discussions of whether the definition of genocide can be applied to Australian history, see "Genocide? Australian Aboriginal History in International Perspective," a special section of *Aboriginal History* 25 (2001), and Moses, "An Antipodean Genocide?"

Selected Bibliography

Archives

Archives Office of New South Wales, Sydney. Premier's Letters Received, Premier's Special Bundles: Treatment of Aborigines in NSW 1936–1963, A27/915; Aborigines' Welfare Board Minute Books, 1934–1938, 4/7126-7, 4/8544, 4/8553; Corrective Services, Darlinghurst Gaol: *Condemned Prisoners' Daily Record, 1892–1903*, 5/1739; *Diary Kept by Officer Doing Duty over Jimmy Governor, 6 December 1900–12 January 1901*, 6/1029.

Beinecke Rare Book and Manuscript Library, Yale Collection of Western Americana, Yale University, New Haven, Connnecticut. Richard Henry Pratt Papers.

Department of the Interior Library, Washington DC. *Annual Reports of the Board of Indian Commissioners to the Secretary of the Interior*.

Hampton University Archives, Hampton, Virginia. *Annual Reports of Hampton Institute*; Caroline Andrus Collection; Discipline Books; Faculty Records; Newspaper Clippings; *Southern Workman*; Student Files; *Talks and Thoughts of the Hampton Indian Students*.

Historical Society of Pennsylvania, Philadelphia, Pennsylvania. Indian Rights Association Papers, 1864–1973.

Jones Library, Amherst, Massachusetts. Goodale Family Papers.

Library of Congress, Washington DC. Report of the Lake Mohonk Conference on the Indian and Other Dependent Peoples.

Mitchell Library, Sydney, New South Wales. Australian Board of Missions Papers.

National Archives and Records Administration, Washington DC. Carlisle Indian Industrial School Student Records, 1879–1918, RG 75; and Central Classified files, 1907–39, RG 75.

National Archives of Australia, Canberra, Australian Capital Territory. Home Affairs Department Files, Northern Territory: Marriages with Aboriginals (A1 1912/3519); A. Anderson Appln. Permission to Marry Female Aborigine (Alice)(A1 1932/3578).

National Archives of Australia, North Melbourne, Victoria. Central Board for the Protection of the Aborigines: Correspondence (B313/1); Minutes of Meetings (B314); Letterbooks (B329); and Aboriginal Case Files (B337/0).

New York State Archives, Albany, New York. Society of American Indians Records, 1911–1916.

Sophia Smith Collection of Smith College, Northampton, Massachusetts. Elaine Goodale Eastman Collection.

Victorian Public Record Office, North Melbourne, Victoria. Outward Correspondence–Primary Schools 1868–1938 (VPRS 796); Central Board for the Protection of the Aborigines Correspondence (VPRS 1694); Female Patient Case Books, Kew Asylum (VPRS 7397/P1); Leave of Absence Register of Kew Asylum (VPRS 7451/P1); and Admittance Warrants of Kew Asylum (VPRS 7456/P1).

Published Sources
Adams, David Wallace. *Education for Extinction: American Indians and the Boarding School Experience, 1875–1928.* Lawrence: University of Kansas Press, 1995.
———. "Education in Hues: Red and Black at Hampton Institute, 1878–1893." *South Atlantic Quarterly* 76, no. 2 (Spring 1977): 159–76.
———. "Fundamental Considerations: The Deep Meaning of Native American Schooling, 1880–1900." *Harvard Educational Review* 58, no. 1 (1988): 1–28.
Adas, Michael. "From Settler Colony to Global Hegemony: Integrating the Exceptionalist Narrative of the American Experience into World History." *American Historical Review* 106, no. 5 (December 2001): 1692–1720.
Ahern, Wilbert A. "Assimilationist Racism: The Case of the 'Friends of the Indian.'" *Journal of Ethnic Studies* 4 (Summer 1976): 23–32.
Alexander, Frederick. *Moving Frontiers: An American Theme and Its Application to Australian History* (Carlton: Melbourne University Press, 1947).
Alexander, Ruth Ann. "Elaine Goodale Eastman and the Failure of the Feminist Protestant Ethic." *Great Plains Quarterly* 8 (Spring 1988): 89–101.
———. "Finding Oneself through a Cause: Elaine Goodale Eastman and Indian Reform in the 1880s." *South Dakota History* 22, no. 1 (1992): 1–32.
Allen, Chadwick. *Blood Narrative: Indigenous Identity in American Indian and Maori Literary and Activist Texts.* Durham: Duke University Press, 2002.
Allen, H. C. *Bush and Backwoods: A Comparison of the Frontier in Australia and the United States.* Michigan: Michigan State University Press, 1959.
Anderson, Warwick. *The Cultivation of Whiteness: Science, Health, and Racial Destiny in Australia.* Carlton: Melbourne University Press, 2002.
Archdeacon, Thomas J. *Becoming American: An Ethnic History.* New York: Free Press, 1983.
Austin, Bain. "'In the Name of All My Coloured Brethren and Sisters': A Biography of Bessy Cameron." *Hecate* 7, nos. 1–2 (1986): 9–53.
———. *Simply the Survival of the Fittest: Aboriginal Administration in South Australia's Northern Territory, 1863–1910.* Darwin: Historical Society of the Northern Territory, 1992.
Attwood, Bain, Winifred Burrage, Alan Burrage, and Elsie Stokie. *A Life Together, a Life*

Apart: A History of Relations between Europeans and Aborigines. Carlton: Melbourne University Press, 1994.

Attwood, Bain, and Andrew Markus. *The Struggle for Aboriginal Rights: A Documentary History.* Sydney: Allen and Unwin, 1999.

Austin, Tony. "Cecil Cook, Scientific Thought, and 'Half-Castes' in the Northern Territory, 1927–1939." *Aboriginal History* 14, no. 1 (1990): 104–22.

———. "Genocide and Schooling in Capricornia: Educating the Stolen Generation." *History of Education Review* 29, no. 2 (2000): 47–66.

———. *I Can Picture the Old Home So Clearly: The Commonwealth and 'Half-Caste' Youth in the Northern Territory, 1911–1939.* Canberra: Aboriginal Studies Press, 1993.

Australian Dictionary of Biography, vols. 8, 9, 11, 12. Carlton: Melbourne University Press, 1981, 1983, 1988, 1990, respectively.

Baldwin, M. Page. "Subject to Empire: Married Women and the British Nationality and Status of Aliens Act." *Journal of British Studies* 40, no. 4 (2001): 522–56.

Banton, Michael. *Racial Theories.* 2d ed. Cambridge: Cambridge University Press, 1998.

Barcan, Alan. *A History of Australian Education.* Melbourne: Oxford University Press, 1980.

Barreiro, José. "First Words: When Education Became Ethnocide." *Native Americas: Hemispheric Journal of Indigenous Issues* 17, no. 4 (Winter 2000): 2.

Barwick, Diane. *Rebellion at Coranderrk.* Aboriginal History Monograph 5. Canberra: Aboriginal History Incorporated, 1998.

Bederman, Gail. *Manliness and Civilization: A Cultural History of Gender and Race in the United States, 1880–1917.* Chicago: University of Chicago Press, 1995.

Bell, Genevieve. "Telling Stories Out of School: Remembering the Carlisle Indian School, 1879–1918." PhD dissertation, Stanford University, 1998.

Bender, Thomas. *Rethinking American History in a Global Age.* Berkeley: University of California Press, 2002.

Bennett, Mary Montgomery. *Teaching the Aborigines: Data from Mount Margaret Mission, WA.* Perth: City and Suburban Print, 1935.

Benson, Robert, ed. *Children of the Dragonfly: Native American Voices on Child Custody and Education.* Tucson: University of Arizona Press, 2001.

Beresford, Quentin, and Paul Omaji. *Our State of Mind: Racial Planning and the Stolen Generations.* Fremantle: Fremantle Arts Centre, 1998.

Betzinez, Jason, and Wilbur S. Nye. *I Fought with Geronimo.* Lincoln: University of Nebraska Press, 1959.

Biskup, Peter. *Not Slaves, Not Citizens: The Aboriginal Problem in Western Australia, 1898–1954.* St. Lucia: University of Queensland Press, 1973.

Blake, Les. *Place Names of Victoria.* Adelaide: Rigby, 1977.

Bleakley, J. W. "Aboriginals and Half-Castes of Central Australia and North Australia." *Commonwealth Parliamentary Papers* 2, no. 21 (1929).

———. *The Aborigines of Australia: Their History—Their Habits—Their Assimilation.* Brisbane: Jacaranda, 1961.

Bradfield, Stuart. "From Empires to Genocide Chic: Coming to Terms with the Stolen Generations in Australia." In *Genocide Perspectives II: Essays on Holocaust and Genocide*, ed. Colin Tatz, 243–66. Sydney: Brandl and Schlesinger with the Australian Institute for Holocaust and Genocide Studies, 2003.

Bradley, Ian. *The Call to Seriousness: The Evangelical Impact on the Victorians*. London: Jonathan Cape, 1976.

Brodkin, Karen. *How the Jews Became White Folks and What That Says about Race in America*. New Brunswick: Rutgers University Press, 1998.

Broome, Richard. *Aboriginal Australians: Black Responses to White Dominance, 1788–1980*. Sydney: Allen and Unwin, 1982.

Brown, Kathleen M. *Good Wives, Nasty Wenches, and Anxious Patriarchs: Gender, Race, and Power in Colonial Virginia*. Chapel Hill: University of North Carolina Press, 1996.

Burt, A. L. "If Turner Had Looked at Canada, Australia, and New Zealand When He Wrote about the West." In *The Frontier in Perspective*, ed. W. D. Wyman and C. B. Kroeber, 59–77. Madison: University of Wisconsin Press, 1957.

Campbell, Malcolm. "Irish Nationalism and Immigrant Assimilation: Comparing the United States and Australia." *Australasian Journal of Australian Studies* 16, no. 2 (December 1996): 25–44.

Carter, Patricia A. "'Completely Discouraged': Women Teachers' Resistance in the Bureau of Indian Affairs Schools, 1900–1910." *Frontiers* 15, no. 3 (1995): 53–86.

Cecelski, David S., and Timothy B. Tyson, eds. *Democracy Betrayed: The Wilmington Race Riot of 1898 and Its Legacy*. Chapel Hill: University of North Carolina Press, 1998.

The Chant of Jimmy Blacksmith (film). Fred Schepisi, prod. and dir., Arthouse Productions, 1978.

Chaudhuri, Nupur, and Margaret Strobel, eds. *Western Women and Imperialism: Complicity and Resistance*. Bloomington: Indiana University Press, 1992.

Chesterman, John, and Brian Galligan. *Citizens without Rights: Aborigines and Australian Citizenship*. Melbourne: Cambridge University Press, 1997.

Child, Brenda J. *Boarding School Seasons: American Indian Families, 1900–1940*. Lincoln: University of Nebraska Press, 1998.

Choo, Christine. *Mission Girls: Aboriginal Women on Catholic Missions in the Kimberley, Western Australia, 1900–1950*. Crawley: University of Western Australia Press, 2001.

Christie, Michael F. *Aborigines in Colonial Victoria, 1835–86*. Parramatta: University of Sydney, 1979.

Churchill, Ward. "The Crucible of American Indian Identity: Native Tradition versus Colonial Imposition in Postconquest North America." In *Contemporary Native American Cultural Issues*, ed. Duane Champagne, 39–68. Walnut Creek: AltaMira Press, 1999.

———. *A Little Matter of Genocide: Holocaust and Denial in the Americas, 1492 to the Present*. San Francisco: City Lights Books, 1997.

———. "Nobody's Pet Poodle: Jimmie Durham: An Artist for Native North America." In *From a Native Son: Selected Essays on Indigenism, 1985–1995*, 483–500. Boston: South End Press, 1996.

Clark, Charles Manning Hope. *A History of Australia*, vol. 5, *The People Make Laws, 1888–1915*. Carlton: Melbourne University Press, 1981.

Clune, Frank. *Jimmy Governor*. London: Horowitz, 1959.

Collier, John. "A Reply to Mrs. Eastman." *Christian Century*, August 8, 1934, 1018–20.

Commonwealth of Australia. *Aboriginal Welfare: Initial Conference of Commonwealth and*

State Aboriginal Authorities Held at Canberra, 21st to 23rd April, 1937. Canberra: L. F. Johnston, Commonwealth Government Printer, 1937.

———. *Historical Records of Australia* 7, ser. 1. Sydney: Library Committee of the Commonwealth Parliament, 1916.

———. *Historical Records of Australia* 20, ser. 1. Sydney: Library Committee of the Commonwealth Parliament, 1924.

Coolidge, Grace. *Teepee Neighbors.* 1917. Norman: University of Oklahoma Press, 1984.

Copeland, Marion W. *Charles Alexander Eastman (Ohiyesa).* Boise State University Western Writers Series, vol. 33. Boise: Boise State University, 1978.

"Coranderrk Aboriginal Station: Report of the Board." *Victorian Parliamentary Papers* 2, no. 5 (1882–83).

Cott, Nancy. *The Bonds of Womanhood: "Woman's Sphere" in New England, 1780–1835.* New Haven: Yale University Press, 1977.

———. "Marriage and Women's Citizenship in the United States, 1830–1934." *American Historical Review* 103 (December 1998): 1440–74.

———. *Public Vows: A History of Marriage and the Nation.* Cambridge MA: Harvard University Press, 2000.

Cowlishaw, Gillian. *Black, White, or Brindle: Race in Rural Australia.* Melbourne: Cambridge University Press, 1988.

———. *Love against the Law: The Autobiographies of Tex and Nelly Camfoo.* Canberra: Aboriginal Studies Press, 2000.

Cronin, Kathryn. *Colonial Casualties: Chinese in Early Victoria.* Carlton: Melbourne University Press, 1982.

Darian-Smith, Kate. "'Rescuing' Barbara Thompson and Other White Women: Captivity Narratives on Australian Frontiers." In *Text, Theory, Space: Land, Literature, and History in South Africa and Australia,* ed. Kate Darian-Smith, Liz Gunner, and Sarah Nuttall, 99–114. London: Routledge, 1996.

Davenport, Charles B. *State Laws Limiting Marriage Selection: Examined in the Light of Eugenics.* Eugenics Record Office Bulletin, no. 9. Cold Spring Harbor NY: Eugenics Record Office, 1913.

Deacon, Desley. "Politicizing Gender." *Genders* 6 (Fall 1989): 1–19.

Deloria, Phillip J. *Playing Indian.* New Haven: Yale University Press, 1998.

D'Emilio, John, and Estelle B. Freedman. *Intimate Matters: A History of Sexuality in America.* New York: Harper and Row, 1988.

Devens, Carol. "'If We Get the Girls, We Get the Race': Missionary Education of Native American Girls." *Journal of World History* 3, no. 2 (1992): 219–37.

Diedrich, Maria. *Love across Color Lines: Ottilie Assing and Frederick Douglass.* New York: Hill and Wang, 1999.

Dippie, Brian W. *The Vanishing American: White Attitudes and U.S. Policy.* Middletown: Wesleyan University Press, 1982.

Dobrow, Julie. "White Sister of the Sioux." *Masterkey* 56, no. 3 (1982): 103–6.

Du Bois, W. E. B. *The Souls of Black Folk.* 1903. New York: Dover, 1994.

Dyer, Richard. *White.* London: Routledge, 1997.

Eastman, Charles A. *From the Deep Woods to Civilization: Chapters in the Autobiography of an Indian.* Boston: Little, Brown, 1916.

———. *The Indian To-day: The Past and Future of the First American*. Garden City: Double-day, Page, 1915.

———. *The Soul of the Indian: An Interpretation*. Boston: Houghton Mifflin, 1911.

Eastman, Elaine Goodale. "Does Uncle Sam Foster Paganism?" *Christian Century*, 8 August 1934, 1016–8.

———. "The Ghost Dance War and Wounded Knee Massacre of 1890–91." *Nebraska History* 26 (January–March 1945): 26–42.

———. "The Indian—A Woman among the Indians." In *The Literature of Philanthropy*, ed. Frances Goodale, 129–40. New York: Harper, 1893.

———. *Indian Legends Retold*. Boston: Little, Brown, 1925.

———. *Little Brother o' Dreams*. Boston: Houghton Mifflin, 1910.

———. *The Luck of Oldacres*. New York: Century, 1928.

———. *Pratt: The Red Man's Moses*. Norman: University of Oklahoma Press, 1935.

———. *Sister to the Sioux: The Memoirs of Elaine Goodale Eastman, 1885–1891*, ed. Kay Graber. Lincoln: University of Nebraska Press, 1978.

———. *The Voice at Eve*. Chicago: Bookfellows, 1930.

Elkin, A. P. "Native Education, with Special Reference to the Australian Aborigines." *Oceania* 7, no. 4 (June 1937): 459–501.

"Empires and Intimacies: Lessons from (Post)Colonial Societies." Special section of the *Journal of American History* 88, no. 3 (December 2001).

Evans, Raymond, Kay Saunders, and Kathryn Cronin. *Race Relations in Colonial Queensland: A History of Exclusion, Exploitation and Extermination*. St. Lucia: University of Queensland Press, 1988.

Fanon, Frantz. *Black Skin, White Masks*. Trans. Charles Lam Markmann. London: Paladin, 1970.

Fletcher, Alice. "The Preparation of the Indian for Citizenship." In *The Indian Policy: Papers Read at the Nineteenth Annual Conference of Charities and Correction, Held at Denver, 1892*. National Conference on Social Welfare, 1892.

Fletcher, J. J. *Clean, Clad, and Courteous: A History of Aboriginal Education in New South Wales*. Sydney: J. Fletcher, 1989.

———. *Documents in the History of Aboriginal Education in New South Wales*. Sydney: J. Fletcher, 1989.

Forbes, Jack D. *Africans and Native Americans: The Language of Race and the Evolution of Red-Black Peoples*. 2d ed. Urbana: University of Illinois Press, 1993.

Foreman, Grant. "Reminiscences of Mr. R. P. Vann, East of Webbers Falls, Oklahoma, September 28, 1932." *Chronicles of Oklahoma* 11, no. 2 (June 1933).

Fowler, David H. *Northern Attitudes towards Interracial Marriage: Legislation and Public Opinion in the Middle Atlantic and the States of the Old Northwest, 1780–1930*. New York: Garland, 1987.

Frankenberg, Ruth. *White Women, Race Matters: The Social Construction of Whiteness*. Minneapolis: University of Minnesota Press, 1993.

Fraser, Joseph. *Husbands: How to Select Them, How to Manage Them, How to Keep Them*. Melbourne: E. W. Cole, 1900.

Fraser, Malcolm A. C. *Western Australian Year-Book for 1902–04*. 13th ed. Perth: Government Printer, 1906.

Fredrickson, George M. "Comparative History." In *The Past before Us: Contemporary His-

torical Writing in the United States, ed. Michael Kammen. Ithaca: Cornell University Press, 1980.

Gale, Fay, *A Study of Assimilation: Part-Aborigines in South Australia.* Adelaide: Libraries Board of South Australia, 1964.

Ganter, Regina. "Living an Immoral Life—'Colored' Women and the Paternalistic State." *Hecate* 24, no. 1 (1998): 13–40.

Garrett, Philip C. "The Indian Policy in Its Relations to Crime and Pauperism." In *The Indian Policy: Papers Read at the Nineteenth Annual Conference of Charities and Correction, Held at Denver, 1892.* National Conference on Social Welfare, 1892.

Garrett, Philip C., and Herbert Welsh. *Letter to the Members of the Fifty-fourth Congress, February 13, 1897.* Philadelphia: Indian Rights Association, 1897.

Garton, Stephen. "Writing Eugenics: A History of Classifying Practices." In *"A Race for Place": Eugenics, Darwinism, and Social Thought and Practice in Australia,* ed. Martin Crotty, John Germov, and Grant Rodwell, 9–18. Proceedings of the History and Sociology of Eugenics Conference. University of Newcastle: Faculty of Arts and Social Science, 2000.

"Genocide? Australian Aboriginal History in International Perspective." Special section of *Aboriginal History* 25 (2001).

Georgi-Findlay, Brigitte. *The Frontiers of Women's Writing: Women's Narratives and the Rhetoric of Westward Expansion.* Tucson: University of Arizona, 1996.

Gerstle, Gary. *American Crucible: Race and Nation in the Twentieth Century.* Princeton: Princeton University Press, 2001.

Giese, H. C. "A Brief Study of Aboriginal Education in the Northern Territory." In *Aborigines and Education,* ed. S. S. Dunn and M. Tatz, 73–99. Melbourne: Sun Books, 1969.

Goodale, Elaine. "How to Americanize the Indian." *New Englander and Yale Review* 52 (May 1890): 452–55.

———. *Journal of a Farmer's Daughter.* New York: G. P. Putnam's Sons, 1881.

Goodall, Heather. *Invasion to Embassy: Land in Aboriginal Politics in New South Wales, 1770–1972.* Sydney: Allen and Unwin, 1996.

Goode, William J. *The Family.* Foundations of Modern Sociology, ed. Alex Inkeles. Englewood Cliffs NJ: Prentice-Hall, 1964.

Goodman, David. *Gold Seeking: Victoria and California in the 1850s.* St. Leonards: Allen and Unwin, 1994.

Gould, Stephen Jay. *The Mismeasure of Man.* New York: W. W. Norton, 1981.

Grew, Raymond. "The Comparative Weakness of American History." *Journal of Interdisciplinary History* 16, no. 1 (Summer 1985): 87–101.

Grimshaw, Patricia. "Interracial Marriages and Colonial Regimes in Victoria and Aetearoa/ New Zealand." *Frontiers* 23, no. 3 (2000): 2–28.

———. *Paths of Duty: American Mission Wives in Nineteenth-Century Hawaii.* Honolulu: University of Hawaii Press, 1989.

———. "Reading the Silences: Suffrage Activists and Race in Nineteenth-Century Settler Societies." In *Citizenship, Women, and Social Justice: International Historical Perspectives,* ed. Joy Damousi and Katherine Ellinghaus, 30–42. Melbourne: Department of History, University of Melbourne and the Australian Network for Research in Women's History, 1999.

————. "Writing about White Women in New Societies: Americans in Hawaii, Anglo-Australians in Colonial Victoria." *Australasian Journal of American Studies* 9 (December 1990): 20–32.

Haebich, Anna. *For Their Own Good: Aborigines and Government in the Southwest of Western Australia, 1900–1940.* Nedlands: University of Western Australia Press, 1988.

————. "Imagining Assimilation." *Australian Historical Studies* 118 (2002): 61–70.

Halse, Christine M. "The Reverend Ernest Gribble and Race Relations in Northern Australia." PhD, University of Queensland, 1992.

Harmon, Alexandra. "When Is an Indian Not an Indian? The 'Friends of the Indian' and the Problems of Indian Identity." *Journal of Ethnic Studies* 18 (Summer 1990): 95–123.

Harris, John. *One Blood: Two Hundred Years of Aboriginal Encounter with Christianity: A Story of Hope.* Sutherland NSW: Albatross Books, 1990.

Harrison, J. B. *The Latest Studies on Indian Reservations.* Philadelphia: Indian Rights Association, 1887.

Haskins, Victoria, and John Maynard. "Sex, Race, and Power: Aboriginal Men and White Women in Australian History." *Australian Historical Studies* 36, no. 126 (2005): 191–216.

Henningham, Nikki. "Perhaps If There Had Been More Women in the North, the Story Would Have Been Different: Gender and the History of White Settlement in North Queensland, 1840–1930." PhD, University of Melbourne, 2000.

Hertzberg, Hazel. *The Search for an American Indian Identity: Modern Pan-Indian Movements.* Syracuse NY: Syracuse University Press, 1972.

Higginbotham, A. Leon, and Barbara K. Kopytoff. "Racial Purity and Interracial Sex in the Law of Colonial and Antebellum Virginia." *Georgetown Law Journal* 77 (August 1989): 1967–2029.

Hilden, Patricia Penn. *When Nickels Were Indians.* Washington DC: Smithsonian Institute Press, 1995.

Hill, Ernestine. *The Great Australian Loneliness.* London: Jarrolds, 1937.

————. "The Strange Case of Mrs. Widgety." *Sunday Guardian Sun,* December 18, 1932. National Library of Australia.

Hodes, Martha. *White Women, Black Men: Illicit Sex in the Nineteenth-Century South.* New Haven: Yale University Press, 1997.

Horner, Jack. *Vote Ferguson for Aboriginal Freedom.* Brookvale: Australian and New Zealand Book, 1974.

Horner, Jack, and Marcia Langton. "The Day of Mourning" in *Australians 1938,* ed. Bill Gammage and Peter Spearitt, 29–33. Broadway, NSW: Fairfax, Syme, and Weldon, 1987.

Horowitz, Helen Lefkowitz, and Kathy Peiss, eds. *Love across the Color Line: The Letters of Alice Hanley to Channing Lewis.* Amherst: University of Massachusetts Press, 1996.

Howard, Michael C. *Aboriginal Politics in Southwestern Australia.* Nedlands: University of Western Australia Press, 1981.

Hoxie, Frederick E. "Exploring a Cultural Borderland: Native American Journeys of Discovery in the Early Twentieth Century." *Journal of American History* 79, no. 3 (December 1992): 969–95.

———. *A Final Promise: The Campaign to Assimilate the Indians, 1880–1920*. Cambridge MA: Cambridge University Press, 1995.

Huggins, Jackie, and Thom Blake. "Protection or Persecution? Gender Relations in the Era of Racial Segregation." In *Gender Relations in Australia: Domination and Negotiation*, ed. Kay Saunders and Raymond Evans, 42–58. Sydney: Harcourt Brace Jovanovich, 1992.

Hulme, Peter, and Ludmilla Jordanova, eds. *The Enlightenment and Its Shadows*. London: Routledge, 1990.

Hultgren, Mary Lou, and Paulette Fairbanks Molin. *To Lead and to Serve: American Indian Education at Hampton Institute, 1878–1923*. Virginia Beach: Virginia Foundation for the Humanities and Public Policy, 1989.

Human Rights and Equal Opportunity Commission. *Bringing Them Home: Report of the National Inquiry into the Separation of Aboriginal and Torres Strait Islander Children from Their Families*. Sydney: Commonwealth of Australia, 1997.

Hurtado, Albert L. *Intimate Frontiers: Sex, Gender, and Culture in Old California*. Albuquerque: University of New Mexico Press, 1999.

Ignatiev, Noel. *How the Irish Became White*. New York: Routledge, 1995.

Iverson, Peter. *Carlos Montezuma and the Changing World of American Indians*. Albuquerque: University of New Mexico Press, 1982.

Jackson, W. Turrentine. "A Brief Message for the Young and/or Ambitious: Comparative Frontiers as a Field for Investigation." *Western Historical Quarterly* 9, no. 1 (January 1978): 5–18.

Jacobs, Margaret. "The Eastmans and the Luhans: Interracial Marriage between White Women and Native American Men, 1875–1935." *Frontiers* 23, no. 3 (2002): 29–54.

Jacobson, Matthew Frye. *Whiteness of a Different Color: European Immigrants and the Alchemy of Race*. Cambridge MA: Harvard University Press, 1998.

Jaimes, M. Annette "Federal Indian Identification Policy: A Usurpation of Indigenous Sovereignty in North America." In *The State of Native America: Genocide, Colonization, and Resistance*, ed. M. Annette Jaimes, 123–38. Boston: South End, 1992.

Johnson, Franklin. *The Development of State Legislation Concerning the Free Negro*. New York: Arbor, 1918.

Johnson, Walton R., and D. Michael Warren, eds. *Inside the Mixed Marriage: Accounts of Changing Attitudes, Patterns, and Perceptions of Cross-Cultural and Interracial Marriages*. Lanham: University Press of America, 1994.

Johnston, James Hugo. *Race Relations in Virginia and Miscegenation in the South, 1776–1860*. Amherst: University of Massachusetts Press, 1970.

Jordan, Winthrop D. *White over Black: American Attitudes toward the Negro, 1550–1812*. Baltimore: Penguin, 1969.

Katz, Michael B. *Reconstructing American Education*. Cambridge MA: Harvard University Press, 1987.

Katznelson, Ira, and Margaret Weir. *Schooling for All: Class, Race, and the Decline of the Democratic Ideal*. New York: Basic, 1985.

Kazal, Russell A. "Revisiting Assimilation: The Rise, Fall, and Reappraisal of a Concept in American Ethnic History." *American Historical Review* 100, no. 2 (April 1995): 437–71.

Keneally, Thomas. *The Chant of Jimmy Blacksmith*. Sydney: Angus and Robertson, 1972.

———. "Doing Research for Historical Novels." *Australian Author* (January 1975): 27–29.

Kennedy, Randall. *Interracial Intimacies: Sex, Marriage, Identity, and Adoption*. New York: Pantheon, 2003.

Kerber, Linda K. "The Meanings of Citizenship." *Journal of American History* 84 (December 1997): 833–54.

Kimmel, Michael. *Manhood in America: A Cultural History*. New York: Free Press, 1996.

Kolodny, Annette. "Letting Go Our Grand Obsessions: Notes toward a New Literary History of American Frontiers." *American Literature* 64, no. 1 (March 1992): 1–18.

Kraditor, Aileen S., ed. *Up from the Pedestal: Selected Writings in the History of Feminism*. New York: Quadrangle/New York Times Book, 1975.

Krupat, Arnold, ed. *Native American Autobiography: An Anthology*. Madison: University of Wisconsin, 1994.

———. *Red Matters: Native American Studies*. Philadelphia: University of Pennsylvania Press, 2002.

Laidlaw, Zoë. "Integrating Metropolitan, Colonial, and Imperial Histories: The Aborigines Select Committee of 1835–37." In *Writing Comparative Colonial History*, ed. Julie Evans and Tracey Banivanua Mar. Melbourne: Department of History Conference Paper Series, University of Melbourne, 2002.

Laird, Carobeth. *Encounter with an Angry God: Recollections of My Life with John Peabody Harrington*. Albuquerque: University of New Mexico Press, 1975.

———. *Limbo*. Novato CA: Chandler and Sharp, 1979.

———. *Mirror and Pattern: George Laird's World of Chemehuevi Mythology*. Banning CA: Malki Museum, 1984. Microfilm.

Larner, John William, ed. *The Papers of Carlos Montezuma, M.D., Including the Papers of Maria Keller Montezuma Moore and the Papers of Joseph W. Latimer*. Wilmington: Scholarly Resources, 1984.

Lester, Robert E., ed. *Records of the Bureau of Indian Affairs: Central Classified Files, 1907–1939*. Bethesda: University Publications of America, 1995.

Leupp, Francis E. *The Indian and His Problem*. New York: Charles Scribner's Sons, 1910.

Leupp, Francis E., and Herbert Welsh. *Let There Be No Backward Step*. Philadelphia: Indian Rights Association, 1897.

Limerick, Patricia Nelson. *The Legacy of Conquest: The Unbroken Past of the American West*. New York: W. W. Norton, 1987.

———. "Turnerians All: The Dream of a Helpful History in an Intelligible World." *American Historical Review* 100, no. 3 (1995): 697–716.

Lindsey, Donal F. *Indians at Hampton Institute, 1877–1923*. Urbana: University of Illinois Press, 1995.

Littlefield, Alice. "Learning to Labor: Native American Education in the United States, 1880–1930." In *The Political Economy of North American Indians*, ed. John H. Moore, 43–59. Norman: University of Oklahoma Press, 1993.

Loomba, Ania. *Colonialism/Postcolonialism*. New York: Routledge, 1998.

Lord, J. E. C. "Furneaux Islands: Report upon the State of the Islands, the Condition and Mode of Living of Half-Castes, the Existing Methods of Regulating the Reserves, and Suggesting Lines for Future Administration." *Tasmanian Parliamentary Papers* 59, no. 57 (1908).

Manne, Robert. "The Stolen Generations." In Manne, *The Way We Live Now: Controversies of the Nineties*, 15–41. Melbourne: Text Publishing, 1998.

Marcus, Julie. "The Beauty, Simplicity, and Honour of Truth: Olive Pink in the 1940s." In *First in Their Field: Women and Australian Anthropology*, ed. Julie Marcus, 111–36. Carlton: Melbourne University Press, 1993.

Markus, Andrew. *Australian Race Relations, 1788–1993*. Sydney: Allen and Unwin, 1994.

———. *Blood from a Stone: William Cooper and the Australian Aborigines' League*. Sydney: Allen and Unwin, 1988.

Mathes, Valerie Sherer. "Nineteenth-Century Women and Reform: The Women's National Indian Association." *American Indian Quarterly* 14, no. 1 (Winter 1990): 1–18.

McGrath, Ann. "White Brides: Images of Marriages across Colonizing Boundaries." *Frontiers* 23, no. 3 (2002): 76–108.

McGregor, Russell. "'Breed Out the Colour,' or the Importance of Being White." *Australian Historical Studies* 33, no. 120 (October 2002): 286–307.

———. *Imagined Destinies: Aboriginal Australians and the Doomed Race Theory, 1880–1939*. Carlton: Melbourne University Press, 1997.

Meyer, Melissa L. "American Indian Blood Quantum Requirements: Blood Is Thicker than Family." In *Over the Edge: Remapping the American West*, ed. Valerie J. Matsumoto and Blake Allmendinger, 231–49. Berkeley: University of California Press, 1999.

Midgley, Clare, ed. *Gender and Imperialism*. Manchester: Manchester University Press, 1998.

Mihesuah, Devon A. "American Indian Identities: Issues of Individual Choices and Development." In *Contemporary Native American Cultural Issues*, ed. Duane Champagne, 13–38. Walnut Creek: AltaMira Press, 1999.

———. *Cultivating the Rosebuds: The Education of Women at the Cherokee Female Seminary, 1851–1909*. Urbana: University of Illinois Press, 1993.

Milnes, Peter. "A History of Aboriginal Education in the Goldfields District of Western Australia since 1927." PhD, University of New England, 1985.

Moran, Rachel F. *Interracial Intimacy: The Regulation of Race and Romance*. Chicago: University of Chicago Press, 2003.

Morris, Barry. *Domesticating Resistance: The Dhan-Gadi Aborigines and the Australian State*. Oxford: Berg, 1989.

Moses, A. Dirk. "An Antipodean Genocide? The Origins of the Genocidal Moment in the Colonisation of Australia." *Journal of Genocide Research* 2, no. 1 (2000): 86–107.

———, ed. *Genocide and Settler Society: Frontier Violence and Stolen Indigenous Children in Australian History*. New York: Berghahn Books, 2004.

Mumford, Kevin J. *Interzones: Black/White Sex Districts in Chicago and New York in the Early Twentieth Century*. New York: Columbia University Press, 1997.

Nash, Gary B. *Red, White, and Black: The Peoples of Early North America*. 3d ed. Englewood Cliffs NJ: Prentice Hall, 1992.

Native Americans and the New Deal: The Office Files of John Collier, 1933–1945. Bethesda MD: University Microfilm Publications of America, 1994.

Neville, Auber O. *Australia's Coloured Minority: Its Place in the Community*. Sydney: Currawong, 1947.

Newman, Louise Michele. *White Women's Rights: The Racial Origins of Feminism in the United States*. New York: Oxford University Press, 1999.

Niezen, Ronald. *Spirit Wars: Native North American Religions in the Age of Nation Building*. Berkeley: University of California Press, 2000.

Noriega, Jorge. "American Indian Education in the United States: Indoctrination for Subordination to Colonialism." In *The State of Native America: Genocide, Colonization, and Resistance*, ed. M. Annette Jaimes, 371–402. Boston: South End, 1992.

Papers Respecting the Treatment of Aboriginal Natives in Western Australia. Perth: Government Printer, 1887.

Partington, Gary, ed. *Perspectives of Aboriginal and Torres Strait Islander Education*. Katoomba: Social Science Press, 1998.

Pascoe, Peggy. "Miscegenation Law, Court Cases, and Ideologies of 'Race' in Twentieth-Century America." *Journal of American History* 83, no. 1 (1996): 44–69.

———. "Race, Gender, and Intercultural Relations: The Case of Interracial Marriage." *Frontiers* 22, no. 1 (1991): 5–18.

———. "Race, Gender, and the Privileges of Property: On the Significance of Miscegenation Law in the U.S. West." In *Over the Edge: Remapping the American West*, ed. Valerie J. Matsumoto and Blake Allmendinger, 215–30. Berkeley: University of California Press, 1999.

———. *Relations of Rescue: The Search for Female Moral Authority in the American West, 1874–1939*. New York: Oxford University Press, 1990.

Patten, J. T., and W. Ferguson. "Citizen Rights for Aborigines! Official Statement on Behalf of the Aborigines Progressive Association." *Publicist* 19 (January 1, 1938): 7.

Peabody, Francis Greenwood. *Founder's Day at Hampton: An Address in Memory of Samuel Chapman Armstrong, January 30, 1898*. Cambridge: Riverside, 1898.

Peterson, Erik. "'An Indian . . . an American': Ethnicity, Assimilation, and Balance in Charles Eastman's *From the Deep Woods to Civilization*." In *Early Native American Writing: New Critical Essays*, ed. Helen Jaskoski, 173–89. Cambridge: Cambridge University Press, 1996.

Pettman, Jan Jindy. "Race, Ethnicity, and Gender in Australia." In *Unsettling Settler Societies: Articulations of Gender, Race, Ethnicity, and Class*, ed. Daiva Stasilulis and Nira Yuval-Davis, 65–94. London: Sage, 1995.

Porter, Andrew, ed. *The Oxford History of the British Empire*. Vol. 3: *The Nineteenth Century*, 198–246. Oxford: Oxford University Press, 1999.

Powell, Alan. *Far Country: A Short History of the Northern Territory*. Carlton: Melbourne University Press, 1996.

"Progress Report of the Royal Commission on the Aborigines." *South Australian Parliamentary Papers* 2, no. 26 (1913).

Prucha, Francis Paul. *The Great Father: The United States Government and the American Indians*. 2 vols. Lincoln: University of Nebraska Press, 1984.

Quarterly Journal of the Society of American Indians (later the *American Indian Magazine*). Washington DC: Huntington Free Library/Museum of the American Indian Clearwater Publishing, 1981. Microfilm.

Rabbit-Proof Fence (film). Phillip Noyce, dir., Miramax, 2001.

Rajkowski, Pamela. *Linden Girl: A Story of Outlawed Lives*. Nedlands: University of Western Australia Press, 1995.

Ramson, W. S., ed. *The Australian National Dictionary: A Dictionary of Australianisms on His-torical Principles*. Melbourne: Oxford University Press, 1988.

Read, Peter. *A Hundred Years' War: The Wiradjuri People and the State*. Rushcutter's Bay: Aus-tralian National University Press, 1988.

———. "The Return of the Stolen Generation." *Journal of Australian Studies* 59 (1998): 8–19.

Report of the Parliamentary Select Committee on Aboriginal Tribes (British Settlements). Lon-don: Aborigines Protection Society, 1837.

Report of the Royal Commission on the Condition of the Natives. Perth: Government Print-er, 1905.

"Report of the Royal Commissioner Appointed to Investigate, Report, and Advise upon Matters in Relation to the Condition and Treatment of Aborigines." *Western Australian Votes and Proceedings* 2 (1936).

"Report of the Select Committee of the Legislative Council on the Aborigines Bill." *South Australian Parliamentary Papers* 2, no. 77a (1899).

Reynolds, Henry. *Black Pioneers*. Ringwood: Penguin, 2000.

———. *An Indelible Stain? The Question of Genocide in Australia's History*. Ringwood: Viking, 2001.

———. "Jimmy Governor and Jimmy Blacksmith." *Australian Literary Studies* 9, no. 1 (May 1979): 14–25.

———. *This Whispering in Our Hearts*. St. Leonards: Allen and Unwin, 1998.

———. *With the White People: The Crucial Role of Aborigines in the Exploration and Develop-ment of Australia*. Ringwood: Penguin, 1990.

Rideout, Henry M. *William Jones, Indian, Cowboy, American Scholar, and Anthropologist in the Field*. New York: Frederick A. Stokes, 1912.

Riley, Glenda. *Women and Indians on the Frontier, 1825–1915*. Albuquerque: University of New Mexico Press, 1984.

Roediger, David. *The Wages of Whiteness: Race and the Making of the Working Class*. Lon-don: Verso, 1991.

Rolls, Eric. *A Million Wild Acres: Two Hundred Years of Man and an Australian Forest*. Mel-bourne: Nelson 1981.

Romano, Renee. *Race Mixing: Black-White Marriages in Postwar America*. Cambridge: Har-vard University Press, 2003.

Roth, Walter E. "Royal Commission on the Condition of the Natives." *Western Australian Minutes and Votes and Proceedings of Parliament* 1, no. 5 (1905).

Roy, Cameron, and Kathielyn Job. *Around the Black Stump: The History of the Coolah-Dune-doo-Mendooran*. Coolah: Council of the Shire of Coolah, 1993.

"Royal Commission on the Aborigines." *Victorian Parliamentary Papers* 3 (1877–78).

Russo, David J. *American History from a Global Perspective: An Interpretation*. Westport: Praeger, 2000.

Ryan, Jan. "'She Lives with a Chinaman': Orient-ing 'White' Women in the Courts of Law." *Journal of Australian Studies* 60 (1999): 149–59.

Ryan, Lyndall. *The Aboriginal Tasmanians*. 2d ed. St. Leonards: Allen and Unwin, 1996.

Ryan, Mary. *Womanhood in America: From Colonial Times to the Present*. 3d ed. New York: Franklin Watts, 1983.

Senier, Siobhan. *Voices of American Indian Assimilation and Resistance: Helen Hunt Jack-son, Sarah Winnemucca, and Victoria Howard*. Norman: University of Oklaho-ma Press, 2001.

Shirley, Glenn. *Belle Starr and Her Times: The Literature, the Facts, and the Legends*. Norman: University of Oklahoma Press, 1982.

Sleeper-Smith, Susan. "Women, Kin, and Catholicism: New Perspectives on the Fur Trade." *Ethnohistory* 47, no. 2 (Spring 2000): 423–52.

Smith, Sherry L. *The View from Officer's Row: Army Perceptions of Western Indians*. Tucson: University of Arizona Press, 1990.

Smits, David D. "'Abominable Mixture': Toward the Repudiation of Anglo-Indian Intermarriage in Seventeenth-Century Virginia." *Virginia Magazine of History and Biography* 95, no. 2 (April 1987): 157–92.

———. "'Squaw Men,' 'Half-Breeds,' and Amalgamators: Late-Nineteenth-Century Anglo-American Attitudes toward Indian-White Race-Mixing." *American Indian Culture and Research Journal* 15, no. 3 (1991): 29–61.

Spack, Ruth. "Dis/engagement: Zitkala-Ša's Letters to Carlos Montezuma, 1901–1902." *Melus* 26, no. 1 (Spring 2001): 173–204.

Spencer, Tracy. "The Lives of Jim Page and Rebecca Forbes in the Adnyamathanha Community." PhD dissertation, Flinders University, forthcoming.

Spencer, W. Baldwin. "Preliminary Report on the Aboriginals of the Northern Territory." *Commonwealth Parliamentary Papers* 3 (1913).

Spickard, Paul R. *Mixed Blood: Intermarriage and Ethnic Identity in Twentieth-Century America*. Madison: University of Wisconsin Press, 1989.

Stanley, Brian. *The Bible and the Flag: Protestant Missions and British Imperialism in the Nineteenth and Twentieth Centuries*. Leicester: Apollos, 1992.

Statistical Register of Western Australia for 1901 and Previous Years. Perth: Government Printer, 1903.

Stensland, Anna Lee. "Charles Alexander Eastman: Sioux Storyteller and Historian." *American Indian Quarterly* 3, no. 3 (Autumn 1977): 199–208.

Stoler, Ann Laura. "Carnal Knowledge and Imperial Power: Gender, Race, and Morality in Colonial Asia." In *Gender at the Crossroads of Knowledge: Feminist Anthropology in the Postmodern Era*, ed. Micaela di Leonardo, 51–101. Oxford: University of California Press, 1991.

———. "Sexual Affronts and Racial Frontiers: European Identities and Cultural Politics of Exclusion in Colonial Southeast Asia." In *Tensions of Empire: Colonial Cultures in a Bourgeois World*, ed. Frederick Cooper and Ann Laura Stoler, 198–237. Berkeley: University of California Press, 1997.

———. "Tense and Tender Ties: The Politics of Comparison in North American History and (Post)Colonial Studies." *Journal of American History* 88, no. 3 (December 2001): 829–65.

Strobel, Margaret. *European Women and the Second British Empire*. Bloomington: Indiana University Press, 1991.

Sturm, Circe. *Blood Politics: Race, Culture, and Identity in the Cherokee Nation of Oklahoma*. Berkeley: University of California Press, 2002.

Summerhayes, Martha. *Vanished Arizona: Recollections of the Army Life of a New England Woman*. 1911. Lincoln: University of Nebraska Press, 1979.

Ten Years' Work for Indians at Hampton Institute, Virginia, 1878–1888. Hampton: Normal School Press, 1888.

Thomson, Judy, ed. *Reaching Back: Queensland Aboriginal People Recall Early Days at Yarra-bah Mission*. Canberra: Aboriginal Studies Press, 1989.

Tiffin, Chris. "Victims Black and White: Thomas Keneally's *The Chant of Jimmy Blacksmith*." In *Studies in the Recent Australian Novel*, ed. K. G. Hamilton, 121–40. St Lucia: University of Queensland Press, 1978.

Tilton, Robert S. *Pocahontas: The Evolution of an American Narrative*. New York: Cambridge University Press, 1994.

Tindale, Norman B. "Growth of a People: Formation and Development of a Hybrid Aboriginal and White Stock on the Islands of Bass Strait, Tasmania, 1815–1949: Results of the Harvard–Adelaide Universities Anthropological Expedition, 1938–1939." In *Records of the Queen Victoria Museum, Launceston*, ed. Frank Ellis. Launceston: Museum Committee, Launceston City Council, 1953.

Tingey, Joseph Willard. "Indians and Blacks Together: An Experiment in Biracial Education at Hampton Institute (1878–1923)." PhD dissertation, Columbia University Teachers College, 1978.

Trudinger, R. M. "Education of Aborigines, Eastern Australia, 1788–1888." Master's thesis, University of Sydney, 1973.

Twenty-two Years' Work of the Hampton Normal and Agricultural Institute at Hampton, Virginia: Records of Negro and Indian Graduates and Ex-Students. Hampton: Normal School Press, 1893.

Tyrrell, Ian. "American Exceptionalism in an Age of International History." *American Historical Review* 96, no. 4 (1991): 1031–55.

———. "Comparing Comparative Histories: Australian and American Modes of Comparative Analysis." *Australasian Journal of American Studies* 9 (December 1990): 1–11.

———. "Making Nations/Making States: American Historians in the Context of Empire." *Journal of American History* 86 (December 1999): 1015–44.

———. "Peripheral Visions: Californian-Australian Environmental Contacts, c. 1850s–1910s." *Journal of World History* 8, no. 2 (1997): 275–302.

———. *True Gardens of the Gods: Californian-Australian Environmental Reform, 1860–1930*. Berkeley: University of California Press, 1999.

———. *Woman's World/Woman's Empire: The Woman's Christian Temperance Union in International Perspective*. Chapel Hill: University of North Carolina Press, 1991.

U.S. Congress. Senate. *Correspondence on Sioux Mixed Bloods*. 53d Cong., 2d sess., 1894.

———. Senate. *Memorial of Wilbur F. Bryant, in case of Louis Riel, on Naturalization of Persons of Mixed Indian and White Blood*. 50th Cong., 2d sess., 1888.

———. Senate. *Report by Mr. Allen from the Committee on Indian Affairs*. 52d Cong., 1st sess., 1896.

Vanden Driesen, I. H., ed. *Essays on Immigration Policy and Population in Western Australia, 1850–1901*. Nedlands: University of Western Australia Press, 1986.

Van Kirk, Sylvia. *Many Tender Ties: Women in Fur-Trade Society, 1670–1870*. Norman: University of Oklahoma Press, 1983.

Wadlington, Walter. "The Loving Case: Virginia's Antimiscegenation Statute in Historical Perspective." *Virginia Law Review* 52 (October 1966): 1189–223.

Wallenstein, Peter. "Native Americans Are White, African Americans Are Not: Racial Identity, Marriage, Inheritance, and the Law in Oklahoma, 1907–1967." *Journal of the West* 39, no. 1 (2000): 55–63.

————. "Race, Marriage, and the Law of Freedom: Alabama and Virginia, 1860s–1960s." *Chicago-Kent Law Review* 70, no. 2 (1994): 371–437.

————. *Tell the Court I Love My Wife: Race, Marriage, and Law—An American History.* New York: Palgrave Macmillan, 2002.

Ward, Russel. *The Australian Legend.* Melbourne: Oxford University Press, 1958.

Ware, Vron. *Beyond the Pale: White Women, Racism, and History.* London: Verso, 1992.

Welsh, Herbert. *Four Weeks among Some of the Sioux Tribes of Dakota and Nebraska Together with a Brief Consideration of the Indian Problem.* Germantown, PA: Horace F. McCann, 1882.

Welter, Barbara. *Dimity Convictions: The American Woman in the Nineteenth Century.* Athens: Ohio University Press, 1976.

Williamson, Joel. *New People: Miscegenation and Mulattoes in the United States.* New York: Free Press, 1980.

Wilson, Raymond. *Ohiyesa: Charles Eastman, Santee Sioux.* Urbana: University of Illinois Press, 1983.

Winks, Robin W. *The Myth of the American Frontier: Its Relevance to America, Canada, and Australia.* Leicester: Leicester University Press, 1971.

Wolfe, Patrick. "Land, Labor, and Difference: Elementary Structures of Race." *American Historical Review* 106, no. 3 (June 2001): 866–905.

————. "Nation and MiscegeNation: Discursive Continuity in the Post-Mabo Era." *Social Analysis* 36 (October 1994): 93–152.

————. *Settler Colonialism and the Transformation of Anthropology: The Politics and Poetics of an Ethnographic Event.* London: Cassell, 1999.

Women's National Indian Association. *Fourth Annual Report of the Women's National Indian Association.* Philadelphia: Grant and Faires, 1884.

————. *Our Work—What? How? Why? The Work of the Women's National Indian Association.* Philadelphia: Women's National Indian Association, 1893.

Wood, Marilyn. "The 'Breelong Blacks.'" In *Race Matters: Indigenous Australians and "Our" Society,* ed. Gillian Cowlishaw and Barry Morris, 97–120. Canberra: Aboriginal Studies Press, 1997.

Yarrabah, Church of England Aboriginal Mission. Rules and Regulations. Yarrabah: Australian Board of Missions, n.d.

Young, Robert J. C. *Colonial Desire: Hybridity in Theory, Culture, and Race.* London: Routledge, 1995.

Zitkala-Ša. *American Indian Stories.* 1921. Reprint, Lincoln: University of Nebraska Press, 1985.

————. *Old Indian Legends.* 1901. Reprint, Lincoln: University of Nebraska Press, 1985.

Index

White Bear, Russel, 37

white men: married to Native American women, 32–33, 34, 177–80; masculinity of, 65; in relationships with Aboriginal women, x, 191

white women: archival evidence of experiences of, xiii–xvi, 150; citizenship of, xi, 225n9, 227n53; as civilizing angels, 82–86; femininity of, 81–84, 95; married to Aboriginal men, xiv, 108, 122–23, 129–47, 149–66, 241n19; married to indigenous men, ix–xvi, 220; married to Native American men, xiii, 2–4, 14, 22–3, 25, 26, 46, 64–65, 84–87, 149; as oddities, 73–74, 108, 150–62, 166; perceived as threat, 165–66; role in colonialism of, xii, 220; as sexually attracted to Native American men, 102–3; and vocation as reformers, 82–84

Winnebago Indians, 30, 63

Woiworung (Aboriginal people). *See* Briggs, George Wright

Women's National Indian Association, xxi, 15, 41, 82, 86

Wondunna, Ethel (née Gribble) and Fred, 162–65

Wounded Knee Massacre, 58, 61

Wyandotte (people from northeast U.S.), 39

Yarrabah (Queensland Mission), 162–63, 245n38

Yavapai Indians, 47

Yellow Robe, Chauncey, 43–5

Yellow Robe, Lillian (née Springer), *44*

Youle, George, *130*, 241n19

Yuma Indians, 31

Zitkala-Ša (Gertrude Simmons), 68–71

www.ingramcontent.com/pod-product-compliance
Ingram Content Group UK Ltd.
Pitfield, Milton Keynes, MK11 3LW, UK
UKHW041909060225
454777UK00001B/180